Hoover Institution Publications

Hungary and the Superpowers

HUNGARY AND THE SUPERPOWERS

The 1956 Revolution and Realpolitik

János Radványi

Hoover Institution Press
Stanford University
Stanford, California

Hoover Institution Publication 111
Standard Book Number 8179-1111-1
Library of Congress Card Number 71-170208
Printed in the United States of America
© 1972 by the Board of Trustees of the
Leland Stanford Junior University

To

Julianna

Why do a thousand torpid wishes
Fail to fuse in one strong will
While Magyar, Slav, Wallach grief
Remains one sorrow still?

Shall we ever be united?
Shall we speak in one sole strain?
We, the oppressed and downtrodden,
Non-Magyars and Magyars all.

Endre Ady (1877-1919)
(Trans. by J. R.)

Contents

FOREWORD

by Zbigniew Brzezinski

Janos Radványi's book is an unusual combination of personal recollections and historical insight. A former diplomat of Hungary's Communist government, the author was first participant and observer, and then chronicler of the events described and analyzed in this book.

Even a close student of East European politics will find in this book much that is new as well as much that is relevant to a broad understanding of international affairs in general. For one thing, the author has had an unusual opportunity to scrutinize carefully some of the principal actors in the Hungarian drama, and his descriptions of their personal characteristics and styles of behavior are unique. Moreover, through his service in foreign posts, he was in a position to observe in action such diverse and indirect participants in the Hungarian affair as the Chinese Communist leaders and the policymakers in the Department of State in Washington.

I read with particular interest the author's account of Mao Tse-tung's reaction to the Hungarian events. It is a significant contribution to our understanding of the critical October-November 1956 period to learn that Mao Tse-tung personally urged Soviet Premier Khrushchev to take the decision to intervene decisively, and by force of arms, in order to suppress the Imre Nagy government in Hungary. This account presents us with important confirmation of a suspicion that some of us have entertained but could not heretofore fully document.

Even more striking and provocative is the author's account of the closed meeting that Soviet Deputy Premier Mikoyan held with Communist ambassadors in Washington shortly after the Cuban missile crisis. Mikoyan offered his allies a revealing interpretation of the Soviet motives for placing offensive missiles in Cuba, an explanation much at variance with the official Soviet record. Mikoyan's statement to the effect that the principal Soviet purpose was to upset the balance of power between the United States and the Soviet Union is of particular relevance to contemporary affairs, for it suggests that the Soviet effort to erase American nuclear superiority anteceded, not followed, the Cuban missile crisis.

Finally, to students of American diplomacy the book offers revealing insights into discreet American efforts to ameliorate internal conditions in Hungary even after the imposition of Soviet control over that helpless country. One thus learns of quiet, persistent, and eventually effective American efforts to obtain from the new Kádár government pledges of internal improvement in exchange for American willingness to remove the Hungarian issue from the United Nations agenda. Though actions of this sort could do little to alter the overall situation of Hungary, they do indicate nonetheless the ability of the United States to exercise subtle, and ultimately effective, leverage even in conditions in which its direct power and influence are limited. Dr. Radványi's book thus stands as a useful reminder of the fact that Eastern Europe remains an area of American political interest, and that it is ahistorical to assume that this vital part of Europe must be considered forever part of a watertight empire exclusively in the Soviet sphere of influence.

Acknowledgments

The preparation and completion of this work would have been beyond my powers without a great deal of help and encouragement over a long period from many quarters. I assume full responsibility, however, for all opinions expressed in the book and for any errors that may have crept into it. I first discussed the project with Professor Zbigniew K. Brzezinski and with Professor Gordon A. Craig, who encouraged me to undertake it.

Among the many friends and colleagues who read the manuscript at different stages and who made valuable suggestions, I am especially grateful to Professors Alexander Dallin, Ivo J. Lederer, and John W. Lewis, and to Dr. Lewis H. Gann. The comments and scholarly criticisms of Professors Richard A. Brody, György Heltai, and Ferenc A. Váli, and of Dr. Peter J. Duignan and Mrs. Adele Rosenzweig have been extremely helpful. I appreciate also the courtesies and guidance in research and library matters provided by Mrs. Ann Fitzpatrick, Miss Paula E. Howe, Mrs. Edith S. Levin, and Mr. John T. Ma. Mrs. Anne K. Laskow deserves many thanks for the careful typing of the manuscript.

To Messrs. Alan H. Belmont and Brien Benson, Mrs. Carole H. Norton, and Miss Liselotte Hofmann of the Hoover Institution I am grateful for help in seeing the book through publication. In addition I should like to thank Mrs. Edna Halperin, who did the editing—with unfailing good judgment and good humor. For their continued support and interest in my work I am indebted to Professor Carl B. Spaeth of Stanford, to Professor Eugene P. Wigner of Princeton, and to Dr. W. Glenn Campbell and Dr. Richard F. Staar of the Hoover Institution. Mr. David C. Wilson, executive editor of the *China Quarterly*, kindly gave permission to reprint parts of my article, "The Hungarian Revolution and the Hundred Flowers Campaign," which had appeared in the July-September 1970 issue.

For generous financial support I should like to express my gratitude to the Center for Research in International Studies, Stanford University, and to the Hoover Institution on War, Revolution and Peace.

Finally, to my wife, who was always at my side and always willing to share with me the burdens of writing a book, I am most thankful.

János Radványi

Stanford University, 1971

Introduction

On 1 November 1956 Imre Nagy, leader of the Hungarian Revolution, demanded of Yuri Andropov, Soviet ambassador to Budapest, the immediate removal from Hungary of the recently arrived Russian troops. He agreed at the same time to accept a promise of the gradual withdrawal of the remaining Soviet armed forces. Yet the influx of troops and military hardware continued. Nagy now followed up his demand by declaring Hungary's neutrality and by announcing his country's withdrawal from the Warsaw Pact. In addition, he requested Secretary-General Dag Hammarskjold of the United Nations to include on the agenda of the world organization the question of Hungarian neutrality.

But before the cumbersome machinery of the United Nations could be geared for action, Soviet tanks were rumbling through the streets of Budapest. Imre Nagy's desperate attempt to stave off Soviet military intervention had failed completely. The United States, despite rhetorical pronouncements about rolling back the iron curtain, actually had no commitment to Hungary; and the attention of the Western powers was at the moment diverted from Hungary by the explosion over Suez. By 4 November, when the Emergency Special Session of the General Assembly to consider "the situation in Hungary" had been convened, it was faced with a Soviet *fait accompli*. The question of Hungarian neutrality became instead the complex "Question of Hungary."

Six years later, on 20 October 1962, U.S. Assistant Undersecretary of State Richard Davis handed to the Hungarian chargé d'affaires in Washington a two-page memorandum. This short document, based on a series of lengthy discussions initiated several months earlier, made the following two points:

1. It was hoped the Hungarian government would either take convincing public steps or would issue an authoritative statement giving assurance that the consequences of the 1956 events would be erased.

2. The government of the United States would exercise its influence at the United Nations to end the debate on the Hungarian question and to have the credentials of the representatives of the Hungarian government recognized.

Though no formal acknowledgment of the memorandum was ever made, the document in itself represented a diplomatic step of major importance. It was to form the basis for a tacit understanding between the United States, the Soviet Union, and Hungary. The Hungarians and the Americans soon took action. On 20 November 1962 János Kádár, first secretary of the Hungarian Socialist Workers' Party and prime minister, publicly stated that 95 percent of those persons sentenced for "counterrevolutionary crimes" had been released, and implied that further concessions might be made if the United States withdrew the "Question of Hungary" from the agenda of the U.N. General Assembly. At the meeting of the Special Committee of the United Nations on 18 December 1962, Carl T. Rowan, the U.S. representative to the General Assembly, expressed the necessity for a "fresh approach" to the question and submitted a draft resolution requesting Secretary-General U Thant to "take any initiative that he deems helpful in relation to the question of Hungary." With this diplomatic formula, the "Question of Hungary" was dropped from the agenda of the United Nations. Following the suppression of the 1956 uprising, both the Soviets and the newly established Kádár government had set about consolidating Hungary's internal situation. They applied exceptional measures to end resistance and to recharge the economy. At that stage neither the United States nor any other member of the United Nations was in a position to affect decisions made inside the Soviet or the Hungarian Politburo. But once pro-Soviet communist rule had been restored in Hungary, the interaction between foreign policy and internal politics became again a factor in decision making. The Kádár government, wanting to break out of international isolation, recognized that it had to improve its image. It wished also to achieve more stability and greater popular support at home. Neither of these aims could be achieved without some degree of internal liberalization.

This process of liberalization was bound to be welcomed by the West. Two years later, in fact, Secretary of State Dean Rusk expressed the belief that the United States should encourage evolution within the communist world toward national independence, peaceful cooperation, and open societies. He pointed out that the United States could best promote these objectives by adjusting its policies to the differing societies of the various communist states—or to the evolving patterns within these states (*Department of State Bulletin* 50, 16 March 1964). In this framework U.S. policy makers, as they assessed the changing situation in Hungary, came to the conclusion that it would be to their own country's interest to reappraise U.S. relations with the Kádár regime. This American attitude, coupled with the increasing sense of security felt by the Hungarian communist leadership, opened the way for the first genuine attempts at reconciliation between the two countries since 1956.

In the aftermath of the Cuban missile crisis the Soviet leadership, too, sought an all-around relaxation of tensions. Khrushchev was now ready to consider seriously a nuclear test-ban treaty. The "hot line" between Moscow and Washington was installed as a safety device for use in future crises. In this atmosphere of détente Moscow could not but acquiesce in a compromise over the Hungarian question in the United Nations.

The existing literature on the 1956 revolution is rich and extensive. Six bibliographies have been published, as well as some four hundred books and over a thousand articles. Documents, collected testimonies, memoirs, and other sources provide ample data for a complete picture of what actually happened before, during, and immediately after the crisis in Hungary. Previous scholarly works, however, have not dealt in depth with the international implications of the Hungarian revolution; they focused mainly on the political, socioeconomic, cultural, and human aspects of the problem. The present study takes a different approach. I treat the Hungarian question primarily in its international framework, extending the analysis beyond the usual cut-off point of 1958. I attempt, further, to portray the decisions and actions of the participants in the events that began with the course pursued by Imre Nagy and that culminated in the U.N. acceptance in 1963 of the Hungarian credentials.

Some twenty years of diplomatic experience in the communist world has given me the opportunity to observe at first hand the ways in which the foreign policies of communist countries are conceived and carried out. Also, I was one of the participants in the negotiations between the United States and Hungary in 1962. In the course of the narrative, therefore, I report to the reader—in addition to previously unpublished details of these events—my own observations, my own actions and reactions. I attempt to offer some insight into the conduct of diplomatic negotiations between the states of East and West and into the motivations underlying high-level policy decisions. I sincerely hope that this study may serve to narrow the gap in our present knowledge between the theory and the practice of decision making, and may thus contribute to a deeper understanding of communist foreign policy.

Hungary and the Superpowers

— 1 —

The Hungarian Uprising and
Emergency Diplomacy

At 11 a.m. on 27 October 1956 a black limousine stopped at the main entrance of the State Department Building in Washington, D.C. A Hungarian diplomat stepped out of the car and hastened through the glass doors to the elevator. In a few minutes he was sitting in the office of Deputy Undersecretary Robert Murphy. Though he greeted the deputy undersecretary in the conventional manner, the face of Tibor Zádor, the highest-ranking diplomat of the Hungarian legation in Washington, was gloomy and drained of color; and there was no concealing the fact that he was fatigued and tense. Murphy, too, the veteran diplomat of the Second World War, the "diplomat among warriors,"[1] was near exhaustion. Ever since the Hungarian Revolution had erupted he had been working round the clock to keep up with events and to keep President Eisenhower informed on current developments.

The undersecretary had asked Zádor to come in because, like everyone else in Washington, he was confused about the situation in Hungary. Neither he nor anyone else in the administration had expected the anti-Soviet revolution that was apparently in progress. Washington was not alone in its surprise and confusion: the Hungarian upsurge of 1956 was equally unexpected even by some of the most interested parties—the Soviet-appointed authorities in Budapest and the Presidium of the Communist Party of the Soviet Union.

Just over a hundred years earlier, Tocqueville had observed in connection with the 1848 revolutions that the laws of physics do not always apply to politics, that explosion in human affairs often occurs not when the pressure is the greatest but when it already has begun to subside.[2] Events in Hungary now seemed to justify Tocqueville's dictum. The international confusion stemmed both from a general failure on the part of statesmen to recognize the unique character of the sociopolitical forces operative in Hungary at the time and

3

from their inability to foresee the impact of the political thaw which had begun in the Soviet Union and in East Europe during the period of uncertainty following Stalin's death. The post-Stalin leadership in the U.S.S.R. evidently realized the necessity for changes both at home and abroad. Nikita S. Khrushchev's reconciliation with Josip Broz Tito, the "Declaration of Belgrade," which emphasized every communist party's right to choose its own road to socialism, indicated the changing Soviet mood in foreign policy. The promise of a consumer-oriented economy in which the needs of the populace would be the central determinant signaled a new trend in Soviet economic policy.

BACKGROUND OF THE CRISIS AND WORLD DIPLOMACY

Events in Hungary followed the pattern of those in the Soviet Union. The first step was a division of powers exercised by the prime minister and the first secretary of the Communist Party. On 4 July 1953 Imre Nagy replaced Mátyás Rákosi, Stalin's satrap, as prime minister; Rákosi remained the party leader.

My first meeting with Imre Nagy occurred during President Tito's visit to Budapest in 1947, when Nagy was serving as president of the Parliament. Although I did not have the opportunity to become well acquainted with him, his manner impressed me as quiet and unassuming. He seemed to resemble rather the fictional image of the old college professor than the popular concept of a smooth politician. His career in politics began in the 1920s, when he was an organizer in the Hungarian agrarian labor movement. After two years' imprisonment for communist activity[3] he went to Moscow, where he worked at the International Agronomy Institute. During World War II he was editor-in-chief of Radio Kossuth, which broadcast programs in Hungarian from the Soviet capital. Once hostilities had ended he returned to Hungary, where, as minister for agriculture, he planned and directed the distribution of land.

Nagy's first serious disputes with Rákosi and his clique date from 1948. Because he disagreed with the timetable and the overzealous implementation of the Moscow-dictated collectivization campaign, he was removed from the party Politburo "for his revisionist views." Dismissed from political life, Nagy seemed more than content to accept a post at the newly established University for Economic Sciences in Budapest. Here he could once more devote all his energy to studying the problems of the peasantry. It may very well be that the post-Stalin leadership, in recalling him from the academic world, hoped to reap great benefit from his economic expertise and from his fast-growing popularity.[4]

In his first speech to the nation, Nagy outlined his "New Course."[5] He promised more consumer goods and more food. He announced that the peasants would be permitted to leave the collective farms. He declared that the concentration camps were to be closed. After much bitter contention with Rákosi, Nagy did succeed in decreasing the planned output of heavy industry. A large-scale exodus of peasants from collective farms took place. The concentration camps were abolished and about ten thousand victims of the communist regimes were freed. In addition, many leading Hungarian political prisoners, among them János Kádár, were released.

Kádár was a very different person in every way from Imre Nagy. He was simple and direct, strong in his convictions, a worker turned politician, but handicapped by lack of knowledge concerning international politics and world affairs. However, he did know his native Hungary well; and when it came to exercising power he was forceful and able, a born tactician. During his youth, at the instigation of his friend János Bojti[6] he had joined the then illegal Communist Party. Advancing rapidly in the party hierarchy, he became the secretary of the Communist Party during the war and was one of the leaders of the anti-Nazi resistance movement in Hungary.[7] After the war he organized the police and headed the cadre department of the Central Committee. He was appointed secretary of the influential Budapest party organization and became deputy general secretary of the party and minister of Interior. Then, in the middle of May 1951, without any official or semi-official announcement, Kádár suddenly disappeared from public life. Only a few high officials were aware at the time that he had been arrested and tried for treason and conspiracy against the state. In the midst of growing terror it would have been imprudent even to mention the name of the highest-ranking representative of the so-called home communists.

For Kádár the experiences of his detention and trial had been excruciating. He often remarked afterward in private that the interrogators of the A.V.H. (the communist State Security Police) had tortured him physically and mentally more savagely than the anti-communist police agents of the pre-war Horthy regime. He left prison in poor health, but after months of treatment recovered and was rehabilitated at the end of 1954. Though Kádár may have become anti-Stalinist, throughout his life he remained a staunch advocate of the pro-Moscow course.

After Kádár's release from prison in October 1954, his place in the prison cell was taken by General Gábor Péter, the former head of Rákosi's State Security Police. At the end of 1954, however, the progress of the New Course ended abruptly. Rákosi was able to exploit the post-Stalin power struggle within the Soviet leadership to regain influence in Moscow. Nagy was branded a "right-wing deviationist" and expelled from the party.[8] The new prime minister, András Hegedüs, modified the New Course so that again, as in Stalin's time, emphasis was given to the development of heavy industry and to farm collectivization. To ease the resulting economic burden, the Hungarian armed forces were reduced by some twenty thousand men. As a political gesture, Cardinal Mindszenty, who had been tried on trumped-up charges and had been sentenced to life imprisonment in 1949, was released from his cell and placed under house arrest, while other church dignitaries were granted amnesty.

Mid-October 1955 saw the beginnings of rebellion. Communist writers, scientists, and artists forwarded a "memorandum" to the Party Central Committee objecting to Rákosi's attempts to restore a rule of force. These intellectuals, who only a few years before had wholeheartedly supported the communist cause, now declared themselves involuntary accomplices in grave crimes. No self-justification, they asserted, could any longer ease their consciences. Rákosi was too cynical to recognize the deep psychological changes that had taken place among the party elite and too power-hungry to condone any accommodation. He attempted to restore unity by disciplinary action, with the leading writers as his prime target. But he had misread the political climate and lost ground rapidly.

In February 1956 Khrushchev delivered his famous report, the "Secret Speech," to the Twentieth Congress of the Communist Party of the Soviet Union.[9] His revelations concerning Stalin's crimes and misuse of power could not, of course, be kept secret. Details rapidly became known all over the world. In Hungary the party bureaucracy reacted with consternation, and in the process opposition to Rákosi became stronger and more vocal. On 27 June 1956 the Writers' Union, student organizations, and other leading intellectuals in the Petöfi Circle asked not only for political and economic reforms, but also for the resignation of the Hungarian Stalinist leader. The opposition bluntly demanded that he be punished. Moscow, sensing the danger of the Hungarian situation, which indeed was beginning to show some similarities to the Polish workers' rebellion in Poznan on 28 June, attempted to undercut the momentum of the movement. Unannounced, the representative of the Soviet Party, Anastas Mikoyan, appeared at the July 1956 Politburo meeting of the Hungarian Workers' Party and replaced Rákosi with another Muscovite, Ernö Gerö.[10] Furthermore, the Soviet government granted a 100-million-ruble loan to rescue the shattered Hungarian economy. But it was already too late. Developments in Hungary were moving rapidly toward their climax.

On 6 October a silent demonstration swept through the Hungarian capital as 200,000 people attended the reinterment of László Rajk and several other rehabilitated victims of the Stalinist era. In the ensuing days the reformist and national Communist Party opposition clamored for the return of Imre Nagy to the premiership and the appointment of János Kádár to the post of first secretary of the party.

On 22 October students, writers, and members of the Petöfi Circle met separately. Each group drafted its own set of resolutions demanding internal economic reforms, the right to strike, freedom of speech and freedom of the press, a system of socialist democracy, readjustment of political and economic relations with the Soviet Union, evacuation of all Soviet troops from Hungarian territory, and guaranteed respect for Hungary's national sovereignty.[11]

On 23 October students, writers, factory workers, and soldiers in uniform took part in militant demonstrations in Budapest.

More than a hundred thousand demonstrators gathered in front of the Polish embassy to express sympathy for the Polish reform movement. Then the milling crowd moved to Stalin Square and in a symbolic gesture pulled down a huge statue of Stalin. Sporadic fighting between demonstrators and security forces broke out around Radio Budapest headquarters. The same day Party Chief Gerö and Prime Minister Hegedüs requested Soviet armed assistance to put down the civil strife. Soviet tanks appeared in the streets of Budapest, but their intervention was not decisive; the local Soviet military command was without clear directives from Moscow and uncertain how to act.

On 24 October the Central Committee of the Hungarian Workers' Party appointed the popular Imre Nagy prime minister of Hungary. That same day Mikoyan and Suslov of the Soviet Party Presidium arrived in Budapest. They backed Nagy's appeal for an end to the fighting, dismissed Gerö and installed Kádár as party chief, then flew back to Moscow to report their findings. What particularly alarmed the two emissaries was the fact that after eight years of uncontested control, in a matter of days the Hungarian Workers' Party had completely lost its influence. Equally menacing was the growing popular demand that Hungary pull out of the Warsaw Pact and proclaim her neutrality.

Meanwhile the fighting had spread all over Hungary and Revolutionary Councils and Workers' Councils had been spontaneously organized. Nagy and Kádár pleaded for the restoration of order. In response to the mounting pressure of revolutionary forces, the Nagy government dissolved the security police, abolished the one-party system, and promised free elections. Gradually the fighting stopped. The tide of reform was at its flood. But it would soon turn.

On 27 October, when the Murphy-Zádor meeting was taking place in Washington, internal developments in Hungary were still unclear. So were Soviet intentions. The U.S. undersecretary hoped the Hungarian diplomat could apprise him of the general situation in Hungary and assure him of the safety of the American diplomatic staff in Budapest; communication with the State Department had been cut off. Zádor regarded his host with only partially concealed surprise. Why, he wondered, was Murphy asking him for this information? He, Zádor, knew nothing of what was going on either in Budapest or in the Hungarian countryside; his own headquarters had sent him no information about the situation. Besides, his main concern was to get some news from his ailing father and his brother.[12]

Since some answer was obviously expected, the Hungarian replied simply that his legation was not in direct contact with Budapest but had communicated with the Hungarian legation in London and had received confirmation that a new government, headed by Imre Nagy, had been formed. This answer was apparently not satisfactory to Murphy, who cited reports of street fighting in Budapest and elsewhere and said that the United States deplored the intervention of Soviet military forces. Zádor at first tried to avoid a direct reply. He acknowledged having heard that the reports of fighting were true. He referred vaguely to a "riot" in Budapest but added that he had no information of any military operations in the provinces.

Pressed for details about the riot, Zádor stared first at the ceiling, then at the open window, as though searching for an escape from the room, and finally said in a somewhat defensive tone that the students had demanded certain changes, which had been made, but that "fascists" had taken advantage of the situation. The deputy undersecretary, not wanting to argue about the "fascists" at this point, inquired whether the workers had made the same demands as the students, to which Zádor replied that they had.

A minute or two passed in silence while Murphy wondered whether it was worth while to continue this discussion with a diplomat who most probably had neither information nor directives, and who was cut off from his superiors in the same way that the Americans in Budapest were cut off from the State Department. He decided he would at least try to ascertain the personal reaction of this young man to the Soviet military intervention. Citing reports of the number of Hungarians who had been killed by the Soviet military action, he invited Zádor to explain his position in the light of these events. To this approach Zádor's response was unimpeachably correct: the Soviet military action was quite legal under the provisions of the Warsaw Pact.

Murphy abandoned further questioning. He expressed the U.S. concern about the humanitarian aspects of the situation in Hungary, noting the fact that the American Red Cross and fifteen other national Red Cross societies had made offers of assistance through the International Red Cross, but had not been able to contact the Hungarian government. As the State Department record of the meeting shows, Murphy closed the conversation "by lodging a firm protest about the fact that our diplomatic representative in Hungary is completely cut off from communication with his government."[13]

THE DEVELOPING HUNGARIAN SITUATION
IN THE UNITED NATIONS

While Murphy was following events from Washington, Henry Cabot Lodge, the permanent representative of the United States to the United Nations, was in constant communication in New York with his counterparts from France and Great Britain, Bernard Cornut-Gentille and Sir Pierson Dixon. Their problem was to coordinate their efforts in the United Nations to try to put an end to the Russian armed intervention in Hungary of 23-24 October. Lodge, to be sure, was in close touch also with President Eisenhower and Secretary of State John Foster Dulles.

On the afternoon of 27 October France, the United Kingdom, and the United States undertook concerted diplomatic action at the United Nations. The three representatives addressed a letter to the president of the Security Council urgently requesting that the Council discuss the Soviet military intervention in Hungary. They invoked Article 34 of the United Nations Charter, which empowers the Security Council to investigate a situation that may lead to international friction or may be likely to endanger the maintenance of international peace and security, and stated:

> The Governments of France, the United Kingdom of Great Britain and Northern Ireland, and the United States of America request the inclusion in the agenda of the Security Council of an item entitled: "The situation in Hungary," and request further that you convene an urgent meeting of the Security Council for the consideration of this item.[14]

On Sunday, 28 October, shortly before the Council was to meet, Dr. Péter Kós, then Hungary's permanent representative to the United Nations, transmitted the text of a declaration by his government:

> The Government of the Hungarian People's Republic categorically protests against placing on the agenda the consideration of any question concerning the domestic affairs of Hungary, since the consideration of such questions in the United Nations would mean serious violation of the sovereignty of the Hungarian People's Republic and would obviously be in contradiction with the principles laid down in the Charter of the United Nations.[15]

The moment the Council meeting began, Arkady A. Sobolev of the U.S.S.R. vehemently objected to consideration of the events in Hungary. As might be expected, his main argument was the same as that of Dr. Kós. He argued that the United Nations had no jurisdiction over Hungary's internal affairs. He was more explicit than the Hungarian, describing the events in Hungary as an "uprising of criminal elements of a fascist type against the legal Government of Hungary." Consequently, he maintained, requesting assistance from the Soviet Union to suppress these fascist elements was an internal Hungarian matter.[16]

Henry Cabot Lodge offered a different picture. Taking his stand on the basis of public information that had been confirmed by official Hungarian government sources, he pointed out that on 23 October a peaceful demonstration had taken place in Budapest. The assemblage had made several demands, including the withdrawal of Soviet troops from Hungary. Hungarian political police units and Soviet tanks had opened fire on the civilians, and the resulting fighting had spread beyond the Hungarian capital, reaching the Austrian frontier.

The British and French ambassadors followed up Lodge's charges by presenting further evidence that Soviet troops had intervened on a massive scale. Sir Pierson told the Council that he had just received information indicating that an additional Soviet army corps had entered Hungary from Rumania. The situation was worsening. In the absence of Soviet assurance that the conflict would be quickly resolved, it appeared that the Security Council would have to act. The French and British representatives, together with those of Cuba, Peru, Nationalist China, Australia, and Belgium, supported the U.S. stand that all members of the United Nations should "give the tragic situation in Hungary their earnest and active consideration."[17]

While the Security Council was in session, Radio Budapest carried a proclamation by Imre Nagy.[18] For the first time since the revolt had begun, Nagy publicly rejected the view that the popular upsurge was a counterrevolution. He promised political and economic reforms and announced an immediate cease-fire to avoid further bloodshed. Finally, he stated his government was opening negotiations with Moscow to review relations between Hungary and the U.S.S.R. These talks would include the question of withdrawing Soviet troops from the country.

The announcement of Nagy's proclamation caused much excitement in the Security Council. Dr. E. Ronald Walker of Australia read aloud part of Nagy's broadcast. Sobolev continued to insist that Soviet military units, stationed in Hungary in conformity with the Warsaw Pact, had only gone to help the Hungarian workers. Dr. Kós expressed his regret that the Security Council had decided to consider "the situation in Hungary" despite the fact that this was an internal Hungarian affair.[19] But in the absence of further instructions from his government he reserved the right to speak on the substance of the question at another time. Since there were no other speakers, the Council adjourned without introducing any resolution, thereby leaving it to the discretion of the president to reconvene when necessary.

During the three ensuing days the Security Council concentrated solely on the Suez crisis. On 29 October the United States informed the Security Council that the armed forces of Israel had penetrated deep into Egyptian territory in the Sinai Peninsula.[20] On 30 October the Security Council was in session all day. The United States proposed an immediate cease-fire. The United Kingdom and France countered with a proposal that an ultimatum be issued to both Israel and Egypt. The British representative emphasized that both Britain and France were resolved to safeguard passage through the Canal. Unless hostilities between Israel and Egypt ceased within twelve hours, therefore, Anglo-French forces would occupy key positions at Port Said, Ismailia, and Suez.[21]

Surprised by the ultimatum, the American representative introduced a resolution calling upon Israel to withdraw behind the established armistice lines. Moreover, the resolution called upon all states to refrain from the use of force or threat of force in the area, and to refrain from giving any military, economic, or financial assistance to Israel as long as it did not comply with this resolution.[22] Great Britain and France vetoed the resolution. The following day British and French aircraft attacked Egyptian airfields and various military targets, while Nasser had a ship sunk in the Canal to prevent passage through it. The Sinai Peninsula was aflame.[23]

The Hungarian public learned about events in the Middle East through the Free Hungarian Press and through Free Radio Kossuth. In the streets, however, people were too preoccupied with internal events to pay close attention to the Suez crisis. Many seemed puzzled as to why Great Britain, France, and Israel had launched the invasion just at this juncture. Could they not have waited until the Russians had withdrawn their troops and tanks from Hungary?

Inside the Parliament building, however, where the Hungarian revolutionary government was in constant session, Imre Nagy and his close collaborators followed the Suez crisis with the greatest care. It was evident that from their angle the Middle East eruption had taken place at a most inopportune time. Tensely alert to every Soviet reaction, they feared that with the West divided over Suez the Kremlin would have free rein to place still greater pressure on Hungary. They hoped, however, that the United States would put an end to the Western intervention in the Middle East and that the Eisenhower administration could then open discussions with the Soviet Union regarding the immediate evacuation of Soviet troops from Hungary.[24] As events showed, Nagy's concern was fully warranted, but his hopes were not fulfilled. American pressure combined with strong internal opposition in London and Paris did put an early end to the Anglo-French venture. On the other hand, the Western powers failed to use the occasion to bargain with the Kremlin. In the final analysis, then, the Suez crisis did at least facilitate the Soviet decision to crush the Hungarian rebellion.

Soviet leadership, however, was as much concerned about American response to the Soviet intervention in Hungary as it was about the crisis in the Middle East. Exactly how far would the Eisenhower administration pursue its oft-stated policy of "rolling back the iron curtain"? Although Khrushchev had never considered as a real threat the Dulles plan of building up and assisting East European resistance movements, he did take seriously the American nuclear deterrent. In the course of private conversations at which I was present, the Soviet premier always felt it necessary to explain that the Soviet leadership had to take into account the possible effect on Soviet actions of the U.S. nuclear striking capability. Khrushchev probably remembered that Eisenhower had used the nuclear threat successfully at the end of the Korean conflict in order to achieve favorable terms for an armistice.[25] While the Soviet leadership thus appears to have considered the possibility that Eisenhower and Dulles might use the nuclear stratagem, the White House on this occasion acted with extreme caution. President Eisenhower thought it possible that the Soviet Union might be tempted "to resort to extreme measures, even to start a world war," to prevent the collapse of its East European security system.[26] Furthermore, having no direct commitment vis-à-vis Imre Nagy, the Eisenhower administration found no basis for granting or extending American military aid to Hungary.[27]

In these circumstances, at a National Security Council meeting Eisenhower asked for a position paper which emphasized that the Soviets had to be reassured that the United States would not attempt to make Hungary a military ally.[28]

This American intention was communicated to the Russians on three separate occasions in rapid succession. The first occurred the day after the Security Council meeting, when Dulles addressed the Council on World Affairs in Dallas. Speaking about the East European situation, particularly as it concerned Hungary and Poland, Dulles pointed out that "we do not look upon these nations as potential military allies."[29] The following day, 28 October, Ambassador Lodge called the attention of the Security Council to Dulles's remarks in Dallas. He quoted Dulles's formula that "we do not look upon these nations as potential military allies," and expressed the hope that the Soviet Union would not misunderstand American intentions with regard to the changing situation in Hungary.[30] On 29 October Charles Bohlen, the American ambassador in Moscow, was instructed to assure the Russians officially that Dulles's remarks in Dallas had been approved by President Eisenhower.[31] This series of statements gave ample reassurance to the Soviets that the United States had no intention of getting involved in the Hungarian affair.

THE SOVIET DOUBLE GAME AND THE INVASION OF HUNGARY

During these crucial days of October 1956, the Soviet Presidium was meeting in full session, attempting to reach a decision on a situation that was becoming more and more confused and unfavorable for the Kremlin. Undoubtedly to the Soviet Union the Hungarian uprising represented one of the gravest intra-bloc crises of the postwar era. While the possible loss of Hungary constituted in and of itself the most immediate danger, the resulting widespread unrest in the Eastern bloc soon demonstrated an even more serious consequence. The Rumanian party head, Gheorghe Gheorghiu-Dej, and Czechoslovakia's Antonin Novotny sent distress signals warning of imminent uprisings of their Hungarian minorities, and East Germany's Walter Ulbricht nervously reminded Moscow of the East Berlin workers' insurrection of 1953 and warned that a similar revolt could break out at any moment. At the same time, the leadership of the Chinese Communist Party manifested a real interest in East European affairs. In the final days of October 1956, Mao Tse-tung became convinced that the leaders of the Communist Party of the Soviet Union had committed grave errors when they "intended to adopt a policy of capitulation and abandon socialist Hungary to counterrevolution."[32] Chairman Mao was certain, as we shall demonstrate, that only military intervention could save the situation. Accordingly, he sent urgent messages to the Kremlin asking Khrushchev and the Soviet Party Presidium for quick action "to smash the counterrevolutionary rebellion in Hungary."

As all these elements crystallized, the Soviet party leadership, taking advantage also of the clearly stated U.S. determination to steer clear of involvement in Hungary, arrived at the firm decision to invade Hungary, to abolish the Imre Nagy government, and to place János Kádár in power. On 30 October Mikoyan and Suslov once more took off for Budapest, where they held a lengthy discussion with Prime Minister Imre Nagy, the head of the Communist Party, János Kádár, and the leader of the newly reorganized bourgeois Smallholders' Party, Zoltán Tildy. The two emissaries from Moscow indicated that they did not object to the formation of a coalition government nor to the return to a multiparty system. They agreed further that a gradual withdrawal of Soviet troops from Hungary should begin. But they warned that the old capitalist regime must not be restored and that Hungary must not become an anti-Soviet base.[33] The following day Mikoyan and Suslov returned to Moscow; and that night (1 November), together with Minister of Interior Ferenc Münnich, Kádár disappeared from the Hungarian capital. Kádár and Münnich had broken with the Nagy government and had sought sanctuary in the Soviet Union. Three days later the world learned of the formation of a countergovernment headed by Kádár.[34]

On the same day that Mikoyan and Suslov left Moscow for Budapest (30 October) the Soviet government issued a declaration of the U.S.S.R. government on the bases for "developing and further strengthening of friendship and cooperation between the Soviet Union and other socialist states."[35] On the one hand, this move represented a final attempt by the Soviets to assuage, and perhaps at the same time to intimidate, the leaders of the Hungarian Revolution. On the other, it was intended to make the Western powers believe that Soviet intentions with regard to Hungary were honorable.

The statement set forth that the Twentieth Congress of the Communist Party of the Soviet Union had created the conditions "for further strengthening cooperation among socialist countries ... on the inviolable basis of maintaining complete sovereignty of each socialist state." The Soviet Union desired to re-examine, in consultation with the other socialist countries, the necessity for stationing Soviet specialists and military advisers in Eastern Europe. Moreover, the Kremlin expressed its readiness to negotiate with the Nagy government and the other Warsaw Pact nations on the presence of Soviet troops in Hungary.[36]

Confusion regarding Soviet intentions increased as, on the night of 31 October, the Russians began to withdraw their troops from Budapest and at the same time new Soviet contingents and special security detachments crossed the Soviet-Hungarian border in substantial numbers, systematically occupying airfields and other strategic points. Budapest was quickly surrounded. Khrushchev, when asked pointblank by U.S. Ambassador Bohlen at a reception in Moscow about this time why the U.S.S.R. was sending troops into Hungary, had replied somewhat nervously and defensively, "Eto ne shutka" (this is no laughing matter). Imre Nagy on his part asked Soviet Ambassador Andropov for an explanation of the Soviet moves. Andropov assured Nagy that the Soviet government's statement issued the previous day presaged a general withdrawal of all Soviet forces from Hungary.

In spite of Soviet reassurances the influx of troops continued. Nagy once more called in Andropov and strongly protested the new military intervention. It was a futile effort, of course; the Kremlin had by then decided to crush the rebellion. As a last attempt to avert the Russian take-over, the Nagy cabinet proclaimed Hungary's neutrality and its withdrawal from the Warsaw Treaty Organization. The Hungarian prime minister notified the secretary-general of the United Nations of this and requested that the question of Hungary's neutrality and the defense of this neutrality by the four great powers be placed promptly on the agenda of the forthcoming U.N. General Assembly.[37]

While Soviet military units rolled on toward Budapest, the Hungarian Permanent Mission in New York transmitted Imre Nagy's second urgent letter to the secretary-general. Once again he requested that Hammarskjöld call upon the great powers to recognize the neutrality of Hungary. In contrast to his first communication, however, he now asked the Security Council to instruct the Soviet Union to start immediate negotiations with his government on the termination of the Warsaw Treaty and the withdrawal of the Soviet troops from Hungary.[38]

The Secretariat distributed Nagy's letter at the close of the 2 November meeting at 8:50 p.m. The following day Henry Cabot Lodge introduced a draft resolution calling upon the U.S.S.R. to desist forthwith from any form of intervention in Hungary.[39] The statement also expressed the hope that the U.S.S.R. would withdraw all Soviet forces from Hungary without delay. It seemed then that the Security Council might act decisively, though the draft carefully avoided recognizing, much less guaranteeing, the declared neutrality of Hungary. But those who hoped that the United Nations would be effective in stopping the Russian military action were soon to be disappointed. Instead of voting, the Council became involved in a lengthy debate.

In this confused situation, Dr. János Szabó, a career diplomat who had been temporarily appointed by Imre Nagy, was prepared on the one hand to transmit to Secretary-General Hammarskjöld the communications of the prime minister. But in addition he relayed to the Security Council and later to the Emergency Special Session of the General Assembly whatever he had been told by the Soviet mission to the United Nations in New York. (Under normal circumstances Soviet diplomatic missions do not give instructions to the diplomatic representatives of any of the East European communist countries; coordination of policy is customarily arranged between the capitals of the bloc countries and Moscow. The 1956 situation, however, was far from normal and required special emergency treatment.) Szabó spent his days in New York under a special type of house arrest: he was guarded day and night in his apartment by two Hungarian security agents. He was escorted to and from U.N. headquarters and was never left alone in the conference rooms. He was well aware of the fact that he might be physically eliminated if he failed to follow instructions. Ironically, he was not unwilling to comply with Soviet demands; yet the Soviets did not trust him.

To clarify the situation in Hungary, Ambassador Lodge asked Dr. Szabó to provide the Security Council with details concerning recent events.[40] He also asked Sobolev, the Soviet representative, whether additional troops had entered Hungary. In addition, he questioned both representatives about fresh reports that a mixed Hungarian-Soviet commission was presumably negotiating in Budapest with regard to the withdrawal of Soviet forces.[41] The Yugoslav representative, Ambassador Joza Brilej, also inquired about the situation in Hungary—more specifically about the reports that negotiations had begun in Budapest.

In reply to Cabot Lodge's question Szabó said that representatives of the Hungarian and Soviet armed forces had indeed met on 3 November to discuss "technical questions involved in withdrawing the Soviet troops." He added that "according to the Soviet proposal, no more troops will cross the border until an agreement is reached."[42] Sobolev repeated what Szabó had already said, merely confirming the reports of the discussions. The Security Council adjourned without arriving at a decision. Five days passed with no further Security Council meeting on Hungary despite repeated attempts by the British government to bring one about. Embittered by the U.S. government policy in the Middle East, Sir Anthony Eden tore into the Eisenhower administration:

> The United States representative was reluctant, and voiced his suspicion that we were urging the Hungarian situation to divert attention from Suez. The United States Government appeared in no hurry to move. Their attitude provided a damaging contrast to the alacrity they were showing in arraigning the French and ourselves.[43]

It was not until Soviet troops had attacked and occupied Budapest and other major cities in Hungary (4 November) that the Security Council began to deal in earnest with the crisis. When questioned about the second intervention, Ambassador Sobolev stated that his delegation had received no official information about this new development and recommended that the Security Council postpone consideration of the question until reliable information was available. Szabó told the Security Council that he could not make contact with Budapest although he had been unofficially informed that "a new government had been formed under the leadership of Mr. János Kádár, president of the Council of Ministers."[44] The Security Council decided to take action.

In Moscow, meanwhile, the Soviet Foreign Ministry, profiting from the lesson of the Korean crisis, reminded the Soviet Party Presidium that at the outbreak of the Korean War in 1950 the Truman administration had recommended military action against North Korea in the U.N. Security Council while the U.S.S.R. was temporarily boycotting the meetings of the world organization.

In an internal report to the Party Presidium, the Soviet Foreign Ministry predicted that the United States would again call for an emergency special session of the General Assembly under the "Uniting for Peace" resolution adopted during the Korean conflict.[45] The report emphasized that the Soviet U.N. delegate could not block recourse to this procedure. And the U.N. General Assembly might recommend economic sanctions or military intervention to the member states. Such measures could be implemented, however, only by voluntary action of the members pursuant to the General Assembly recommendations. The U.S.S.R. had to make certain, therefore, that its delegation, even if under attack, was present during the debate on the Hungarian situation so that it could negate any possible Security Council action by its veto. This is precisely what happened. After discussion and the proposal of the U.S. draft resolution the Security Council voted to call upon the U.S.S.R. to introduce no additional troops into Hungary and to withdraw, without delay, all its forces from that country. But the Soviet Union vetoed the resolution of the Security Council.[46]

Immediately after the veto Cabot Lodge introduced a motion to call an emergency special session of the General Assembly under the Uniting for Peace procedure. With the exception of Sobolev, the members of the Security Council voted in favor of adopting the U.S. draft resolution. On the same day a special emergency session—the first to be called on the Hungarian question—convened to consider "the situation in Hungary."

At the 4 November Emergency Session, the Soviet Union defended its position without much difficulty. Sobolev announced that the Imre Nagy government had collapsed and that the new Hungarian Revolutionary Workers' and Peasants' government objected to the discussion of the Hungarian situation in the United Nations. Three days later Dr. János Szabó, the Hungarian representative, declared that recent events in Hungary must be considered as an internal Hungarian affair, and he therefore protested sharply the consideration of "the situation of Hungary" by the General Assembly.[47]

From that time on, the question of Hungarian neutrality became the complex "question of Hungary." The world organization passed approximately sixteen resolutions dealing with Hungary, condemning Soviet aggression and calling for an end to the suppression of human rights and for the restoration of freedom to the Hungarian people. The Soviet Union, however, not only defied these resolutions but resolutely maintained its position that the United Nations had no right to interfere in the internal affairs of Hungary. Aware that collective security could not operate effectively against one of the two nuclear superpowers unless the other was ready to move to the brink of war,[48] the Soviet leaders paid little attention to verbal attacks from the United States and the other member states. For public consumption, they branded Western views as "reactionary cold-war propaganda."

The new Kádár regime followed the Soviet position in the United Nations with consequences that were far more serious for Hungary than for the U.S.S.R.

As a result of this policy Hungary's relations with the West were frozen for years. Even a number of Afro-Asian states were reluctant to recognize the new regime, and the United Nations itself refused to accept the credentials of the Hungarian delegates. Unlike their Soviet counterparts, the Hungarian leaders were not in a position to disregard world opinion and to endure international isolation. Because Kádár was considered a puppet of the Kremlin, the stabilization of his regime required a constant fight for international acceptance. In order to normalize its relations with the United States and with the United Nations, the Kádár government was forced to make political concessions.

INTRODUCTION OF THE
NONRECOGNITION-NONREFUSAL FORMULA

At the Emergency Special Session of the General Assembly on 4 November 1956 a number of representatives questioned whether the Hungarian delegate, Dr. János Szabó, represented the people or even the legitimate government of Hungary. Representative Lodge went even farther. In condemning the Soviet act of aggression he said:

> A small group of Soviet straw men announced their own formation as a government at the moment Soviet troops began their attack. We have seen no passage of governmental authority from one Hungarian government to another, but only the creation of a puppet clique and the overthrow of a liberal socialist government responsive to popular will in their desire to see these troops go.[49]

When Szabó told the Emergency Special Session that life in his country was returning to normal, that transportation was functioning and that the schools had reopened, Emilio Nuñez Portuondo of Cuba replied passionately: "A young man comes here to give his blessing to the murder of over 65,000 of his fellow countrymen and tells us that nothing has happened in Hungary." He added that for Cuba, Szabó represented neither the people nor the government of Hungary.[50] Carl J. Eskelund, the representative of Denmark, raised a point of order in connection with the Hungarian's statement. He recalled to the Assembly that two days earlier Szabó had spoken in the Security Council on behalf of the Imre Nagy government. For this reason he wanted information from the secretary-general "concerning the credentials of the gentleman who spoke here as a representative of Hungary."[51]

Louis de Guiringaud, the French representative, not only condemned the Soviet aggression but severely criticized the failure of the United Nations to assist Hungary. He emphasized that those members of the world organization who had based their views on Soviet statements were naive and those who believed Szabó were in error.[52]

In this heated atmosphere the Credentials Committee of the Emergency Session convened on 8 November. This committee, which from its inception had played only an administrative role, now became a battleground of international diplomacy. During the debate the representative of France first raised the question of the validity of the Hungarian representative's cabled credentials since, in his opinion, Russian military intervention alone had created the Kádár government. The Soviet representative immediately rejected the charges, maintaining that the Hungarian credentials had been issued in accordance with the rules of procedure of the General Assembly. The representatives of Indonesia and Afghanistan expressed agreement with the Soviet views. Australia, Colombia, and the United States supported a Dominican Republic proposal that, pending further clarification, the Credentials Committee should take no decision on the Hungarian delegate's credentials at that time. In spite of Soviet objections the Credentials Committee decided to delay any decision on the Hungarian credentials. The next day the General Assembly unanimously approved the report of the Credentials Committee.[53]

In explaining their affirmative votes, the Soviet and Ukrainian representatives expressed reservations in connection with the adverse ruling on the credentials of the People's Republic of China, which was also under U.N. debate. They avoided mentioning, however, the delicate question of the Hungarian credentials. Sobolev expected that at the next regular session of the General Assembly the Credentials Committee would accept without difficulty a written accreditation of the Hungarian delegation.[54] The Soviet calculation, however, proved unrealistic. With the transfer of the question of Hungary from the Emergency Special Session to the regular Eleventh Session of the General Assembly, the credentials of the Hungarian representatives were again challenged. This time the United States introduced a motion that "the Committee take no decision regarding the credentials submitted on behalf of the representatives of Hungary." As did the French objection, the American pointed out that "these credentials had been issued by authorities established as a result of military intervention by a foreign power."[55] The Soviet representative emphatically opposed the American proposal. He emphasized that the lawful government of the Hungarian People's Republic had issued the credentials; the American initiative, therefore, was part of a hostile campaign directed against a socialist state. In spite of the Soviet objection, the Credentials Committee adopted the motion introduced by the United States in a vote of 8 to 1, with the U.S.S.R. casting the negative vote.

As expected, the Kádár government also strongly protested the "discriminatory procedure without precedent in the history of the United Nations Organization."[56] Neither the Soviet nor the Hungarian protest, however, prevented the United States from taking further action. At the next session of the General Assembly, in December 1957, the United States again questioned the representative character of the Hungarian government; and once more no decision was taken regarding the credentials submitted on behalf of the Hungarian representative.[57] In subsequent sessions the General Assembly refused to recognize the Hungarian credentials on the grounds that the Hungarian regime had disregarded the resolutions of the General Assembly.

Few observers at the time followed the credentials question closely. Most were interested in those resolutions that condemned the Soviet Union for its military actions, the delegates calling upon the U.S.S.R. to desist from all armed attacks on the Hungarian people (Resolution 1004 ES-11). A five-power resolution requested that free elections be held in Hungary under the auspices of the United Nations as soon as law and order had been restored (Resolution 1005 ES-11). Emilio Nuñez Portuondo told the Assembly that according to his information the Soviet occupation forces in Hungary were deporting Hungarian men, women, and children. Despite the Kádár government's denial, the Cuban delegate submitted a draft resolution pointing to the principles of Articles 55 and 56 of the United Nations Charter—the Convention on the Prevention and Punishment of the Crime of Genocide. In addition Portuondo demanded the prompt withdrawal of Soviet forces and the dispatch of U.N. observers to Hungary (Resolution 1127 XI).

The General Assembly also devoted time and energy to providing humanitarian assistance to the Hungarian people. It called on member states and on national and international humanitarian and religious organizations to organize emergency relief programs to provide food, medicine, clothing, and textiles. The High Commissioner for Refugees of the United Nations was given overall responsibility for coordinating international action for resettlement, repatriation, care, and maintenance, as well as a tracing service, for the two hundred thousand refugees.[58] During the crisis U.N. representatives visited Hungary on two occasions, neither of which was publicized in Hungary. One group was headed by U.N. Undersecretary Philippe de Seynes, who, with three other U.N. officials, reported to the secretary-general on the relief requirements for Hungary. Maurice Paté, executive director of the U.N. Children's Fund (UNICEF), visited Budapest for the same reason.[59]

When the General Assembly voted on these humanitarian matters, the Soviet-bloc countries abstained, meanwhile expressing their willingness for limited cooperation with the world organization. Foreign Minister Imre Horváth, head of the Hungarian delegation during the Eleventh Session of the General Assembly, declared his readiness to meet with Hammarskjöld, although he made it clear to the secretary-general that his government would not discuss political problems with him or with any of his representatives. He insisted that consideration be given only to relief programs.

Despite Hungarian refusal, the General Assembly continued to press for the admission of U.N. observers into Hungary and requested the secretary-general to visit Budapest. On 11 December the Hungarian representative told the Assembly that a number of delegations had offended his government by acting in a manner incompatible with the sovereignty and the national honor of the Hungarian people. The Hungarian delegation would not, therefore, participate in the work of the Eleventh Session of the General Assembly so long as the discussion of the Hungarian question did not proceed in the spirit of the U.N. Charter.[60] The dramatic walkout of the Hungarian delegation did not change the course of the debate, but it did give the Hungarian government an excuse to postpone indefinitely Hammarskjöld's visit to Budapest.

After all other attempts at resolving the question of Hungary proved fruitless, the General Assembly on 10 January 1957 adopted a 24-power resolution establishing a Special U.N. Observation Committee, composed of representatives of Austria, Ceylon, Denmark, Tunisia, and Uruguay, to study the situation in Hungary.[61] From 1957 on, this committee had extensive but quite impractical plans. Not only did its members want to secure the cooperation of the Hungarian government to interview the former Hungarian prime minister, Imre Nagy, but they also hoped to clarify the origin and significance of Nagy's communications to the United Nations. These elaborate plans, however, were frustrated because the Hungarian government barred the members of the committee and its staff from Hungarian territory. The best they could do was to prepare a long report based on documents and interviews with eyewitnesses. The report of the Observation Committee and the later reports of the U.N. special representative on Hungary, Sir Leslie Munro, did serve to keep interest in the Hungarian cause alive. Yet the sum total of all these efforts in no way altered the Soviet and Hungarian positions. Instead, the introduction before the U.N. Credentials Committee of the nonrecognition, nonrefusal formula that "the Committee take no decision regarding the credentials submitted on behalf of the representatives of Hungary" was crucial to the shaping up of the foreign relations of the Kádár government.

In February 1957, when the Credentials Committee accepted this important ruling, not only the position of the superpowers but the issues involved in the question of Hungary as well became clear. The Soviet Union, knowing that the United Nations was not in a position to recommend sanctions against its action in Hungary, flatly rejected any cooperation with the world organization. On the other hand, the United States had committed itself to using the forum of the United Nations to mobilize the moral forces of world opinion against the Soviet invasion of Hungary. At U.S. insistence, the Credentials Committee was to withhold recognition of the Hungarian representatives' credentials as long as the question of Hungary was being debated on the floor of the world organization. In making use of this new tactic, the United States had demonstrated that one of the superpowers in the United Nations could initiate limited action in opposition to the other superpower with a reasonable expectation of success.

— 2 —

The Hundred Flowers Movement
and the Hungarian Revolution

Looking back at the 1956 Soviet military intervention in Hungary from a vantage point of more than fifteen years, we can only characterize the Kremlin move as the final act of a superpower's emergency diplomacy. Such emergency diplomacy does not, of course, exist in a vacuum; it is directly or indirectly, sometimes even subtly and unwittingly, influenced by events far removed from the origins of the crisis. The Hungarian revolution, for instance, represents the first occasion on which China emerged from her isolation to manifest a real interest in the affairs of Eastern Europe. This interest created an international backdrop for the more immediate diplomatic maneuverings, and it foreshadowed the constantly developing conflict of interest and the deepening rift between China and Russia.

During the fifties China was represented in Budapest by Ambassador Ho Te-ching, a man of supple intellect and considerable diplomatic experience. In 1955 and 1956, when the fortunes of the Stalinist-inclined Rákosi-Gerö group were already clearly on the wane, Ho Te-ching began quietly to establish connections with the opposition, composed of the nationalist communist group within the party. According to the customary practice in the socialist countries, he represented both the Chinese state and the Chinese Communist Party. Not only did he enjoy free access to the highest Hungarian party circles and regular contact with the Foreign Ministry, but he had at his disposal an extensive intelligence apparatus that earned the Chinese embassy the reputation of being the best-informed foreign post in the Hungarian capital. The Chinese cultural attaché, who spoke Hungarian fluently, maintained contact with Hungarian intellectuals. In 1956 correspondents of the New China News Agency and the Chinese exchange students in Budapest reported to their ambassador regularly on activities both of the revolutionary Petöfi Circle and at the universities. The ambassador himself traveled widely in the country, becoming acquainted with the local party secretaries, the councilmen, and other officials in the towns and villages. He was also prominent in the social life of the Hungarian capital, with his two cooks and his staff helping to provide a lavish Oriental atmosphere. While the Soviet embassy made it a practice to invite Hungarian Stakanovists (elite workers) to its receptions, Ho was more interested in entertaining leading writers, artists, economists, and newspapermen, even those who were not outspoken supporters of the regime.

Through these various sources Ho learned in 1956 that Rákosi's leading political opponent, Imre Nagy, was working in forced retirement on a political position paper entitled "In Defense of the New Course."[1] When Nagy forwarded one copy of the document to the Central Committee of the Hungarian Party and another to Yuri Andropov, the Soviet ambassador, Ho Te-ching managed to obtain a copy from a friend who was working in the secretariat at Communist Party headquarters. Understandably, he paid special attention to the chapter dealing with Chinese foreign policy, in which Imre Nagy discussed the Bandung Conference and stated that "the five basic principles of the Bandung Conference (otherwise known as Panch Shila) cannot be limited to the capitalist system or the battle between the two systems, but must be extended to the relations between the countries within the democratic and socialist camp."[2]

By the summer of 1956 Ho had become aware that Mao's Hundred Flowers Movement was arousing widespread pro-Chinese sympathy among Hungarian intellectuals and students and, in order to take full advantage of this growing sentiment, he made a special effort to provide the Hungarian press and radio with plenty of information on the new movement and on developments at the Eighth Congress of the Chinese Communist Party. As a result, many of the dissenting Hungarian intellectuals came to believe sincerely that the slogan of the movement, "Let a hundred flowers bloom, let a hundred schools of thought contend!" was a true reflection of the intentions of the Chinese Communist Party leadership. This delusion led a large percentage of the revolutionaries in Budapest to hope for Chinese support during the uprising. On the streets of Budapest, where people were constantly discussing the turbulent events of the day, the sentiment was echoed and reechoed that "the Chinese are with us." The organ of the revolutionary writers, *Irodalmi Ujság* [Literary Gazette], stated on 2 November that "the West and the East are on our side; America has proclaimed faith in our cause as clearly as have powerful nations like China and India."[3]

Hopes of Chinese support, however, were soon followed by bitter disappointment. As the events of 1956 proved, the Chinese not only supported but advocated Soviet intervention in Hungary. On 23 October, the day the uprising began, the Chinese ambassador ordered the iron-grill gates of his embassy locked and seldom left the building until 4 November, the day the Kádár government arrived in Budapest. Many functionaries of the Rákosi regime, relying on their old friendship with the ambassador, sought refuge at the Chinese embassy during the fighting. Ho Te-ching sent word through his Chinese doorman, however, that they should go to the Soviet embassy instead. The seemingly quiet Chinese embassy was, in fact, in full-scale operation and there is no doubt that Ho not only knew what was happening but was also keeping Peking *au courant*. Observing the situation carefully, Ho was forced to conclude that communist control over Hungary had ceased and that Imre Nagy's policy of coalition with bourgeois parties would lead to the restoration of capitalism. In the final days of October 1956 the ambassador became convinced that Soviet delegate Anastas Mikoyan's dealings with the Imre Nagy government and the Soviet troop withdrawal from the Hungarian capital had been grave miscalculations. He was certain that only military intervention could save the situation. Accordingly, Ho asked Peking to put pressure on the Kremlin for a second Soviet military action against Hungary. Peking shared his view, with the result that Mao Tse-tung sent urgent messages to Khrushchev pressing for prompt action.

On 1 October Ho Te-ching was informed officially of Hungary's withdrawal from the Warsaw Pact, as were the heads of other diplomatic missions accredited in Budapest. The Chinese ambassador was received by Prime Minister Imre Nagy and First Deputy Foreign Minister György Heltai. Closeted with Imre Nagy for two hours, he listened politely while Nagy explained to him that as a consequence of the Soviet violation of the Warsaw Pact his government had decided to withdraw from the Pact and to declare Hungary's neutrality. The ambassador on his part asked detailed questions concerning the new Russian troop movements, the temper of public opinion, the composition of the political parties, and the regime's plans for the future. Once his questions had been answered, Ho promised that he would report immediately to Peking everything he had learned. Taking the whole picture into consideration, Heltai was left with the impression that Ho was sympathetic to the Hungarian cause.[4]

On 4 November, after the revolution had been crushed by the Soviet army, the Chinese ambassador appeared on the scene once more, this time offering China's advice and assistance to the new Hungarian regime. He and his military attaché were especially interested in the rapid formation of the workers' militia and the purge and reorganization of the Hungarian army. The Soviets on the sidelines eyed the Chinese activity with suspicion.

With a keen political sense, Ho had established contact even before the revolution with those communist leaders who had been released from Rákosi's prisons. With unerring instinct the ambassador had singled out in particular János Kádár, who, rehabilitated in 1954, had become first secretary of the party for the thirteenth district of Budapest and later county secretary of Pest. In July 1956 the Kremlin had replaced Rákosi with another of Stalin's former appointees, Ernö Gerö, and had agreed that the anti-Stalinist national faction of the Hungarian communists would be represented in the Politburo by János Kádár.[5]

While Gerö was preoccupied with building up his position within the party, the task of representing the Hungarian party at the Chinese Eighth Party Congress in Peking had fallen to Kádár. Kádár attended also the Chinese National Holiday celebration that followed on 1 October 1956.[6] The Chinese leadership paid special attention to this rising personality in the Hungarian party hierarchy. Kádár was received by Mao Tse-tung himself; and Chou En-lai, Liu Shao-ch'i, Chen I, and Peng Te-huai all held lengthy conversations with him. They displayed a keen interest in his prison experiences and in his views on the current situation in Hungary.

A year later, in October 1957, Kádár once again visited Peking and stood on the right side of Mao Tse-tung before the throngs at Peking's T'ien-an-men (Gate of Heavenly Peace). He had by then become first secretary of the Hungarian Party and the most celebrated East European leader, for he personified the victory of communist rule in Hungary.

Much had taken place in China during the period between Kádár's first and second visits to Peking. The Hundred Flowers Movement, launched by Chairman Mao in early 1956, had bloomed and then wilted. The "forced march" of collectivization, which in the course of one year would affect some 110 million households, was already well on its way.[7] This rapid transformation shook Chinese society to its very foundation and inevitably created a great deal of tension and political dissent. Realizing the gravity of this domestic turmoil, the Chinese communist party leadership labored to bring some degree of stability to the internal situation in the months before embarking on the final collectivization of the countryside.

Chairman Mao had evidently hoped that the Hundred Flowers Movement would release tensions and gain for his regime support of the skeptical intelligentsia. As a matter of fact, during the spring and summer of 1956 the intellectuals did respond, though somewhat cautiously, to Mao's appeal for open criticism of the regime; and the party chairman, seeing the situation well under control, continued to encourage the growth of the movement.[8]

The shattering repercussions of the Soviet Twentieth Party Congress, the Polish events, the Hungarian revolution, and Russia's handling of the crisis in Eastern Europe, however, helped to increase tensions within China. Eventually this mounting pressure led Mao Tse-tung, early in 1957, to supplement the Hundred Flowers with the seemingly liberal Rectification Campaign. Although this venture sounded like a reiteration of Mao's earlier call for open criticism, it was, according to his later testimony, an elaborate plan to ferret out and eliminate the enemies of the regime.

In his February speech initiating the Rectification Campaign, Mao emphasized the fact that the Chinese leadership "had succeeded in suppressing counterrevolution quite thoroughly" following the 1949 take-over. Arguing that historical conditions in China were different from those in other socialist countries, he explained that the Chinese "have been able to keep their mistakes within bounds because it has been their policy to draw a sharp line between their people and their enemies."[9]

By early May 1957, the Hundred Flowers Movement was bringing forth complaints and criticism from intellectuals all over China. As one might expect, dissent was most rampant in university circles. The best-documented anti-party demonstrations occurred at Peking University. In the course of the student debate, the leading figure in this fracas—a student named Lin Hsi-ling—posed several intriguing questions about the "cult of personality" and the falsifications of Soviet communist party history. She also alleged that when "Chairman Mao proposed in his speech the principle regarding the correct handling of contradictions among people, 80 per cent of the high-ranking cadres disapproved of it." Lin Hsi-ling ended with the statement, "Our objective is crystal clear: to establish genuine socialism, to lead the life of real people."[10] Particularly strong criticism came from right-wing students. A group known as the Hundred Flowers Society demanded a "new interpretation of capitalism."[11] Voicing the opinion of this group, Ko Pei-chi, a scholar at China People's University, went so far as to say, "The masses want to overthrow the party and kill the communists."[12]

The fiercest anti-party criticism, however, came from the students and professors at Shanghai and Wuhan Universities.[13] Organizing themselves into an anti-party force, the students at Wuhan University, backed by many of the faculty, published the *Ho-yen pao* [Fire Journal]. According to Nationalist Chinese sources, the Wuhan University Students' Association posted slogans on the streets publicizing the aims of their movement.[14] On 5 June the Dean of the University, Liu Chen, tried to arrest the rightist elements, but the students launched a strike that subsequently spread to the Wuhan Commercial School and other schools. A week later, street demonstrations followed in which students shouted "Down with Chairman Mao," "Welcome the return of the Kuomintang," and "Russians, get out." Finally, the students rushed to the party committee headquarters of Hanyang City,[15] beat up cadres, and destroyed the offices. They left a huge Chinese Nationalist flag drawn on the school grounds.[16]

The next day, following a futile attempt to enter the arsenal, the students organized fighting groups and tried to kidnap the Hanyang party secretary. Traveling to the countryside to mobilize support among the peasants, one group of students distributed literature bearing such titles as "The Manifesto to the People of the Nation" and "The Manifesto to the People of Wuhan." The students also sent delegations to the second and third high schools of Hanyang and to various other schools in Wuchang and Hankow in order to gain support. They had planned to attack the prison, where the revolutionaries hoped to seize arms and ammunition for the assault and to further their struggle. The Wuhan communist party organization, however, mobilized workers and retired soldiers (probably the People's Militia) and forced the students back to their campuses. All public buildings and factories in Wuhan were fully guarded throughout the night. Step by step the rebellious students were quelled. In the months that followed, an anti-rightist campaign methodically and ruthlessly crushed all signs of dissent here and throughout the country.

When Hungarian First Party Secretary János Kádár paid his second visit to Peking on 1 October 1957 to participate in the National Day celebration, he openly endorsed the suppression of rightist elements in China. He represented himself as a hard-line revolutionary who had learned the lesson of class struggle from the "imperialist attack" of 1956. He stated accordingly that in Hungary events had taught the Hungarian people that "the counterrevolution cannot be handled mercifully—one has to fight against it."[17] He added for emphasis that "the international workingclass struggle against the rightists showed the same experience as ours.... Imre Nagy and others of his kind did not care to criticize the mistakes, but opposed the party, attacked the unity of the party as well as the whole system of the dictatorship of the proletariat." In direct reference to the recent suppression of open criticism in China, Kádár underlined Mao Tse-tung's thesis that "the contradictions within the people could become, under certain circumstances, irreconcilable and antagonistic."

Although the crushing of the Wuhan student rebellion marked the end of the Hundred Flowers Movement, the memory of the campaign lived on. Some indication of how Mao viewed the impact of Hungarian events on policies in China during this crucial year was given two years later when a Hungarian party and government delegation, led by Prime Minister Münnich, visited China from 27 April to 7 May 1959.[18] After spending several days in Peking, the delegation flew to Shanghai, Wuhan, and Hankow. The delegation attended the 1 May celebration and held discussions with high officials of the Chinese party and government. The highlight of the program was to be the meeting with Mao. Nobody had the faintest notion, however, when or where the meeting would occur. The Chinese chief of protocol, Yu Pei-wen, when asked where Mao was, simply answered that Comrade Mao was somewhere in the countryside hard at work on ideological and philosophical matters. Károly Kiss, the number two man of the delegation, put similar queries to his opposite number, a member of the Chinese Central Committee, Yeh Chi-chuang, but received the same reply. Toward the end of the visit everyone had given up hope of seeing Mao. Prime Minister Münnich, feeling that mishandling of the affair had been a personal insult, was in a gloomy mood. Even Stalin, "the living god," he noted, had been less mysterious than Mao.

On the third day before the visit came to an end, 5 May, no official program had been planned for the Hungarian delegation. The Chinese deputy foreign minister, Tseng Yung-chuan, and Ambassador Ho Te-ching took the visitors on a sightseeing tour around Peking. At noontime everyone went to a popular restaurant for Peking duck. Suddenly, in the midst of the meal, ten or fifteen Chinese security officers rushed into the dining room (for security reasons it had been cleared of other guests before the arrival of the foreign visitors). The leader of the group whispered something to Tseng, who told Münnich that Chairman Mao was waiting for the delegation. With visible displeasure the old Hungarian statesman, who had a long-standing reputation as a gourmet, replied: "The boss can wait a few minutes. I waited long enough to hear from him." The security officers, however, took a somewhat different view of the matter, and in two minutes the delegation was on its way toward the Tien-an-men. In another few minutes it had passed through the gardens of the palace and at least six or seven well-guarded gates to be greeted by Mao Tse-tung at his residence in the Chung-nan-hai.

Mao Tse-tung first presented his entourage. "We have a new president," he said, pointing toward Liu Shao-ch'i, who stood up.[19] After Mao had introduced Chou En-lai, Chen I, and the other Chinese present, Münnich did the same for his party. Tea was served to the guests, but Mao and the Chinese leaders drank only hot water. "We are used to drinking hot water since the time of the Long March," he explained.

The conversation began somewhat haltingly. Münnich conveyed greetings from Kádár and from the Hungarian people and expressed the gratitude of the Hungarian party and government for the economic and moral support given by Mao Tse-tung. Then he explained that the situation in Hungary had stabilized and that the remnants of the "1956 counterrevolution" had been liquidated. He noted that the Hungarian communists had caused serious problems for the socialist camp and that without their friends they could not have averted a capitalist take-over.

Mao replied by insisting that, on the contrary, the Hungarian communists had done a great service to the international communist movement and that the Chinese had profited from their experiences. He noted that the Chinese leadership had watched the 1956 events closely and had evaluated them daily. Mao Tse-tung pointed to Ho Te-ching, who was sitting behind Foreign Minister Chen I, and declared that the ambassador's reports and recommendations had been most helpful in assessing and dealing with the rapidly developing situation in Hungary during 1956. He recalled that at the end of October of that year the Chinese embassy in Budapest had reported that the counterrevolution was gaining ground at an alarming rate, and had warned that if the Soviet Union should fail to liquidate the Imre Nagy government, the restoration of capitalism in Hungary would be inevitable. On the basis of this and other information received from the various East European communist parties, Mao had sent an urgent message to the Kremlin asking Khrushchev for quick military action against the Hungarian revisionists. Mao mentioned that he had discounted the danger of any foreign intervention, or an American nuclear threat, for America was, after all, a paper tiger.[20]

The Chinese leadership had remained in close touch with the Soviet Presidium and had been relieved by the news that additional Soviet armed forces had been dispatched "to put Hungarian affairs in order." Mao said that he had endorsed the installation of Kádár because he had complete confidence in Kádár's ability and political judgment. He appreciated in particular the fact that Kádár had been the leader of the Hungarian communists during the Second World War. During this discussion Mao described his long-standing argument with Stalin over the question of leadership in Eastern Europe. Stalin preferred to install leaders like Rákosi who had lived for many years in the Soviet Union and had lost contact with the realities of their homelands, while Mao considered local leaders like Kádár to be the most effective.

Mao spoke in a low voice in the Hunan dialect, using short, crisp sentences. His interpreter, a young girl who had studied Hungarian literary history in Budapest for several years, was also from Hunan Province and translated Mao's words with amazing clarity, a fact which the Hungarian delegation's own translator noted.

Following his remarks about the Hungarian situation, Mao spoke at length about the Hundred Flowers Movement. He described the campaign as a long and complicated process designed to release the tension that had been building up in Chinese society after the death of Stalin. He claimed that originally the movement had produced good results: constructive criticism and lively debates had mobilized the masses and intellectuals. According to his interpretation, however, rightist elements, hidden in the masses, were only rarely attempting to make their voices heard. During the movement's early stages, the party could not be sure who were its enemies and who were its supporters. The outcome of the Hungarian "counterrevolution" and the events in Poland had convinced him that in such a state of affairs, contradictions among the people "must be handled in a correct way." He continued to refer frequently to the interrelationship between Eastern Europe and China.

Following the Twentieth Soviet Party Congress, Mao explained, the Chinese leadership had been forced to pay attention to the Chinese right wing, and he added that the only way to flush them from their hiding places was to push the Hundred Flowers Movement to its fullest extent. During the first few months of 1957, the party repeatedly asked the intellectuals for criticism; and eventually the rightists, voicing their anti-party propaganda, began to appear openly in the public debate. Some of the local party leaders wanted to cut short this controversy, seeing Kuomintang agents everywhere, but Mao decided to wait for a while and see. In his opinion, Chiang Kai-shek was not powerful enough to influence any mass movement in China.

With great self-confidence Mao explained how in 1957 the party had launched the Rectification Campaign at Peking University and in Wuhan. In Wuhan, he said, some students and professors had attempted to transform the discussions into street fights, hoping to capture the party building, to open the prisons, and to capture arms, just as the "counterrevolutionaries" had done in Hungary. Profiting from the Hungarian experience, however, the party leadership retained full control of the masses and quickly isolated the rebels. As Mao noted, the comrades in Wuhan had known what to do. They had simply explained to the workers in the big factories the danger of counterrevolution, reminding them of their miserable past when foreign imperialists and Chiang Kai-shek had exploited them, and when famine had killed countless numbers of the Chinese people.[21] The Wuhan party leaders had also been able to mobilize the workers to crush the uprising in a two-day long street fight without calling for intervention from the special police or army units. The "little Hungary," as Mao called the Wuhan incident, should be considered important for the light it shed on the contradictions within the people. As he pointed out, the Chinese leadership had learned not only who the friends and enemies of the regime were, but that discussions must be conducted only "in the interest of the people."

— 3 —

Deterioration of Hungarian-American Relations

The conversation between Murphy of the United States and Zádor of Hungary on 27 October 1956 was the last diplomatic exchange of views between the two governments for several years. After the Soviet military intervention in 1956, high-ranking officials of the U.S. State Department received no Hungarian diplomats, and U.S. diplomats in Hungary had no access to officials there. It was only when protest notes were to be handed over that American diplomats were invited to the Hungarian Foreign Ministry, and the same rule applied to the Hungarians in Washington. And just as U.S. contacts with the Kádár regime were channeled through the Foreign Ministry's protocol department, the Hungarian diplomats communicated with Washington only through the State Department's Hungarian desk officer.

The U.S. legation in Budapest was constantly surrounded by plainclothes agents who checked and interrogated everybody who entered the building. In the hope that Cardinal Mindszenty might give up his self-imposed exile and leave his refuge there,[1] two, sometimes three, carloads of secret police waited patiently at the entrances. By these and other police tactics the U.S. diplomats in Budapest were almost hermetically sealed off from the outside world.

Nor was the life of the Hungarian diplomats in the United States an easy one. Surrounded by hostile Americans, they were continually taunted by the man on the street demanding to know why the Russians had raped Hungary. At the United Nations American and Hungarian officials avoided one another. The guest list at social functions of the Hungarian legation was made up for the most part of gas station employees who serviced the legation's cars, some members of the Communist Party of the U.S.A., Khrushchev's American "friend" Cyrus Eaton, a few newspapermen, and diplomats of the socialist countries stationed in Washington. The Hungarian Mission to the United Nations in New York was picketed on every possible occasion by Hungarian refugees and by members of the Organization of the Captive Nations.

At the same time, in Budapest, harassments and petty incidents, as well as major political confrontations, were contributing almost daily to the already tense situation in Hungarian-U.S. relations. Some of the employees of the Budapest Central Post Office, for example, who wanted to prove their loyalty to the new Kádár regime and their "international solidarity" with the Soviet Union, often interrupted, without instructions, the American legation's telegraphic communication line and refused to transmit coded material. After a strong State Department protest, this practice was stopped by higher Hungarian authorities.[2]

Hungarian postal authorities created still another diplomatic *affaire*. They discovered that personal letters coming from the United States bore the stamp "Support your crusade for freedom." On the recommendation of the Minister of Posts and Communication and with the approval of party headquarters, the Foreign Ministry addressed a protest note to the American legation in Budapest. The Hungarian protest note stated that the American stamps were "obviously intended to incite the counterrevolutionary elements defeated last November to further subversive activity." The American legation rejected the charge.[3]

An additional source of friction arose when the Foreign Ministry, at the urging of Hungarian counterintelligence, pressed for a one-third reduction in the American legation's diplomatic and administrative personnel. The Hungarians particularly wished to get rid of the legation's marine guard, which patrolled the corridors and offices of the building after working hours, making it virtually impossible to install wiretapping devices. Fearing American retaliation, the Hungarian military and civilian intelligence opposed this plan, since a decrease in their agents working abroad under diplomatic cover would handicap their activity, too.

After an interministerial debate, the counterintelligence service, which enjoyed Soviet support, prevailed. Emphasizing the importance of the internal security of the country and the "dangerous subversive activity" of the U.S. legation, the minister of the Interior and the foreign minister worked out a joint draft proposal for the Politburo. This draft, favoring a reduction in personnel, the Politburo accepted without change. Hence on 25 May 1957 the Foreign Ministry received instructions from party headquarters to deliver the note to the American legation. Washington was left with no choice but to comply with this embarrassing and unfriendly request.[4]

In the spring of 1957 both Americans and Hungarians regarded as routine matters the expulsion from Hungary of Assistant Military Attaché Captain Thomas R. Gleason and from the United States of Assistant Military and Air Attaché First Lieutenant Károly Mészáros.[5] The accusation of "open espionage" made against the American captain—couched in routine phrases—simply meant that the American assistant military attaché had come too close to Soviet barracks and military bases installed in Hungarian territory.

On 9 April, the same day that the Hungarian expulsion note was handed over, Mészáros received instructions from Budapest to prepare to leave. It was assumed that he, being of the same rank as the captain, would be declared persona non grata by the Americans—an expectation that proved correct. American retaliation came soon.[6] Despite public excitement, however, this incident had no special effect on American-Hungarian relations. More disturbing to the Hungarian government were the annual White House, State Department, and other official statements commemorating the October 23 revolution.

On 23 October 1957 the internal situation in Hungary was still fluid. The open hostility of the population to the Soviet occupation and to the Kádár regime forced the Soviet and Hungarian authorities to take special measures. On the first anniversary of the Hungarian revolution, the Soviet forces stationed in Hungary were put on alert, and border guards received orders to prevent, at all costs, the infiltration of foreign agents across the Austrian-Hungarian and Yugoslav-Hungarian borders. Hungarian legations all over the world were instructed to deny or postpone, with few exceptions, the visa requests of foreign correspondents and Western diplomats. Reinforced police and workers' militia units patrolled the streets of Budapest and other cities in Hungary day and night. Official buildings, including the radio station where the uprising had started a year before, were heavily guarded. Special security forces were dispatched to the neighborhoods of universities, industrial centers, churches, and cemeteries. In addition, Western legations were under careful surveillance, and the jamming of Hungarian language programs on the Voice of America, Radio Free Europe, and the BBC was stepped up.

At this time when internal tensions were high, the statements of President Eisenhower and of the American U.N. representative, Henry Cabot Lodge, commemorating the first anniversary of the 23 October revolution understandably irritated Hungarian party and government circles.[7] The party headquarters promptly instructed the Foreign Ministry to study the White House statement carefully and to prepare an answer. Without delay the leaders of the Foreign Ministry unanimously agreed that a sharp protest note should be delivered to the U.S. government. The Foreign Ministry hard liners at the department level wanted to sever diplomatic relations with the United States, but their extreme view was discounted by Kádár. Instead the text of the originally planned protest note was worked out. The draft pointed out that the Hungarian government had learned with indignation of President Eisenhower's 23 October statement. The Hungarian government considered it an attempt to encourage counterrevolutionary elements in the country and another instance of U.S. interference in the internal affairs of Hungary. It was on this second point that the Ministry of Foreign Affairs proposed to lodge its strongest protest, asking for guarantees from the American government that such provocation would not be repeated in the future. If such guarantees were not given, the United States would have to bear responsibility for the consequences.

This draft was forwarded to party headquarters, where the Department of International Relations coordinated the matter with the Soviet embassy in Budapest.[8] Soviet officials concurred regarding the gravity of the American President's "provocative act." They expressed the view, however, that a Hungarian protest would only underline the importance of Eisenhower's statement and might hamper negotiations that were then in progress for a new cultural, technical, and educational exchange agreement between the United States and the Soviet Union—the first such projected program since the 1956 events in Hungary.[9] The Soviet argument prevailed, the draft note was shelved, and instead of filing a diplomatic complaint the Hungarian U. N. mission in New York was instructed to issue a communiqué in which only Henry Cabot Lodge's 23 October commemorative statement was condemned as an intervention in the internal affairs of Hungary. President Eisenhower was not mentioned at all.[10]

The most serious in this sequence of diplomatic incidents involved the American minister to Hungary, Edward Thomson Wailes, who became a victim of circumstance and was forced to leave Budapest as a result of Hungarian pressure. Wailes had arrived in the Hungarian capital on 2 November 1956 with instructions to present his credentials to the Hungarian government. At that time Imre Nagy was still prime minister and most of the Soviet troops had been withdrawn from Budapest. When two days later the Soviet forces ousted the Nagy government and installed Kádár, the American minister refrained from presenting his credentials as a form of political protest. During the next three months Hungarian Foreign Ministry officials often inquired when Wailes would present his letter of accreditation. The most aggressive official in this regard was Károly Csatordai, the chief of protocol, who had been indecisive during the days of the 1956 "counterrevolution" but who afterward demonstrated open personal hostility toward the American diplomats. The U.S. legation replied evasively that the minister had not as yet received instructions from Washington.

This ambiguous situation finally came to an end. On 21 February 1957 the U.N. General Assembly approved the U.S. motion that "the Credentials Committee take no decision regarding the credentials submitted on behalf of the representative of Hungary."[11] The next day the Kádár government "requested the Government of the United States of America to remove Mr. Wailes from the Territory of Hungary if he does not wish to present his letter of credence."[12] On 27 February Minister Wailes left Budapest; subsequently, in a note, the U.S. legation reminded the Foreign Ministry that in New York the U.N. General Assembly had "taken no action to accept the credentials of the Hungarian delegation."[13]

The U.S. government's action at the United Nations in regard to the Hungarian delegation's credentials and the departure of Wailes from Budapest indicated that Hungarian-American relations had reached a new low. From that time on, the American legation in Budapest, as well as the Hungarian legation in Washington, continued to function under a chargé d'affaires *ad interim*.

— 4 —

Summit Conference Diplomacy and the Execution of Imre Nagy

Although Hungarian-American relations continued at a low ebb, the prospect for easing international tensions seemed somewhat brighter in early 1958. The voluminous correspondence between the U.S.S.R. and the Western powers for an East-West summit conference, initiated in 1957 by Premier Nikolai A. Bulganin, continued. Thousands of words were exchanged between the head of the Soviet government and President Eisenhower, Prime Minister Harold Macmillan, and other Western leaders. In mid-December 1957, Bulganin sent notes to all U.N. member nations, and also separately to the fifteen NATO countries and to Switzerland, setting forth the Soviet government's proposals for the suspension of nuclear tests, for a demilitarized zone in Central Europe, and for a nonaggression pact between NATO and the Warsaw Treaty Organization. He followed this up in January 1958 with further notes to the NATO countries and to neutral Austria and Sweden, as well as to nonaligned India and Egypt, proposing a summit conference of heads of government, preferably in Switzerland during the early months of 1958.[1]

Observers in the West watched the "Soviet peace offensive" with caution. Many East Europeans hoped that a nonaggression pact between NATO and the Warsaw Treaty Organization would lead to a collective security arrangement in Europe, and that a demilitarized zone in Central Europe would lead to a Soviet troop withdrawal from their occupied countries. For the same reason, the creation of an atom-free zone in Germany, Poland, and Czechoslovakia, proposed by Polish Foreign Minister Adam Rapacki, received official endorsement and popular support in the other bloc countries. At the same time, East European diplomats in Peking learned from high officials of the Chinese Foreign Ministry that the Chinese leadership suspected the Soviet Union of conspiring to sell out China's interests by excluding her from a summit conference.

On the other hand, the Western powers stressed the points they were interested in bringing up for discussion. In a letter dated 12 January 1958 President Eisenhower suggested to the Soviet premier that the United States and the U.S.S.R. agree to relinquish the veto power in the Security Council; that they proceed toward bringing about the reunification of Germany by free elections; that the promise given to the people of Eastern Europe by the Yalta Agreement, that they would be given the opportunity to choose their own form of government, be fulfilled; that the United States and the U.S.S.R. agree that outer space may be used only for peaceful purposes; and that steps be taken toward nuclear disarmament and the cessation of nuclear arms production, under effective safeguards and inspection.[2]

Premier Bulganin expressed disappointment at the U.S. proposal to abandon the veto power. He considered this suggestion a ''departure from the unanimity principle of the Great Powers in the Security Council'' (which was, in the view of the Soviet government, the mainstay of the very existence of the United Nations). Bulganin disagreed with the American proposals relating to Germany and Eastern Europe, insisting that the reunification of Germany could be achieved only by a rapprochement between the two German states—the German Democratic Republic and the Federal Republic of Germany—and that ''the position of the Soviet Government does not require any kind of clarification'' and ''any kind of polemics on this question would not be of any benefit.''[3]

Despite the distrust and unwillingness to negotiate a compromise so evident in the diplomatic correspondence, neither side wanted to cut the dialogue short. In March 1958, after three months of bargaining, the Soviet government reversed its previous stand and consented to a foreign ministers' meeting preparatory to the summit conference.[4] The long preparatory discussions of the foreign ministers' meeting resulted only in an exchange of memorandums and a restatement of already known positions.[5] To break the deadlock, the Kremlin policy makers decided at the Warsaw Treaty Organization Political Consultative Committee meeting in May 1958 to reduce their armed forces by 119,000 men. As a further gesture, the Soviet Union withdrew all its troops from Rumania and one division from Hungary.[6] The West, however, was apparently not influenced by the Russian action.

On 11 June Khrushchev, in one of a series of letters to Eisenhower, asked the United States again for a joint effort to ''prevent disruption of the Summit Conference and clear the way to it of artificial obstacles.''[7] This message, like all the Soviet notes that had preceded it, stressed that Eastern Europe could not be a subject of discussion. ''We have repeatedly stated that we consider it impossible to raise such a question at an international conference,'' Khrushchev wrote to President Eisenhower. Khrushchev opposed also the discussion of German reunification at the summit meeting. However, the Soviet leader hoped that the United States would be ready for discussion of a nonaggression pact, as had recently been proposed to the NATO countries by the Warsaw Treaty Organization.

Eisenhower, Macmillan, and de Gaulle still considered the circumstances unfavorable for a summit conference despite the Soviet leader's written message. Had a summit meeting materialized somewhere along the way, the last in the long series of Hungarian tragedies might have been averted.

THE "CASE" AGAINST IMRE NAGY

Five days after President Eisenhower received the letter from Khrushchev, 16 June, the Hungarian Wire Service (MTI) and Radio Budapest announced: "Hungarian legal authorities have concluded the proceeding in the case of the leading group of persons who, on 23 October 1956, started a counterrevolutionary armed uprising against the legitimate order of the Hungarian People's Republic." The People's Tribunal of the Supreme Court had found the defendants guilty and passed the following sentences: Imre Nagy (former prime minister), Pál Maléter (former defense minister), Miklós Gimes, and József Szilágyi (both close associates of Imre Nagy) were sentenced to death. Sándor Kopácsi (former police chief of Budapest) was sentenced to life imprisonment. Sentences ranging from five to twelve years were passed upon Zoltán Tildy (former president of the Republic), Ferenc Donáth (close friend and associate of Nagy), Ferenc Jánosi (clergyman, son-in-law of Imre Nagy), and Miklós Vásárhelyi (journalist). "No appeals were admissible. The death sentences have been carried out."[8]

The Hungarian Foreign Ministry immediately dispatched to its legations and embassies abroad an abbreviated version of the communiqué. The cable was to serve as a general guideline for the ministry's diplomatic personnel. It reported the case as follows:

Twenty months of intensive investigation of the Imre Nagy group's role had revealed its conspiratorial activity before, during, and after the counterrevolution.

1. The Imre Nagy group had started its anti-state activity as early as 1955.

2. The court had examined the secret documents written by Imre Nagy himself[9] and found that he had characterized the people's democracy as "degenerated bonapartist power." He had advocated the restoration of the multi-party system, and had undermined Hungary's defense alliance by withdrawing from the Warsaw Pact.

3. Imre Nagy and his accomplices had organized a political club (the Petöfi Club) through secret channels. Here they had provoked anti-regime discussion to prepare the counterrevolution.

4. The Imre Nagy group had initiated the well-known 23 October demonstration. The group members had directed the armed rebellion.

5. Imre Nagy had formed an alliance with the most reactionary fascist elements. He had rehabilitated the condemned Cardinal József Mindszenty.

6. The conspirators' group had been in contact with the British military attaché in Budapest, who had taken part in the direction of the counterrevolution. The Americans

had smuggled small arms into the country with the help of the Red Cross.

7. Imre Nagy had eliminated the legal authorities and had created revolutionary committees and workers' councils with the help of "bourgeois fascist elements."

8. The judiciary proceedings proved that Imre Nagy had instigated the continuation of armed resistance. He had instructed the Central Workers' Council—from the Yugoslav embassy in Budapest, where he had fled after his regime collapsed—to hamper the normalization of the situation by strikes.

9. The Imre Nagy group had disorganized the Hungarian army on 4 November 1956 and had asked openly for the Western powers' armed intervention.

The head of each Hungarian diplomatic mission received instructions to hold staff meetings at which he would provide background information concerning the trial and sentences. The ambassadors received orders to brief the local communist party's leadership, loyal émigré groups, intellectual circles, and other friendly groups. In anticipation of hostile demonstrations special security measures were taken, and diplomats and other embassy personnel were not allowed to go into the cities without protection. Legations in the Arab world were supplied with additional information about Imre Nagy's "Jewish origin." The Hungarian representatives in the Third World were to convince the politicians and intellectuals that Nagy had coordinated the timing of the counterrevolution with the tripartite aggression of the colonialist and neocolonialist powers against the Suez Canal so as to divert world attention from this strike. Finally, the diplomatic missions in the West were called upon to show "firmness and revolutionary vigilance against expected imperialist provocation."

WORLD REACTION TO THE EXECUTION

The judicial murder of the leader of the Hungarian revolution caused worldwide indignation and demonstrations against the Soviet Union and the Hungarian regime. Leading politicians from Washington to New Delhi reacted strongly. Labor leaders and intellectuals called the execution the starting point of a revival of Stalinist terror. Students in Paris held protest meetings, and demonstrators broke the windows of the Soviet embassies in the Scandinavian countries, in Bonn, and elsewhere. In a vigorous protest note to Budapest, the Yugoslav government charged that the Kádár regime had twice violated its guarantee of safe conduct to Nagy and his associates (the first time on 22 November 1956, when they were kidnapped upon emerging from the Yugoslav embassy in Budapest and sent into forced exile in Rumania, and now with the executions).[10]

The State Department in Washington issued a strong statement: "By this act the Soviet Union and the Soviet-imposed regime in Hungary have once more violated every principle of decency and must stand in judgment before the conscience of mankind."[11] Ambassador Henry Cabot Lodge compared the execution with the bloodiest days of Stalin. The United Nations Special Committee on the Problem of Hungary pointed out:

> The secret trials and executions were evidence of continued disregard for the General Assembly resolutions and for human rights. The record clearly showed that the action of the Hungarian Government in bringing Imre Nagy to trial was contrary to solemn assurances which János Kadar had previously given on behalf of the Hungarian Government, including those confirmed by letter to the Yugoslav Government.[12]

The wave of indignation and anger brought into the open the question of the Soviet Union's dependability in international politics. President Eisenhower declared that "the execution of Nagy and Maléter should alert the free world to the lack of confidence we are compelled to feel in the words and actions of these Communist imperialists."[13] U.S. legislators of both parties agreed with Senate Republican Leader William F. Knowland that the execution was further evidence that the West could not rely upon communist promises.[14] In London, Foreign Secretary Selwyn Lloyd deplored the execution of Imre Nagy and General Pál Maléter, declaring that the executions should be considered proof that in dealings with the Soviet Union "good faith has to be proved by deeds and not by words." He referred to the preparatory negotiations for the foreign ministers' meeting between the Western powers and the Soviet Union. "Our caution is now perhaps a little better understood," said the Foreign Secretary.[15]

The Kremlin seemed not too concerned about diplomatic reactions. Disregarding the numerous sharp attacks on the execution of Imre Nagy, Foreign Minister Gromyko selected for comment the relatively mild remarks made by Attorney General William P. Rogers at a youth rally in Chicago. Gromyko's complaint in this case took the form of an oral protest to U.S. Ambassador Llewellyn Thompson, charging that Rogers was trying to "ascribe to the Soviet Union interference in the activity of Hungarian organs of justice" and that the attorney general's statement exacerbated "the cold war."[16] When the State Department simply brushed aside the accusation, Soviet diplomacy did not press the matter.

At the United Nations, however, the Soviet stand was different. The executions revived the currently fading question of Hungary. On 21 June 1958, the Special Committee on the Problem of Hungary not only issued a statement concerning the execution of Imre Nagy, Pál Maléter, and two of their associates, but published a supplementary report on the circumstances of these executions.[17] Because the Soviet Union was blamed along with the Kádár regime for the repressive measures, Soviet diplomacy was compelled to step up its support of the representative of the Hungarian government at the United Nations.

Inside Hungary a deadly quiet prevailed. The population would neither revolt nor protest, for the memory of the crushed rebellion was too fresh.

Nevertheless, as concealed hostility against the foreign invader grew, the deep rift between the regime and the people widened. Many in the West questioned whether the Kremlin or the new regime really needed to take such brutal action two years after all resistance had ended. Was it not a miscalculation on the part of the Soviet and Hungarian communists to create a martyr, a national hero? Was it a shortsighted act of revenge, or a warning to other potential deviationists?

One consideration that may have been largely responsible for the decision to hold off the execution of the leaders of the revolution (i.e., from 1956 to 1958) was the developing power struggle that broke out inside the Kremlin in 1957. Between them, Malenkov, Molotov, and Shepilov opposed and outvoted Khrushchev and Mikoyan in the Presidium. During the course of the debate Malenkov sharply attacked Khrushchev, charging that Khrushchev had completely disrupted the international labor movement with his well-known anti-Stalin speech at the Twentieth Party Congress, and had thus triggered the Poznan riots and the Budapest uprising. There is certainly some merit in Malenkov's accusation, for Khrushchev's encouragement of liberalization in Hungary, as well as his attempt to prove that Stalinist leadership was no longer effective in Eastern Europe did stimulate the hopes of those who desired more changes both inside and outside the party. The Malenkov group, however, neglected to follow through with any immediate action against Khrushchev following the Presidium meeting. Taking quick advantage of the breathing space afforded him by this slip, Khrushchev arranged to have Marshal Zhukov transport the members of the Central Committee from all over the country to Moscow in military planes. While the Central Committee session was in progress inside the Kremlin, the tanks of Zhukov surrounded the meeting place and Khrushchev emerged triumphant. Malenkov, Molotov, Kaganovich, and Shepilov were expelled from the Presidium and from the Central Committee. Malenkov became a power station director in Siberia; Molotov was exiled to Outer Mongolia "as Soviet ambassador." Shepilov and Kaganovich also disappeared from public life. Throughout this period the Soviet leaders were too preoccupied with their own struggles for survival to concern themselves with the fate of Imre Nagy.

Khrushchev's "peace offensive" for a summit meeting was also an important factor in the postponement. Indeed, if plans for a summit conference had materialized, there is little chance that the execution would have taken place at all, at least in 1958. Because of the outbreak of Soviet-sponsored guerrilla warfare in Lebanon (which rapidly expanded into a Middle East crisis),[18] Eisenhower and the Western powers did not regard the circumstances as very propitious for a summit meeting. The stage was finally set to act out the last scene in the Hungarian tragedy.

It was true that these harsh measures resulted partly from the pressure of the hard liners in the international communist movement. But they derived mainly from the need to create a *memento mori* for Soviet supremacy in Eastern Europe. As Kádár explained in 1957 to an American senator: "The Russians were in mortal fear that Hungary would fall into the hands of the West ... and Hungary might be used by the West as a base to attack Russia."[19]

— 5 —

Kádár's Two-Pronged Plan of Action

During the summer of 1958 the party leadership in Hungary was fully aware that despite the explosive Middle East situation and other pressing international problems, the Hungarian question would be debated at length at the fall session of the United Nations General Assembly. The execution of Imre Nagy was bound to provoke violent attacks against the Hungarian regime. In anticipation of these reactions the Hungarian Politburo began intensive preliminary discussions aimed at setting the most effective course for influencing Hungarian as well as world opinion. The classical solution would have been to take no action at all and to maintain complete silence concerning the political trials. A second possibility would have been to discredit the Americans by exposing the "espionage work" in which the American legation at Budapest was still supposedly engaged. The Counterintelligence Service of the Ministry of the Interior had, indeed, made a habit of assembling precisely such "evidence" to be produced at opportune moments. The third choice involved the "soft line." This implied an end to political persecution in order to convince world opinion that the 1956 affair was about to become a closed issue. To this last course the "hard liners" in the Hungarian Politburo objected. They argued that it would create an impression of weakness and that the communist leadership in Budapest would appear to be caving in under hostile Western pressure. They feared internal disturbances also. Kádár, however, whose opinion always prevailed, felt that Hungary should combine two lines of action: (1) expose the Americans, and (2) assure the world organization in New York that with the execution of Imre Nagy all investigations and legal proceedings were henceforth terminated. The Politburo voted unanimously in favor of Kádár's middle-of-the-road position.[1]

42

THE CAMPAIGN AGAINST THE AMERICANS

Following this policy decision and high-level coordination with the Soviets, the state apparatus was set in motion. The Administrative Department of the Central Committee ordered the minister of the Interior to work out a plan for a press conference at which the government spokesman would detail to newsmen the illegal activities of American diplomats stationed in Budapest. Plans were made at the same time to set up an exhibition in the Parliament building where spy equipment, photos, and documents would be displayed. The Ministry of Foreign Affairs received instructions from the Central Committee's Department of International Relations to draft a protest note to the American legation. "Bem Square," as the Ministry of Foreign Affairs is called in Budapest, was also busy preparing Foreign Minister Dr. Endre Sik's speech for the coming U.N. General Assembly.

After several meetings the Ministry of the Interior, the Foreign Ministry, and the Government Information Bureau agreed on the timing of the various phases of action. The press conference was scheduled for 13 September, the protest note was to be delivered on the 20th, and the speech was to be given by the foreign minister at the U.N. shortly thereafter.[2] To avoid any leak, the American desk officer in the Foreign Ministry was not informed of the planned press conference, nor were the Government Information Bureau's officers aware of the protest note. The entire affair was handled at a high level. Only members of the Politburo, the head of the Department of International Relations of the Party, and the ministers and their deputies had a full picture of the plan. The Soviet chief adviser sitting in the Ministry of the Interior and the Soviet ambassador in Budapest were among the few persons involved in the action.

On 13 September László Gyáros, the permanent spokesman of the government, invited representatives of the Hungarian and foreign press to the Parliament building. There he read a prepared statement which elaborated at great length upon the subversive activities of Colonel Welwyn F. Dallam, Jr., Colonel James C. Todd, and his deputy, Thomas R. Gleason.

According to the statement, the American military and air attachés had directed a spy ring in Hungary and had made several secret reconnaissance trips around military barracks and airfields. Gyáros told about a Hungarian, Gábor Illési, who had spied for the Americans, but who had been captured, tried, and sentenced to death. Then he presented to the newsmen a Hungarian citizen, József Karsai, who allegedly had been trained in West Germany by the Americans and smuggled into Hungary. Karsai, "having a guilty conscience, gave himself up to the Hungarian authorities" when he crossed the border and then helped to capture other American spies. "Of course Karsai was pardoned," said Gyáros. "But traitors in American pay have been severely punished according to Hungarian law." The spokesman went on to "expose" several American spy centers in West Germany and Austria, among them the American History Research Institute in Munich.

To support his story, Gyáros asked several persons present, who had supposedly been recruited for or were to be included in American spy rings, to tell of their own experiences with the Americans. These people explained how they had been bribed by the American intelligence services and how some had been successfully recruited. The spy exhibit adjoining the press conference served the same purpose. Radio transmitters and receivers, pocket cameras, false identity cards, arms, and other objects—"all confiscated from captured spies"—were on display.

Stressing the importance of the entire exposé, Gyáros announced at the end of his press conference:

> The hostile spy activity is an integral part of the foreign policy of American aggressive circles. This policy tends to maintain and increase tension. Together with the Hungarian people, we condemn this warlike foreign policy and we denounce the Americans' subversive activity with indignation.[3]

A week later the Hungarian Ministry of Foreign Affairs delivered the protest note to the American Legation in Budapest. It read:

> The foreign policy of the government of the Hungarian People's Democracy is based on the peaceful coexistence of states with different social structures. Guided by this principle, the Hungarian Government strives to improve its relations with the United States.

The note declared that this aim could not be accomplished because of the hostile American policy toward Hungary. All of the complaints of the Ministry of Foreign Affairs were then enumerated. The Hungarian government charged that "the Americans have of late intensified their espionage and subversive activity against the Hungarian People's Democracy and on several occasions have attempted to intervene in the internal affairs of Hungary." At this point the note referred to the Gyáros press conference, which "offered proof" of these hostile acts.

The note further accused the American government of conducting an "open propaganda war against Hungary." Leading American officials and government organs, it charged, constantly issued statements attacking the lawful Hungarian government. "The Voice of America and Radio Free Europe, financed by Americans, incited the Hungarian population." The note went on to describe a few examples in which the American authorities had refused to grant visas to Hungarian sportsmen and scientists. The State Department had even refused to permit Hungarian participation in the 1959 New York World's Fair. The detailed note ended with the statement that the Hungarian government was ready to normalize relations with the United States. As a precondition, however, it demanded the termination of the discriminatory policy of the United States against the People's Republic of Hungary, as well as of its espionage and subversive activity.[4]

For a whole month the U.S. State Department allowed the note to remain unacknowledged, then rejected out of hand the Hungarian charges concerning the improper activities of the United States.[5] The reply maintained first of all that the United States, as one of the principal signatories of the United Nations Declaration, the Yalta Declaration on Liberated Europe, the Charter of the United Nations, and the Treaty of Peace with Hungary, bore clear responsibilities toward the Hungarian people's basic human rights and national independence. The State Department then went on to point out that it was not the United States but the Soviet Union who had intervened in the internal affairs of Hungary. Furthermore, the Hungarian government had acquiesced in the Soviet domination and had actively supported the Soviet objectives. The note referred to the execution of Imre Nagy and other leaders of the 1956 revolution.

The State Department agreed with the Hungarian Foreign Ministry that relations between the United States and Hungary were not "normal." However, in the opinion of the United States government any real improvement would depend upon the willingness of the Hungarian government "to live up to its international obligation under the United Nations Charter and the Treaty of Peace."

The U.S. note did not, of course, surprise the officials of Budapest. They were fully prepared for the answer they received. No analytical consideration was given to the U.S. policy statement, which was regarded purely and simply as a hostile deliberation, a form of interference in the internal affairs of Hungary. It was clear that for years to come the position of the Hungarian government and that of the United States would remain diametrically opposed.

The implementation of the second, "soft" phase of the Kádár plan—which was intended to improve the image of his regime—was more complex, for a painful interchange between Ambassador Henry Cabot Lodge and Ambassador Péter Mód had recently intensified the difficulties of the Hungarian delegation at the United Nations. On 17 December 1957, in the course of the U.N. debate on the question of Hungary, Ambassador Lodge had reported that the members of the Hungarian military delegation (Major General Pál Maléter, Major General István Kovács, and Colonel Miklós Szücs) appointed by the Imre Nagy government to negotiate with the Soviet delegation on the question of withdrawal of Soviet troops from Hungary, had been arrested and brought to trial.[6] Lodge had told the General Assembly that the United States might well call for a special session on Hungary should the situation there appear to warrant such action.

The statement of the U.S. delegate stirred the assembled delegates. Representatives of the Latin American countries called for clemency. Dr. Pacifico Montero de Vargas of Paraguay, the chairman of the Latin American group, met Ambassador Mód and asked him to forward to the Hungarian government "the group's appeal for clemency."[7] The same day the Hungarian Mission, in an attempt to find at least temporary relief from the mounting pressure, issued a hastily written press release to the effect that if the U.S. representative were "really interested in ascertaining what was happening in Hungary, he had the opportunity to ask for authentic information through the proper channels."[8] Not surprisingly, U.S. Representative Lodge and his deputy, James T. Wadsworth, took advantage of the opportunity. On 11 February 1958 Wadsworth sent a personal letter to the Hungarian ambassador to the United Nations, Péter Mód, politely inquiring about the circumstances of Maléter, Kovács, and Szücs. Wadsworth further requested information on the whereabouts of Imre Nagy and his closest associates, who had taken refuge at the Yugoslav embassy in Budapest after the Soviet troops had moved into the city. He wanted to know also what had happened to Sándor Kopácsi, the former chief of the Budapest police, to Dominik Kosáry, the well-known professor of history at Budapest University, and to Istvan Bibó, minister of State of the Nagy government. Wadsworth pointed out that his questions "pertain only to a small number of individuals whose fate is being followed with particular interest because of their prominence or the circumstances connected with their disappearance from public life."[9]

Ambassador Mód was not, of course, in a position to answer the questions, and asked Budapest for instructions. The Ministry of Foreign Affairs replied: acknowledge receipt of the American ambassador's letter and promise that it will be forwarded to the competent Hungarian authorities. Ambassador Mód acted accordingly. The Americans waited almost two months. Finally Henry Cabot Lodge reminded his Hungarian colleague that he was still awaiting a reply to the inquiry: "I would like therefore to take this occasion to express again my earnest hope that a reply will be forthcoming in the near future."[10]

On 13 March 1958 Ambassador Mód offered a complicated explanation in which he "recognized an American endeavor to correct the mistake" made in the statement of the American delegation at the Twelfth Session of the General Assembly of the United Nations (in 1957). According to Mód, however, Henry Cabot Lodge had failed "to take note of the fact that by making use in a distorted way of the questions involved," the U.S. Mission "tried to incite hostile public sentiment against Hungary on the basis of unconfirmed rumors. This mistake, naturally, cannot be considered as cancelled in view of subsequent inquiry." Mód ended his letter by charging that the wording of Lodge's questions "makes it appear as if your mission wanted to interfere in the domestic affairs of Hungary.'' For this reason Mód was refusing to cooperate with the American ambassador. ·

It is probable that Ambassador Mód, like the heads of Hungarian diplomatic missions in other countries, had not been officially informed at the time about the impending fate of Major General Maléter, Major General Kovács, or Colonel Szücs. He knew only what had been reported about them in the Western press. It is quite possible that Mód was not even informed of what had happened to Imre Nagy and his associates during the spring of 1958. The Foreign Ministry provided Mód and other heads of missions with the well-known version—that is, that Nagy and his group, after leaving the Yugoslav embassy in Budapest, had been transported to Rumania. Mód could have made a fairly accurate guess about the fate of Kopácsi, Kosáry, or Bibó. He knew his regime. But whether he actually knew the truth was not important so far as his answer to Lodge's letter was concerned. For the time being, all he was expected to do, or indeed could do, was to translate into English the Hungarian text he had received in the diplomatic pouch from Budapest.

In April the State Department published the exchange of letters. On 16 June 1958, as already mentioned, the world learned from the Hungarian press of the execution of Imre Nagy and Pál Maléter, proving ''the hostile rumors of Henry Cabot Lodge'' to be true. Ambassador Mód found himself in a very awkward position at the United Nations. In September, when Foreign Minister Sik arrived in New York, hostile feelings against the Hungarian regime were intensified. Everyone knew that a heated debate would develop on the Hungarian question.

The sixty-seven-year-old Hungarian diplomat had undergone so much in his lifetime that the prospect of a confrontation in the United Nations did not disturb him. Born into a middle-class Jewish family in Hungary in 1891, Endre Sik had fought as an officer of the Austro-Hungarian Monarchy in World War I and had been captured by the Russians on the Eastern Front. His long years as a prisoner of war in Siberia ended when the October Revolution opened the gates of his camp. He sided with the Bolsheviks and stayed in Russia until 1945. As a professor of history at the Moscow Eastern University, he had specialized in African studies and had written a general history of Africa curiously old-fashioned and Eurocentric in its general approach.[11] Many of the leaders who govern Africa today, among them Jomo Kenyatta, had been enrolled in his classes. Luckily, he had avoided the purges of Stalin.

After World War II he had returned to Hungary with the Muscovite émigrés, where Mátyás Rákosi set him to work in the Foreign Ministry and later, in 1946, in Washington. He was not eager to become involved in diplomatic work, for he preferred the quiet life of a scholar teaching diplomatic history. In those days, however, few asked his opinion. From 1949 until 1957 Sik was deputy foreign minister. He organized a high-level Diplomatic Academy in Budapest where he spent more time than in his ministerial office. He used to say that Maksim Litvinov's chief accomplishment was not what he had done as Soviet foreign minister, but what he did after he had become head of the diplomatic academy of the Soviet Foreign Ministry.

After the sudden death of Foreign Minister Imre Horváth in 1958, the Politburo quickly appointed Sik foreign minister and later made him a member of the party's Central Committee. With his new post he was well pleased not only because the appointment guaranteed him a position in the Hungarian state and party hierarchy but also because it allowed him more personal freedom. Besides, it made it possible for him to enjoy more frequent visits with his brother Sándor Sik without being shadowed by the secret police. Sándor Sik was a well-known Hungarian literary scholar who lived in semi-retirement in the university town of Szeged. He was the Provincial of the Piarist Teaching Order after World War II,[12] the founder of the Hungarian Boy Scout movement, and the author of a prayer book for youth which was used as a textbook in religious education.

Dr. Sik liked the post of foreign minister especially because it provided him with the opportunity to come to New York each year to attend the U.N. General Assembly. Those were golden days for him—no bureaucratic duties, no cabinet meetings, and time to spend on research for his African book in the Schomburg Collection at the New York Public Library. He charged the younger members of the delegation with the task of writing his speeches and went to U.N. headquarters only to have lunch with other diplomats or when it was absolutely necessary. He was the only Hungarian foreign minister who dared to invite Israeli Foreign Minister Golda Meir to his table.[13]

THE "SOFT SELL"

On 22 September Charles Malik, the distinguished foreign minister of Lebanon and president of the Thirteenth Regular Session of the U.N. General Assembly, declared: "We come now to item sixty-nine concerning the situation in Hungary." The General Assembly was faced with the decision whether or not to place the Hungarian question on its agenda. Sik, the old, white-haired professor and Hungary's foreign minister, immediately took the floor as the first speaker. He seemed to be completely realistic when he said: "Surely no one will be surprised when I declare that we know beforehand the outcome of the voting which is to take place now."[14] Then he repeated the well-worn arguments of his government as to why the Hungarian question should not be placed on the agenda. He spoke at great length about delegates who "were not in a position to grasp the whole truth about Hungary." He said that he understood the attitude of those delegates who were "misguided" or "whose governments were bound to the government of the United States by certain ties of interest." Naturally, Sik attacked U.S. foreign policy, asserting that the Hungarians were "utterly disgusted" with what he called the political poison fed by those who wanted to keep the item before the Assembly. These preliminary remarks were necessary before he came to the main point.

"Two immediate aims," he went on, "are prompting the maintenance of this question on the agenda: first, to challenge the presence of Soviet troops in Hungary and, secondly, to call on the Hungarian Government to discontinue certain court proceedings." He was firm on the question of Soviet troops stationed in Hungary. "How long and how many Soviet troops will remain in Hungary," he said, "is the exclusive concern of the Hungarian and Soviet Governments within the framework of the Warsaw Treaty." As far as the court proceedings were concerned, Sik emphasized: *"I am authorized to state that these have been wound up and terminated."* Having stated this, Dr. Sik had carried out the mission with which he had been charged by the Politburo's earlier decision.

The effectiveness of his appearance and of his statement was questionable. No one in the Western camp actually believed that the political trials had ended. Apparently the propaganda efforts of Gyáros and the Hungarian protest note addressed to the Americans had not substantially changed the situation in the United Nations either. Only a few Third World nations altered their previous positions concerning the Hungarian question.

Ambassador Lodge recalled that on 27 November 1956 Kádár had declared: "We have promised not to start any punitive proceedings against Imre Nagy, and we shall keep our word."[15] Lodge then went on to quote a six-day old United Press dispatch from Vienna stating that four more leaders of the aborted Hungarian revolution—Gábor Tánczos, secretary of the Petőfi Circle of intellectuals and writers in Hungary; journalists Sándor Haraszti and György Fazekas; and the former secretary of the Budapest Communist Party Committee, József Surec—had been convicted and sentenced to prison terms ranging from three years to life.[16] The American delegate further referred to the report of the Special Committee on the Problem of Hungary, which had revealed that the Soviet Union and the Hungarian authorities "continue to act in complete defiance of the many resolutions adopted in the General Assembly." For this reason Lodge firmly supported the inclusion of the question of Hungary.[17]

Lodge was followed by the Soviet representative, Valerian Zorin, who in his speech blasted the Americans and leveled irresponsible and unfounded charges about the arms supply and sabotage activity of the U.S. Air Force during the 1956 uprising. He spoke about the "development of armed provocation against the People's Republic of China by the United States and the followers of Chiang Kai-shek," and asserted that the Hungarian question was only "a means of distracting the attention of governments and world public opinion from these provocations."

The Yugoslav delegate, Dobrovoje Vidiç, also voted against inclusion of the item. He expressed the view that the Hungarian question would only produce pointless debate and would not reduce world tension. Ceylon's Sir Claude Corea expressed similar sentiments but abstained. Finland, India, Indonesia, Iraq, Nepal, Saudi Arabia, the United Arab Republic, Yemen, and Afghanistan shared this same point of view and also abstained.

Shortly after his speech Dr. Sik, with not much success behind him, hurried back to Budapest to take part in the festivities commemorating the Russian October Revolution, of which he had so many memories.

In December a joint draft resolution was submitted to the General Assembly over the names of thirty-seven member states. Among other points, it proposed to denounce the execution of Imre Nagy and to appoint Sir Leslie Munro to report to the member states on developments relating to the implementation of the Assembly's resolutions on the Hungarian question. Henry Cabot Lodge pointed out that the most shocking act in the reign of terror was the secret trial and execution of Nagy and Maléter and their companions. Although he severely condemned Soviet rule in Hungary, the American delegate expressed the hope that the Kádár regime would "grant amnesty to those who participated in the stirring events of October and November 1956."[18]

Deputy Foreign Minister János Péter answered. He acknowledged that promises had been made not to bring charges against some of the protagonists of the counterrevolution.[19] Then he explained defensively that at first it had been assumed that Imre Nagy had simply drifted toward his fateful action under the impact of events. Later investigation, he alleged, had brought forth evidence which proved that Imre Nagy "had been conspiring in devious ways for years before to overthrow the legal order of the country and to gamble with the fate of the whole nation." Péter also emphasized that "all these investigations and proceedings were completed a long time ago."

Representatives of the U.S.S.R. and of the socialist countries supported the stand taken by the Hungarian delegate. They argued that the campaign to renew debate on the Hungarian question aimed to divert attention from the growth of national independence movements in Asia and Africa. They branded the joint draft resolution a further attempt to interfere in the domestic affairs of Hungary, and they warned that "these hostile acts" could not lead to any constructive results.

Despite all the efforts and the rhetoric of the Soviet bloc, the majority of the delegations (54) accepted the joint draft resolution. The Soviet camp and Yugoslavia voted against it. The number of abstentions increased from 10 to 16. Ceylon and Greece abstained for different reasons (see Chapter 6). Israel and Yemen were absent.[20] The abstentions and absences did not significantly affect the course of the Hungarian question in the United Nations, as indicated by the fact that the Credentials Committee again adopted the U.S. motion "to take no decision regarding the credentials submitted on behalf of the representatives of Hungary."

At his yearly press conference Péter told newsmen that the U.S. proposal regarding the Hungarian question had received six fewer votes than a year ago and that this decrease reflected "a deeper change of the balance of power in the world organization."[21] This was about the only achievement of the two-line plan of action. The abstentions, however, reflected the extensive efforts of the Soviet and the Kádár regimes to secure international recognition for Hungary.

— 6 —

The Campaign for Recognition
at the United Nations

During the debate at the 1958 session of the United Nations General Assembly, the Soviet diplomats actively lobbied against further discussion of the Hungarian question. There was no doubt that two of Russia's neighbors, Afghanistan and Finland, as well as neutral India, Indonesia, and Nepal, would continue to abstain from voting. Soviet economic assistance played a primary role in convincing the government of Ceylon to withdraw from the five-nation Special Committee investigating the Hungarian question. A trade and economic agreement between Ceylon and the Soviet Union had been signed in Colombo on 8 February 1958. Under the agreement Ceylon's exports to the U.S.S.R. included tea, rubber, coconut oil, copra, spices, etc. The Soviet export list contained, among other items, petroleum products, rolled iron, steel products, etc. A second agreement on U.S.S.R.-Ceylonese economic and technical cooperation, signed in Colombo on 25 February 1958, provided for Soviet participation in implementing Ceylon's economic development plans. Similarly, the Soviet Union had no problem with most of the Arab countries (except Tunisia).

Friendship and collaboration with the Soviet Union proved its worth to Nasser in 1956 when Soviet diplomatic assistance enabled him to survive the tripartite British-French-Israeli intervention, and a Soviet grain shipment averted famine in Egypt. After the Suez crisis Egypt naturally endorsed without reservation the Soviet intervention in Hungary, for Gamal Abdel Nasser urgently needed Moscow's continued economic, military, and political support. Nasser did not fare too badly. Soviet exports to Egypt in 1957 amounted to £18,500,000, and the construction of 65 major industrial projects was begun with Soviet aid. These figures do not include the cost of building the Aswan Dam nor the cost of the ongoing military assistance program.[1] Nasser was able to add

52

to these items substantial assistance from the different East European communist regimes. Hungary alone, for instance, had undertaken to build a bridge on the Nile at Helwan (a suburb of Cairo), to modernize the Egyptian railway with Diesel locomotives, and to provide Nasser's police force with automatic pistols.

In August 1957 Deputy Foreign Minister Károly Szarka, Presidential Council Member and Member of Parliament János Péter, and Director of the Foreign Ministry Pál Rácz toured the nonaligned countries of Asia, as well as Syria, Egypt, and the Sudan, on a goodwill mission. They attempted to convince the leaders of these countries that the Kádár version of the 1956 events was the one and only true picture. Jawaharlal Nehru gave them a cool reception. Syrian President Shukry Kuatly was friendly at his reception of the delegation. Nasser showed some understanding. During the course of this visit Szarka told Nasser that the imperialists had had an obvious interest in creating confusion in Eastern Europe in 1956. At the height of the Suez crisis, he said, the colonial powers, mainly France and Great Britain, had hoped to divert world attention from the Middle East and to tie down Soviet military forces in Hungary. The Hungarian diplomat laid the blame for the 1956 Hungarian events at the door of the United States and its agents in Hungary. Although Nasser did not accept this version (he noted that the Soviet ambassador in Cairo had told him that there had been no U.S. intervention in Hungary), he did stress that he understood Kádár's difficult situation.

At this point the Hungarian deputy foreign minister asked for Egyptian support in the United Nations. President Nasser cautiously agreed that he would gladly instruct the Egyptian U.N. delegate to vote against any hostile resolution on the Hungarian question, but added that he would have to take into consideration the stand of the other Arab countries. He promised that in any case Egypt would demonstrate its solidarity with the new Hungarian regime and the Soviet Union by abstaining, and that he would exercise his influence inside the U.N. Arab bloc in Kádár's behalf. Szarka was disappointed at getting a pledge of only limited support from Nasser, but Soviet diplomats in Cairo explained to him later that more could not be expected from this bourgeois leader who had put Egyptian communists in desert prison camps. Nasser did keep his word, however. In 1957 the Egyptian delegate abstained on the question of Hungary; and in 1958, after the unification with Syria, the U.A.R. delegation secured the abstentions of six more Arab countries when the General Assembly voted on the Thirty-seven Powers draft resolution.

The abstention of Ghana surprised the members of the Hungarian delegation in the United Nations, for they had thought that Britain still dominated Kwame Nkrumah's foreign policy. Remembering in particular Nkrumah's recent visit to the United States to discuss the Volta River project, a plan to develop Ghana's hydroelectric power and aluminum production, the Hungarians were certain that the Ghanaian representative, Ako Adjei, and his British adviser, Charles H. Chapman, would follow the Western camp in the voting. Apparently, however, Nkrumah's visit to Cairo in June 1958 carried more weight. It was on this occasion that the Ghanaian leader had received a full account of Nasser's visit to Moscow and of the economic aid that Egypt was receiving from the Soviets. Unlike the Hungarians, the Soviet delegation was not at all surprised when Ghana abstained, for the Soviets had been fully informed of the results of the Nkrumah-Nasser meeting.

As for the Greek abstention and the fact that Israel was not present at the roll call vote in the United Nations, both of these actions may be attributed to Hungarian diplomatic activities. To understand why Greece, a member of NATO, was not following the policy line of her allies in 1958 and voted differently on the delicate question of Hungary requires some explanation. In March 1948, when the civil war was raging, a great number of Greek children three to fourteen years of age, living in the territory held by partisan troops, were evacuated to several East European communist countries. According to a December 1948 report of the United Nations, 23,696 Greek children remained in these countries, some 3,000 of them in Hungary.[2] After the 1949 defeat of the Communist-led Greek National Liberation Army (ELAS)[3] many of its members and the activists of the Greek Communist Party (KKE) fled to Albania and Bulgaria with their families, forcing a large number of civilians living in the territory controlled by ELAS to go with them.

From 1950 on, the refugees gradually settled all over Eastern Europe. Those Greeks transplanted to Hungary were concentrated in Köbánya (an industrial district of Budapest) and in the western countryside near Stalinváros.[4] Those in the countryside lived in semi-seclusion. Some worked in the big Stalinváros steel plant, along with Hungarian workers, and some families were employed on state farms; but in the evening all were transported back to their village. The affairs of the Greeks living in Hungary were handled by a special department at Hungarian party headquarters, and their movements were strictly controlled by the police.

During the 1956 uprising the great majority of Greeks in Hungary sided with the revolutionaries. After the second Soviet intervention, when they fought with the Hungarian freedom fighters in the Stalinváros area, Soviet troops had to use tanks and heavy artillery to end their resistance. Greek university students (many of them were the children who had been evacuated from Greece in 1948) were also active in Hungarian revolutionary organizations and took part in the Budapest street fighting, despite warnings of the Greek Communist Party organization in Hungary.

The new Kádár regime was disappointed with the Greeks. For their participation in the uprising the police arrested the leaders of the rebels. The Hungarian Politburo ultimately came to the conclusion that many of the Greeks had abused "Hungarian hospitality" and decided to allow Greek citizens to return to their homeland if they wished to do so. In 1958 the Greek envoy in Budapest,

Alexandre T. Sgourdeus, was discreetly informed by the Hungarian Foreign Ministry that the Hungarian authorities would not object to family reunions—in other words, to gradual repatriation. The Hungarian Ministry required that no undue publicity be given to the affair, and that Greece not vote against Hungary in the United Nations. The Greek government accepted both conditions and complied with them.

In 1958 this special matter apparently commanded more importance for the Greeks than NATO solidarity. The following year, however, Greece again voted with the Western powers.[5] It is difficult to say whether this was a result of lobbying by the U.S. delegation or of the fact that the Hungarian Ministry of the Interior had dragged its heels on the repatriation issue.

As for the explanation of Israel's absence during the 12 December 1958 roll call vote and of her abstention in 1959, the story of this, too, goes back to 1956. According to a report of the Hungarian legation in Tel Aviv, an elderly woman who had fled Hungary after the "counterrevolution" visited the legation's consular section. She told the officer on duty that before leaving Hungary she had turned over to the Israeli legation a package containing her jewelry. Now, she explained, she had come to fetch her belongings. At first the Hungarian consular officer did not understand what this lady was talking about, but he listened carefully. The woman said that like so many others of her faith she had gone to the Israeli legation in Budapest and had asked that the remaining family jewelry be forwarded to her in Israel. The consular officer finally understood what the lady was trying to say and asked her to make a list of her jewelry and to sign it. When she had complied, she was informed that she was at the wrong address; she was at the Hungarian legation and should go elsewhere to collect her things.

On the basis of this report, Hungarian counterintelligence started a thorough investigation and dug up additional instances of the Israeli legation's "smuggling activity." When enough evidence had been collected, the Foreign Ministry sent a strong protest note to the Israeli legation in Budapest and presented Israel with a $20 million claim for losses caused by the smuggling activity. As further retaliation, the emigration of Jews to Israel was completely stopped. Israel denied the charges and relations between Israel and Hungary became very strained.

Understandably, the Israeli government was anxious to improve this state of affairs and attempted several times to normalize the situation in order to renew Jewish emigration. In 1958 the Israeli envoy in Budapest, Dr. Mier Tuval, visited Deputy Foreign Minister Szarka and complained about the restrictions preventing Hungarian Jews from emigrating to Israel. He suggested the possibility of concluding a trade agreement advantageous to Hungary and then asked permission for several people to leave the country.

Both his offer and his requests were flatly rejected. Szarka told Tuval that the persons in question were Hungarian citizens and that the Israeli legation had no jurisdiction over them. For that reason Tuval's appeal was considered to be a grave interference in the internal affairs of Hungary. Szarka also mentioned the smuggling affair and told the Israeli envoy that until Israel was ready to pay adequate compensation, normalization of relations could not even be a topic of discussion. Tuval's argument that Israel had been one of the first Western countries to recognize the new Kádár government and to send a minister to Budapest failed to alter Szarka's position.

On several occasions, the latest in September 1958, Tuval had repeated his attempts to reach some sort of agreement. On Tuval's most recent visit Szarka had decided to be less uncompromising, and this time offered his guest a cup of coffee—a gesture extended only to diplomats from friendly countries. In the course of the conversation Szarka developed a new interpretation of the emigration question. He explained to Tuval that the Hungarian government did not in principle oppose the emigration of Hungarian citizens but wanted only to avoid a policy which would encourage people to leave the country. The Passport Department of the Ministry of the Interior, he explained, was presently issuing emigration passports for Hungarian Jews separated from their families and to a limited number of others for humanitarian reasons.

Finding some encouragement in the deputy foreign minister's statement, Tuval produced a long list of names of people who had asked his legation for immigration visas. At this point, Szarka abruptly switched to the Hungarian question in the United Nations and accused the Western powers of interference in the internal affairs of Hungary. Furthermore he asked the envoy how Israel would vote this year on this particular question. Dr. Tuval was not in a position to give an immediate answer but promised to get instructions from Jerusalem. As an indication of Hungarian willingness to negotiate, in October and November a few elderly persons received Hungarian passports and were allowed to emigrate to Israel. The dialogue and interactions between Israel and Hungary continued; and although no agreement had been reached, the Israeli U.N. delegation, as a gesture of goodwill, did absent itself from the December 12 roll call of the General Assembly.

During the first months of 1959 emigration permits were again frozen, and Tuval was told that only an arrangement for the settlement of the smuggling claim could open the way for the consideration of any other question. Apparently the problem of the emigration of the Hungarian Jews was an important issue for the Israeli government. Tuval soon made another attempt. He asked Szarka if the Hungarian Foreign Ministry would issue a visa to the representative of a private Jewish organization who was prepared to come to Budapest from Switzerland to discuss the claim problem with competent Hungarian authorities. This news was immediately reported to party headquarters.

Károly Kiss, member of the Politburo and party secretary responsible for international relations, consulted with the head of the Department of International Relations of the Party, Dezsö Szilágyi, and Foreign Minister Sik. While Kiss and Sik were in favor of entering into negotiations with the Jewish representative, both hoping that the matter would result in a large flow of dollars into the Hungarian treasury, Szilágyi, a Moscow émigré who had been freed from a Russian prison camp only after the end of World War II, was inclined to be more cautious. He was afraid that the Arabs would find out about the purpose of the discussions and would protest to Moscow and Budapest, attacking the Hungarian emigration policy as anti-Arab. Kiss overruled Szilágyi's objections, however; and after clearing the affair with Kádár, with the other members of the Politburo, and with his counterpart in the Soviet party headquarters, he instructed the Foreign Ministry to start negotiations. Kádár's condition was that Israel take at least a neutral position on the Hungarian question at the United Nations. The Russians asked only that the Hungarians avoid publicity, but did not object to the discussions.

A three-man Hungarian team headed by Deputy Foreign Minister Szarka was selected to handle the case. The Israeli representative was issued a tourist visa and duly arrived in Budapest, where, accompanied by the Israeli minister, he presented himself at the Foreign Ministry. It became apparent at the outset that the differences between the two sides were substantial enough to require several months of discussions. The representative of Israel wanted to talk about ensuring the emigration and wanted to know how much compensation the Hungarian government would ask for each Jew. For appearance' sake the Hungarians expressed complete distaste for this approach, stating that they were not prepared to discuss the Hungarian government's emigration policy with representatives of foreign countries; they were authorized to speak only about "the smuggling claim."

After a brief return to Switzerland for further instructions, the Israeli representative reported that his organization would gladly offer a lump-sum payment if the Hungarian government would be more flexible on the emigration question. In reply the Hungarian authorities explained that they could not give priority to persons who wished to emigrate to Israel, but they were ready to consider each case separately and to promote the reunion of families for "humanitarian reasons." The discussion concluded with a financial agreement, and Tuval left with Szarka's promise that the long list of persons who wished to go to Israel would be considered favorably. Szarka made it unmistakably clear, however, that implementation of the informal agreement required at least an abstention by Israel on the Hungarian question. As the 1959 record of the United Nations showed, Israel did indeed abstain.

— 7 —

Reorganization on the Home Front

The years 1957 and 1958 saw decisive steps taken toward the restoration and partial consolidation of the Hungarian Communist regime. During this period the national leaders and the active participants in the 1956 revolution were eliminated by one means or another. The Kádár regime had gradually reassumed charge of the state administrative functions relinquished by the Soviet military administration. The General Headquarters of the Soviet occupation force had ceased to control public order and to dissolve "counterrevolutionary committees," as they had done immediately following the crushing of the revolution.

Considering the situation sufficiently stable to push the new Hungarian regime to the fore, Moscow ordered Mikhail I. Kazakov, the commanding general of the occupation forces, to deal only with Kádár and a few of his close associates. The Soviet advisers reoccupied the offices in the Ministry of the Interior and the Ministry of Defense that they had abandoned during the revolution. Under the name of Department of Political Police, the secret police apparatus was reorganized from the personnel of the discredited Stalinist A.V.H. (Hungarian Secret Police). From this point on, it was the Hungarian, rather than the Soviet, secret police who made arrests, although they had to clear their activity with the Soviet advisers.

Wary of those people who had arrested and tortured him only a few years earlier and who now constituted his secret police, Kádár appointed his close friends Béla Biszku and István Tömpe to the posts of minister and deputy minister of the Interior, respectively. Münnich's protégé, Colonel László Mátyás, a veteran of the Spanish Civil War, who had been a prisoner in Rákosi's jail along with Kádár, became the head of the Department of Political Police.

While this new police institution was being established, the shock troops of the new regime, the so-called Special Armed Forces, were dissolved and their members ordered either back to police duty or to the border-guard units of the Ministry of the Interior. The non-professional members of the shock troops, the party functionaries and activists, were regrouped in the newly created "Workers' Militia." As the 12 February 1957 party resolution indicated quite plainly, they were organized on the county and city level rather than in the factories because the workers refused to follow anyone but their elected leaders, the Workers' Councils.[1]

With the approval of the Kremlin, Kádár applied the method of using a big stick and a little carrot to break the workers' opposition and to dissolve their organizations.[2] After the December 1956 general strike in Budapest, the regime abolished the central organ of the Workers' Councils, the Great Budapest Workers' Council, and arrested its leaders, Sándor Rácz and Sándor Báli. In order to separate the workers from their leaders, the government continued to pay full wages during the strikes. Stripped of all political and economic power, the plant Workers' Councils were permitted to exist "as an experiment" until November 1957, when the government dissolved them officially and instituted, *pro forma*, the shop council.[3]

During this period the party-led trade unions were reactivated. Despite obstacles they became once more the instrument of the party, or, as Lenin had originally designated them, "the transmission belt between the Party and the masses." In November 1957 the Presidential Council, on the proposal of the Party Central Committee, finally repealed the 1956 martial law.[4] The Anti-Strike Decree of 15 January 1957, however, remained in force, making the incitement to or advocacy of industrial strikes punishable by death.[5]

RECONSTITUTION OF THE PARTY APPARATUS

Among the many difficulties confronting the regime, two seemed to require the most urgent attention: the reorganization of the Communist Party and the revitalization of Communist rule in Hungary. The re-creation of the inner circle of the party, the Central Executive Committee and the Central Committee, posed few·serious problems. The key post, that of first secretary of the party, was already held by Kádár. His closest collaborator was Ferenc Münnich, an old Bolshevik and a veteran of the International Brigade in the Spanish Civil War. Münnich had influential friends in high Soviet party circles and in the Soviet intelligence. With their backing he had managed to survive the Stalinist purges despite the fact that during the years 1949-53 he had opposed Hungarian Stalinist leader Rákosi. In 1956, acting for Imre Nagy, he had performed the important task of dissolving the A.V.H. However, at the end of October 1956, he, along with Kádár, broke with Nagy. It was Münnich who had advised his friends in the Kremlin to reinforce Kádár's hold on the leading post of first secretary.

Kádár named to the Executive Committee György Marosán and Gyula Kállai, both of whom had served with him in Rákosi's prison. Marosán was a representative of the left wing of the Social Democratic Party, and Kállai, at least in Kádár's opinion, spoke for the Hungarian Communist intellectuals. In addition the first secretary selected for his team Béla Biszku, who had worked with him in the XIIIth District of Budapest after Kádár's release from prison in 1954. Also appointed to the Executive Committee were the hard liner Károly Kiss and figureheads Miklós Somogyi and Sándor Rónai. Jenö Fock and Antal Apró were recruited as economic experts, while the agricultural post was filled by Lajos Fehér, a well-known expert on rural areas of Hungary. Fehér, because of his former close ties with Imre Nagy, accepted the nomination to the Executive Committee only after prolonged hesitation.[6]

It was more difficult to recruit the rank and file of the party, especially the workers and the intellectuals. The workers listened to their own organization, the still-existing Workers' Council; and the Communist intellectuals generally felt that so long as the country was occupied by foreign military forces, Hungarian political life would have no meaning. Although the Communist Party claimed about 800,000 members before 1956, it numbered only 100,000 in January 1957.[7]

Kádár wanted a relatively small central party apparatus that would control but not duplicate the functions of the state bureaucracy. He was opposed to a complete separation of party and state functions, but he felt that if more authority were given to the ministries and national institutions, the economic and political problems confronting the regime could be solved more readily. As Kádár explained to a group of party employees of the Central Committee in late December 1956, Communists held the leading positions in the state organs; hence there was no need to maintain in the party apparatus a Department of Agriculture, for instance, or a Department of Industry, as had been the case in Rákosi's time. A small, highly centralized party apparatus would guarantee the fulfillment of the most important resolutions of the Politburo.

This concept was understandably unpopular among the party bureaucrats, who feared the loss of their power and influence or even of their jobs. Kádár, ignoring the complaints, fired more than 80 percent of the old personnel. The offended group sought help from the Soviets. Plotting against Kádár, they charged that his reduction and centralization of the party constituted, in fact, a separation of party and state power that could lead eventually to a Hungarian variation of Titoism. The Soviet Party *aparatchicks*, appreciating the dangers inherent in Kádár's policy, exerted pressure. In the course of a year this maneuver, combined with that of the Hungarian Party bureaucrats, resulted in the growth of the central apparatus of the party and the local party administration to approximately the same number as before 1956.

THE NEW IDEOLOGICAL COVER

The matter of personnel was only one of the problems encountered in the attempt to reconstitute the party. The most urgent item of party policy was the development of an ideological cover, a formula explaining the events of 1956. As early as 8 December 1956 the Provisional Central Committee of Kádár's reorganized party had been called together. At that time "the criminal policy of the Rákosi-Gerö clique" was denounced; Imre Nagy too was criticized for his actions during the uprising.

A long communiqué published after the meeting stated that the decisive role in the Central Committee and in the government had been played by Rákosi. His deviation from the basic principles of Marxism-Leninism must be held chiefly responsible for the events of 1956.[8] Kádár's group still considered the activity of the party opposition led by Imre Nagy to have been positive insofar as it had been directed against the policies of the Rákosi-Gerö clique. Nagy's mistake, they asserted, had been to take his legitimate criticism "to the streets," a measure that encouraged reactionary elements and sparked the "counter-revolution."

This somewhat moderate evaluation of the turmoil of October and November did not hold up for very long. With the arrival in Budapest on 1 January 1957 of the leaders of the Soviet, Bulgarian, Czechoslovak, and Rumanian parties and governments, the political evaluation of Kádár and his group changed abruptly. After four days of meeting with Soviet representatives Khrushchev and Malenkov, Kádár and his deputy Münnich agreed to designate the uprising officially as a "counterrevolution," and the label stuck. Bulgarians Todor Zhivkov and General Georgi Damianov, Czechoslovaks Viliam Siroky and Antonín Novotný, and Rumanians Gheorghe Gheorghiu-Dej and General Petre Borila supported the Soviet leaders. The meeting of the representatives of the five countries became, in short, a demonstration of solidarity and sympathy for the interventionist policy of the Soviet Union.

According to the final joint declaration of the meeting, "the attempts to destroy the people's democratic regime and the socialist achievements of the Hungarian people were smashed by the efforts of the Hungarian workers under the leadership of the Hungarian Revolutionary Workers' and Peasants' Government and with the assistance of the Soviet armed forces."[9] "The threat of a fascist dictatorship" in Hungary was thereby averted. The "intrigues of counterrevolutionaries and imperialists" had been turned aside. This time, while the Rákosi-Gerö clique was still criticized for its anti-Leninist methods, Imre Nagy was branded a traitor whose government opened the path before the "fascist counterrevolutionaries."

The Budapest meeting of the representatives of the five Eastern bloc countries was followed a week later by a sudden, unplanned visit from the prime minister of the People's Republic of China, Chou En-lai. The Chinese appearance demonstrated clearly the extent of Peking's interest in the affairs of Eastern Europe. Just shortly before this time, at the end of 1956, the Chinese prime minister had made an extended tour in southeastern Asia. During his stay at Phnom Penh he had told American newspaper men that the time had come to establish better relations between China and the United States, and that American journalists would be welcome to visit China if they could obtain permission from their government. In addition, he suggested that if an agreement were reached between the People's Republic of China and Taiwan, Chiang Kai-shek might get a higher position than that of minister.[10] Chou En-lai recalled the general as "an old friend" with whom he had cooperated before 1927. Later, speaking in Delhi before the Indian Parliament, he paid high tribute to India's peacemaking efforts, emphasizing her contribution to the cease-fire agreement in Korea and to the formulation at the Bandung Conference of the Asian version of peaceful coexistence, better known as the "Five Principles" (Panch Shila). Chou was abruptly recalled from India; then, after a brief stay in Peking, he proceeded to Moscow.

On 7 January 1957 the Chinese premier arrived in the Kremlin with some of his advisers to discuss with the Soviet leadership ways and means of stabilizing the still fluid East European situation. The conferees spent a great deal of time assessing the aftermath of the Hungarian uprising, a problem that was apparently still causing serious difficulties. Three days later Kádár was summoned to Moscow to join in the discussions. He was given reassurance that China supported his regime. Moreover Chou offered the Hungarian premier substantial economic assistance—100 million rubles ($25 million) in credit in convertible currency and 100 million rubles in commodities.[11] On his part Kádár invited the Chinese delegation to come to Budapest and to study the Hungarian situation on the spot.[12]

Arriving in Budapest, Chou En-lai politely conveyed Mao Tse-tung's greetings and emphasized that he had come to Hungary to learn about the 1956 events and to exchange revolutionary experiences. During his meetings with Kádár he listened attentively to Kádár's explanation of the causes of the counterrevolution.

The Chinese leader accepted without reservation Kádár's account of student unrest and of the fatal mistakes made by the dogmatic Rákosi-Gerö clique, mistakes that led to discontent among the masses and later facilitated the outbreak of the revolution. In particular, he showed great understanding when Kádár turned to the role of Imre Nagy. According to Kádár, Imre Nagy was a weak man, driven by events. While the mob was lynching Communists, he had been unable to restore order. Furthermore, he had given up the dictatorship of the proletariat by accepting a multi-party system. Neutralism—which is what Imre Nagy had wanted—would have resulted in the restoration of capitalism in Hungary. For these reasons Kádár and other Hungarian Communists had disassociated themselves from the Imre Nagy group.

Chou En-lai thanked his host for the information and expressed to Kádár the conviction that the Hungarian leaders must act according to their own judgment. Nobody, he added, could evaluate better than Kádár himself the past errors, the actual situation, and the action to be taken. In connection with Imre Nagy, the Chinese prime minister noted that political misjudgments were unpardonable, and that in China the party would have exposed Nagy's crimes and mistakes at length before the masses, sending him to a remote area where he himself would have the opportunity to correct his way of thinking and to practice self-criticism.

The joint communiqué published at the end of Chou En-lai's visit emphasized that "Socialist countries are independent and sovereign states and relations between them are based upon Leninist principles of national equality," and, further, that the goal of leadership in these countries should be "to educate the people in such a way that they distinguish between correct ideas and actions and those which are erroneous, and that they be capable of resisting the enemy."[13]

Chou En-lai's visit aroused the hopes of various groups in Hungary, particularly the intellectuals. Perhaps with Chinese help there would be a reconciliation with the Soviets rather than harsh repression. But those who found hope in the differences of tone between the Chinese statements and the declaration of the five European Communist leaders had apparently missed one of Kádár's remarks concerning his Chinese experience: "I learned in China in 1956 that in this huge country many different flowers bloom for the benefit of the people. Weeds, however, were not to be allowed to flower."[14]

By the end of 1957 the state administration had been formed, the party reorganized. With the dissolution of the Workers' Councils, the last pockets of resistance had been eliminated. This internal consolidation, plus the economic support of the Soviet Union and the encouragement of Chou En-lai, effectively discouraged any open hostility to the Kádár regime. Covert opposition or defeatist resignation, however, remained widespread. Although Communist rule had been reintroduced in Hungary, the political survival of the regime continued to depend on the presence of Soviet troops.

REVITALIZATION OF INDUSTRY AND RECOLLECTIVIZATION

In the wake of the 1956 revolution there followed not only partial political consolidation but revitalization of the economic life of the country as well. With substantial economic assistance from the Soviet bloc, the new Hungarian government ensured the immediate needs of public supply and temporarily halted the growing inflation.[15] The October uprising and the general strike in December, plus the general slowdown in industrial production, however, inflicted a loss on the economy of twenty billion florins,[16] or a reduction of 20 percent in the national income. Thus the government was forced to introduce a whole series of emergency measures. It restricted the consumption of coal and electric energy and drastically cut back the budget of the state administration. It kept government investment to a minimum. At the same time, the regime did not object to a limited development of the private sector of industry and of artisan cooperatives.[17]

On 1 January 1958 a transitional three-year plan was launched. Although the importance of central planning similar to that of the Soviet model was in no sense de-emphasized, Kádár's specialists, Politburo member Jenö Fock and the president of the National Planning Office Árpád Kiss, laid special stress on the specific circumstances and needs of the Hungarian economy. In their judgment the prime objectives were to be a reasonable return on investment, the introduction of advanced technical expertise, and a rapid increase in productivity.[18] In principle, they advocated some of the economic conceptions of Imre Nagy; in practice, however, they did not introduce any basic changes or structural modifications in the economic life of the country.[19] Most important in the recovery was the fact that Hungary did not have to maintain a large army and was not required to purchase sophisticated Soviet armaments until 1961.

The initially liberal treatment of the peasant also proved helpful in restoring the economy. When the fighting ended, the Kádár regime simply took note of the existing situation in the countryside. It accepted the fact that 50 percent of the cooperative farms had ceased to function during the revolution and that 78 percent of the arable land was being cultivated by individual farmers. The party expert on agricultural matters, Politburo member Lajos Fehér, proposed the encouragement of the private sector and opposed the reintroduction of compulsory delivery of agricultural goods.[20] The opportunity to sell their produce on the open market provided the peasants with incentive to increase production.[21] Fearing repercussions in their own countries, the hard liners in the Rumanian and Czechoslovakian Communist parties protested in Moscow and Budapest, but to no avail. The Kremlin did not interfere, at least for the next two years, and the Kádár regime enjoyed relative tranquillity in the countryside, a peace absolutely essential to a government faced with continuing tension in the cities.

By 1958 recollectivization in the agricultural districts became one of the primary concerns of the Politburo. Before taking any major steps in this direction, however, the Hungarian Party leadership sought Soviet advice, consent, and material backing. A good opportunity for consultation arose in April 1958 when a Soviet Party and government delegation headed by First Secretary Khrushchev arrived in Budapest. The official purpose of the visit was to participate in Hungarian National Holiday celebrations, thus repaying an earlier Hungarian visit to the U.S.S.R. Soviet high officials spent seven days in Hungary touring scientific institutions, plants, and showcase cooperative farms. In the course of the visit Khrushchev and his deputy, Frol R. Kozlov, delivered several speeches and concluded a number of agreements with the Kádár regime.

Signing a treaty that "legalized" the status of Soviet forces stationed in Hungary,[22] Khrushchev emphasized that Soviet troops would remain in Hungary only temporarily in accordance with the Warsaw Treaty, not as a Soviet army of occupation. In addition, a consular agreement was reached annulling dual Soviet-Hungarian citizenship. This forced the so-called Muscovite Hungarians (Hungarians who had lived in the U.S.S.R. between the two world wars and who, as political émigrés, had received Soviet citizenship automatically) to make a choice.[23] Finally, the two parties concluded a long-range economic agreement, discussed matters of commercial protocol, and made arrangements for Soviet economic aid to Hungary (the amount was not disclosed).

Besides sharing in the usual round of social engagements and official negotiations, Khrushchev and Kádár found time also for private discussions of other important issues, among them the question of recollectivization. Explaining to the Soviet leader that the political stabilization of his regime was progressing well, Kádár suggested that the time was appropriate to initiate a campaign in the agricultural areas. Khrushchev agreed with Kádár's assessment and advised that he put primary emphasis on developing and reinforcing the State Farm system and the already existing cooperative farms. The Soviet leader warned Kádár of the danger inherent in excessive use of the strong-arm police methods employed by Rákosi in the 1950s. He suggested as an alternative that the Hungarian government offer a wide range of benefits for those peasants who were ready to give up their individual plots and to join the cooperatives. In connection with this proposal he cautioned Kádár about the importance of proceeding somewhat slowly at first, pointing out that the 1957 Chinese failure to collectivize had been occasioned by the excessive tempo of the campaign. The Soviet leader assured Kádár of Soviet support and promised delivery of extra agricultural machinery, seed, and fertilizer. Kádár received from the Soviets full authority for the execution of the program. Khrushchev stipulated only that the "socialist sector" (as opposed to the private sector of individual farmers) should ultimately comprise at least 80 percent of Hungarian agriculture, and that the re-collectivization campaign be fulfilled in approximately three years.

As soon as the Soviet party and government delegation had left Budapest, Kádár summoned the Hungarian Politburo and informed them about his discussion with Khrushchev. The members of the Politburo agreed that the campaign be launched in the coming months. Minister of Agriculture Imre Dögei, although not a Politburo member, attended the meeting as an agricultural expert. Maintaining that the relative prosperity of the individual peasants had reached the point where they had become the "new exploiting class" in Hungarian society, Dögei proposed that a heavy tax burden be levied on the individual peasant to eliminate this danger. Such a measure, he explained, would strip the wealthy peasants of their economic power and hence force them to enter the state-supported collective farms.

Kádár and other Politburo members, however, opposed Dögei's plan, considering it politically and economically impractical first to impoverish the peasants and then to push them into the cooperatives. Lajos Fehér characterized the Dögei plan as illogical and dangerous. Reproaching the minister of Agriculture for having no contact with the peasantry and misunderstanding the entire situation, Fehér explained that the purpose was not to destroy the villages economically but to reorganize them. Like Khrushchev, he warned against repeating Rákosi's mistakes of forcing the peasants into the cooperatives by administrative police methods. As a counterproposal, Fehér advocated a well-prepared program of step-by-step transformation lasting two or even three years. He felt that the party should proceed cautiously with collectivization, setting modest and flexible goals that could be altered according to the initial results. He proposed concentrating initial efforts in areas where the least resistance was likely to occur and starting the recollectivization campaign there.

Without making a final decision the Politburo accepted Fehér's plan in principle and charged him to work out the details with the help of the Department of Agriculture of the Party Central apparatus. In addition, the Politburo decided to convene the Central Committee, the advisory body of the party, on 25 April. For this occasion Kádár planned a Central Committee meeting where the members would not only rubber-stamp the Politburo decision, but would also discuss the recollectivization plan with the county party secretaries of the rural areas whose support would eventually be necessary for the execution of the program.

The April session of the Central Committee followed the usual routine. On behalf of the Politburo, Lajos Fehér delivered the *referata*, informing the Central Committee members of the Politburo discussion of the recollectivization plan. Explaining the Politburo's assessment of the political and economic situation in the farmlands, he announced that the time was ripe to launch a new collectivization drive and proposed that the party apparatus in agricultural districts and villages mobilize for the task. Fehér suggested further that the Department of Agriculture of the party, in collaboration with other Central party departments, work out the details for the next session of the Central Committee to be held in September of the same year.[24] Although the Dögei-Fehér controversy was not officially discussed at the April meeting, it became the topic of many private conversations.

The next Central Committee session, originally scheduled for September, was delayed two months because of the June execution of Imre Nagy. Central Committee members like György Aczél, who had served long prison terms in the 1950s, fearing that persecution of high-ranking party functionaries would follow, nervously requested an explanation from Kádár. The first secretary was able to allay their anxiety only by issuing a party directive to the Ministry of the Interior that members of the Central Committee were not to be arrested for political reasons without the prior knowledge of the Politburo. It took a few months, however, before they felt reassured. Dögei and left-wing elements of the party saw in Nagy's execution a new opportunity to challenge Kádár's power and to demonstrate a hard-line orthodoxy in the policy of collectivization.

Hoping to gain support from some of the Soviet leaders, who seemed at that point to be shifting toward radicalism, the Dögei group started a factional struggle within the party. They aimed at seizing power through the agricultural issue at the coming Central Committee meeting. Kádár again needed a few months to organize his counterattack. He and his close associate, Béla Biszku, interviewed the members of the Dögei group and with threats and promises successfully convinced them to change sides.

In late November 1958 the Politburo endorsed Fehér's two- to three-year plan for recollectivization. It proposed that 500 well-trained agitators from the Central apparatus be sent to the villages with the task of convincing the individual peasant to join a cooperative. According to the Fehér plan, the county party organization was to be reinforced by additional communist activist groups. The National Bank was ordered, through the Ministry of Finance, to open an agricultural monetary fund to support the new cooperatives. In addition, the Ministry of Finance was instructed to lower the taxation of cooperative peasants and the Ministry of Agriculture to work out the details for the reimbursement of the peasants for their land. (This payment turned out to be a nominal ground rent from the cooperative.) The Politburo ordered the ministries of Commerce and Health to reserve consumer food and medical supplies for those areas where communes were to be organized. Following party procedure, the Fehér plan would be presented to the Central Committee for acceptance. The actual decision, however, had been made there in the Politburo.

On 7 December 1958, when the Central Committee finally met, Kádár and the Politburo remained in control of the situation. During the debate, Dögei continued to press for his plan, arguing that after 1956 the individual peasants had become, through black market speculation, capitalist extortionists and, consequently, dangerous opponents of the People's Republic. Therefore, he reasoned, the party should lead a class struggle against the peasants, utilizing economic means in particular. Dögei placed primary emphasis on the state farm rather than on the cooperative; he envisioned the former as an agricultural factory and its workers as new members of the proletariat who would be politically and economically more reliable than the cooperative farm peasants.

At the same meeting various Central Committee members, most of them high party functionaries from urban districts and industrial compounds, expressed genuine fear that an eventual effort to begin a collectivization drive would result in an industrial and agricultural relapse. They proposed that the problem of collectivization be postponed for several years. Enjoying Politburo backing, Fehér restated his moderate position, the position that subsequently received unanimous support from the rural county secretaries. At the end of the session, Kádár summarized the discussion. Labeling Dögei a "sectarian leftist" and those who advocated postponement "revisionists," Kádár proposed that Fehér's position be accepted. The Central Committee voted unanimously in favor of the plan previously endorsed by the Politburo.

Immediately following the 7 December session, Kádár reduced Dögei to a figurehead in the Ministry of Agriculture, working instead through the new deputy minister, István Tömpe, previously Kádár's watchdog in the Ministry of the Interior. In January of the following year Dögei was replaced as minister of Agriculture by Pál Losonczi, chairman of a successful agricultural collective. Finally, in 1962, Dögei was ousted from the Central Committee and appointed city water supply director. He had made the fatal mistake of insisting upon an unpopular and impractical position with very little Central Committee backing.

A month of preparation preceded the carrying out of the Fehér plan. In February 1959 the first cadres arrived in the countryside and joined the local party organization in a campaign of forced collectivization. Utilizing methods far more sophisticated than those employed by Rákosi's hired toughs, they were successful in herding the farmers into the new cooperatives.[25] At party headquarters, meanwhile, Fehér's staff had been working to stabilize the newly organized system. Although Fehér emphasized the strengthening of the rural party organization, he allowed former kulaks (usually the most experienced of the peasants) to become members, and even presidents in some cases, of the collectives. This unorthodox approach caused an uproar, particularly in the neighboring Rumanian and Czechoslovakian Party circles. The new Soviet ambassador, Terentii F. Stikhov, also voiced strong opposition; but Kádár, because he enjoyed Khrushchev's full support, was able to arrange for Stikhov's recall.[26]

During the first two months of recollectivization, both the population of the cooperatives and the arable land doubled. The acreage of the so-called socialist sector (cooperative and state farms together) reached 40 percent. In April the organizational drive was temporarily halted in order to proceed with the normal processes of agricultural production. Then, following harvest, the drive was resumed. The same pattern was applied during the years 1960-62. On 19 February 1961 the party disclosed that the socialist sector comprised approximately 89 percent (14 percent state farms, 75 percent collective farms) and that the total state investment of 16 billion florins had exceeded the original estimate by approximately 75 percent.[27] When the recollectivization drive terminated in the spring of 1962, 95.5 percent of Hungary's arable land was under cultivation by cooperative and state farmers.[28]

Although he fulfilled the aims of the recollectivization campaign, Kádár had to pay a heavy price for his success. As Finance Minister Rezsö Nyers disclosed in his budget report to the National Assembly in February 1962, agricultural production had fallen 8 to 9 percent below the estimates. Furthermore,

Nyers pointed out, the majority of the cooperatives "needed bank loans to tide them over; and in some exceptional cases the solution was found in granting special state assistance."[29] Owing to the decrease in agricultural production during the collectivization campaign, Hungary was forced to import grain from Russia, France, and, in 1963, the United States.

During the first collectivization drive in the 1950s, the peasants had experienced the futility of resistance. They had finally migrated from the rural areas to find jobs in the factories. Similarly, during 1960-63, the young peasants fled to the cities rather than enter the collectives. Official statistics on the division of families according to the social and economic grouping of the head of the family demonstrate dramatically that the extent of peasant migration had reached disastrous proportions. In 1949, 48 percent of the population worked in agriculture. This figure dropped to 33.4 percent in 1960 and in 1963 to 28.9 percent.[30] This phenomenon dealt a serious blow to agricultural production, for it took the regime years to eliminate the labor shortage through mechanization. From the point of view of the regime, however, the situation did have one positive aspect. Since most of the young people had left the farms soon after the initiation of the recollectivization campaign, there was no noticeable political resistance. And social unrest created by the 1960-62 recollectivization drive did not reach nearly the proportion that it had in the 1950s. The Hungarian people as a whole were jolted only momentarily from their apathy. Both the Kremlin and the Hungarian party leadership considered the collectivization of 95 percent of the peasantry "a giant step forward in the building of socialism."

— 8 —

The New Wave of De-Stalinization

It remains the task of a future generation of historians to decide whether the vacuum left by the death of Stalin was ever filled. Perhaps they will assess this question in entirely new terms. But in October 1961, at the time of the Twenty-second Congress of the Communist Party of the Soviet Union (C.P.S.U.), the problem of succession in the Soviet hierachy seemed to be solved. Khrushchev appeared on the speaker's platform of the Congress as the victor. During the years of the long power struggle Khrushchev had step by step, as we have mentioned earlier, eliminated everyone who had opposed his rule. Georgi M. Malenkov, Vyacheslav Molotov, and Lasar Kaganovich, his erstwhile colleagues from Stalin's time, had been defeated in June 1957. His prime minister, Nikolai Bulganin, and the nominal head of state, the president of the Presidium of the Supreme Soviet, Kliment Voroshilov, had also been dismissed. For the first time in Soviet history, Khrushchev had elevated a military man, Marshal Georgy Zhukov, to a post in the Presidium. But when Zhukov's power seemed to have become too great, Khrushchev dismissed him, too. In so doing, Krushchev probably foiled a military takeover. He had methodically removed his opponents and their supporters at every level of the party and state apparatus. Only in Stalin's darkest days had the Soviet Union witnessed such a far-reaching clean-up. In accordance with the new unwritten rules of Khrushchev, the purge was accomplished without trials and executions.[1]

THE RISING POWER OF MAO TSE-TUNG

In the course of events, however, a series of new rivals and opponents proceeded to make their appearance on the scene. Though Khrushchev had

70

temporarily solved the leadership problem in the C.P.S.U., he had not been successful in ensuring his supremacy within the international communist movement. The rising power and authority of Mao Tse-tung were challenging his leading role in the movement. Mao Tse-tung, who during the civil war in China had disregarded Stalin's advice and had emerged victorious, had executed a neat political reversal and was now criticizing the incalculable damage Khrushchev had done to the communist movement by exposing before the world the terror and crimes of Stalin. "The disintegration of a secular faith," as Richard Lowenthal described the aftermath of the destruction of the Stalin myth,[2] really amounted to washing the party's dirty linen in public and contributed to the mounting friction between the Chinese and Soviet leaderships.

Khrushchev's renewed attack against leftism, dogmatism, and Stalinism at the Twenty-second Congress brought into sharp focus not only the personal rivalry but also the clash of national, or in other words, party interests between Russia and China. Though the dispute was couched in ideological rhetoric, there was no concealing the fact that the underlying issues were conflicting national aims. In the first place, China wanted Soviet assistance for its rapid industrialization and agricultural program. In the next place, envisioning herself as a world power China was determined to develop a modern military machine that included nuclear weapons. In pursuance of these goals the People's Republic of China and the U.S.S.R. had in October 1957 signed an "Agreement Concerning the New Technology for National Defense." By this instrument the Soviet Union assumed the obligation to provide China with the latest results of its atomic research and to hand over to China a prototype atom bomb.

With plenty of reason the Kremlin sensed a potential danger to itself in China's rapid development. All available information, in fact, supports the Chinese disclosure that Moscow had backed down on its promise, and in June 1959 had refused to share with Peking the Russian atomic know-how.[3] It is known also that Soviet economic and technical assistance had been drastically cut back. During 1959-60 almost two thousand Soviet economic and military advisers were withdrawn from China. However, just as Stalin's economic measures had failed to bring down Tito's Yugoslavia in 1948, so Khrushchev's economic strategy proved ineffective against Mao.

During and immediately in the wake of the 1956 East European crisis the Chinese Communists were active in "saving and reestablishing" communism in Poland and Hungary. They hoped thus to get a footing in Eastern Europe. Although the Soviet leaders perforce accepted the Chinese presence, they used all possible means to curb the influence of Peking. As far as Hungary and Poland were concerned, the Chinese hopes were soon dashed: party leaders János Kádár and Władisław Gomułka followed without hesitation the lead of the Kremlin.

The path taken by Albania differed significantly from that of Poland and Hungary. Here the leaders of the Albanian Workers' Party (A.W.P.), Enver

Hoxha and Mehmet Shehu, viewing the rapprochement between Moscow and Belgrade, were understandably concerned. They were aware that in 1955 part of Tito's price for improvement of relations between Moscow and Belgrade had been the dismissal of the Stalinists Rákosi in Hungary and Vulko Chervenkov in Bulgaria. The leadership of tiny Albania, when under attack by Khrushchev in 1960, wishing to avoid a fate similar to that of Rákosi and Chervenkov, had taken an unprecedented step. They had sought and received support from China against Russia, whose expansionist aims in Central and Eastern Europe go back many centuries. The clash between Russia and China over the issue of Albania seemed inevitable, therefore, when Chinese Prime Minister Chou En-lai arrived in Moscow in October 1961 to attend the Party Congress.

By the time the Twenty-second Party Congress had convened, Khrushchev had successfully prepared his party's public opinion for the famous program of "building Communism." The draft of the program had been discussed in party organizations throughout the Soviet Union. According to official reports, the rank and file and the local leaders approved the new "Communist Manifesto," including its ambitious twenty-year economic goals. The only duty remaining to the Congress was to cheer and to rubber-stamp a proposal that had already been approved. Khrushchev's opening speech, in which he announced to the delegates that "Socialism had triumphed in the U.S.S.R." and the Soviet society had now "entered upon the period of full-scale communist construction,"[4] was wildly applauded. The Congress demonstrated even greater enthusiasm when the Soviet leader informed them that the dictatorship of the proletariat and the class struggle were no longer required in the Soviet land. All working people would have equal rights because the proletarian dictatorship would be transformed into a state of the "whole people."[5]

Khrushchev managed the Congress with great expertise. The details given concerning Stalinist terror and the great purges provided the delegates with insight into the dimension of suffering endured by the Soviet people. The new leadership's assurances that the abuse of the personality cult would never be repeated was undoubtedly popular. The new wave of de-Stalinization furnished the ideological excuse for the vigorous denunciation of "the anti-party group." The attack against the members of the group, Molotov, Malenkov, Kaganovich, Voroshilov, and others, indicated that Khrushchev was determined to eliminate once and for all the remnants of the Stalinist opposition within the C.P.S.U. leadership.

The condemnation of "the anti-party group" was closely connected with Khrushchev's first public impeachment of the Albanian party's leadership. The carefully staged anti-Albanian show started off with Khrushchev's opening speech. On 17 October the Soviet Party chief criticized the Albanian leaders, expressing the hope that they would correct "their dogmatic errors." Anastas Mikoyan followed Khrushchev by charging that the Albanian leaders had departed from internationalism by backsliding onto the path of nationalism.[6] Mikoyan also quoted Albanian Prime Minister Mehmed Shehu as having said that Stalin had made only two mistakes: he died prematurely, and before his death he should have liquidated the entire present leadership of the C.P.S.U. The attack was stepped up by Dmitry S. Polyansky, Otto V. Kuusinen, and other Presidium members.

Against the Soviet outburst, the Chinese launched a well-conceived counterattack. On 19 October Chou En-lai objected that Chairman Khrushchev unilaterally and in "the face of the enemy" had assaulted the Albanian Workers' (Communist) Party. He argued that such methods "cannot be regarded as a serious Marxist-Leninist attitude." In his view, interparty differences should be resolved through consultation and "on the basis of mutual respect, independence and equality." He warned that "any public, one-sided censure of any fraternal party does not help unity and is not helpful in resolving problems."[7] As was later revealed in Chinese documents,[8] Peking was diametrically opposed to Moscow on all major issues in dispute. Chou En-lai sharply criticized the Soviet commitment to peaceful coexistence, peaceful competition, and peaceful transition. He warned that the renewed and concentrated "onslaught on Stalin" would cause disunity in the international communist movement. Finally, Chou En-lai categorically rejected the Soviet charges leveled against the Albanians.

The day following his speech before the Congress, the Chinese premier visited the Lenin-Stalin mausoleum. By placing two wreaths, one dedicated to Lenin, the other "to Josif Vissarionovich Stalin—the great Marxist Leninist," he unmistakably expressed what the Chinese were thinking about Khrushchev's de-Stalinization policy. In addition to his speech at the Congress and to his public activity in Moscow, the Chinese premier met with Khrushchev and other leaders of the C.P.S.U. in several private sessions. On 23 October he abruptly left Moscow.

Although confused and irritated, the Russians still wanted to maintain the appearance of Soviet-Chinese friendship. At Moscow's Vnukovo Airport an impressive Soviet farewell party headed by Khrushchev wished bon voyage to Chou En-lai, who returned "the courtesy" by sending Khrushchev a message from the plane thanking him for the warm reception and kind attention.[9]

At the closing session of the Congress on 27 October Khrushchev once more took the floor and in a vitriolic speech went so far as to demand openly the overthrow of the Albanian leadership under Enver Hoxha and Mehmed Shehu. But Chou En-Lai's public performance and his secret discussions with the Soviet leaders had had an impact on the Congress. Of the 68 delegates, 44 attacked Albania and 24 refrained. By not mentioning Albania at all, the Asian parties, with the exception of Ceylon, tacitly supported Peking's position. The communist parties of Europe, the Middle East, and Latin America all sided with the C.P.S.U.[10] The East European party chiefs not only voted for the Kremlin but were ready to follow the Soviet leadership in the final break with Albania.

The pro-Soviet attitude of the East European party chiefs was a surprise neither to the Chinese nor to the Albanians. In fact, each of the party leaders had received a copy of Khrushchev's "last warning letter," which reached the Albanian capital on 24 August 1961, two months before the Congress was scheduled to take place.[11] In the name of their Central Committee, the East European bloc leaders also had sent to Tirana letters of "fraternal criticism" that did not differ in substance from the Soviet documents delivered to the Albanian Workers' Party (A.W.P.). Party contacts with Enver Hoxha and Mehmed Shehu had been practically broken off. Also, following the Soviet example, the East European communist regimes had cut off economic aid and had gradually withdrawn their specialists from Albania.

THE OUSTER OF ALBANIA FROM THE BLOC

At the time of the Twenty-second Congress the only question left open was when and how to sever the only remaining formal tie—the diplomatic relations—with Albania. In the course of the behind-the-scene discussions the East European leaders suggested lowering the level of the diplomatic representation to a type of caretaker diplomacy by heading their embassies in Tirana with a chargé d'affaires *ad interim*. While agreeing to the proposal, Khrushchev pointed out that the Soviet Union might go even farther and close its diplomatic and commercial representation in Tirana altogether.

As far as the timing of the action was concerned, Khrushchev seemed desirous of observing correct diplomatic procedure. It appeared that he was taking into account also the growing Chinese influence in the international communist movement when he insisted that the diplomatic action should be put in motion only in the event of a new Albanian provocation. This "Albanian provocation" came soon. On 20 November 1961 the Albanian embassy in Moscow distributed to Soviet institutions and to diplomatic representatives of the countries with which Albania had diplomatic relations, Enver Hoxha's 7 November speech and two declarations of the Central Committee of the A.W.P.[12] The Soviet authorities considered this Albanian version of the Soviet-Albanian differences slanderous. While protesting this hostile and illegal activity, Soviet Deputy Foreign Minister Nikolai P. Firyubin, in a note handed to the Albanian embassy in Moscow on 25 November, demanded the recall of Albanian Ambassador Nesti Nase from Moscow. In a separate note the Soviet Foreign Ministry announced the withdrawal of Soviet Ambassador Josif Shikin from Tirana.[13] As a sign of solidarity with the Soviets, the Hungarian embassy in Moscow, on instruction from its Foreign Ministry, returned the Albanian pamphlet to the Albanian embassy. It is probable that the other East European diplomatic missions did likewise. The die was cast.

In December, after a brief inter-bloc coordination, the Czechoslovak ambassador, then the East German, Hungarian, and Rumanian ambassadors in rapid sucession were recalled from Tirana. In all cases the pattern was similar to Moscow's: the Albanian ambassador was declared *persona non grata* for distributing hostile propaganda materials and was ordered to leave the country. The Chinese ambassador in Budapest and the Chinese representatives in other bloc countries attempted to stop the move. Peking's envoy in Budapest, Tsei Tse-minh, went to the Hungarian party's headquarters and visited the Foreign Ministry, but his interventions on behalf of Albania did not alter the decision already made at the time of the Twenty-second Congress of the C.P.S.U. in Moscow.

While Stalinist East European communists like Walter Ulbricht and Antonín Novotný may have had plenty of reason to be uneasy about their political future, the rise of Khrushchev and the new wave of de-Stalinization launched at the Twenty-second Congress substantially reinforced the position of Hungarian Party Chief János Kádár. Until Khrushchev's leadership had become assured, Kádár was as much concerned with his left opposition within Hungary as Khrushchev had been with the influence of the "anti-party" group remaining in the Soviet party and state apparatus. Although Kádár, with Khrushchev's full support, had already silenced these opponents, he had not been in a position to eliminate them completely from the political forum.[14]

As has already been mentioned, the prominent figures of the Rákosi regime who in fear of their lives had fled to Russia during the 1956 revolution reappeared on the Hungarian political scene after 1957. Salvaged from the ruins of 1956, the officer corps of the dissolved A.V.H. recaptured the leading positions in the newly organized Political Police. The "workers' militia" was in the hands of the left. Several city and county party organizations were controlled by the old Rákosi establishment. István Friss, the Moscow-trained dogmatic economist, headed the Economic Department of the party headquarters.[15] Rightly or wrongly, Politburo member Károly Kiss was regarded as the leading figure in the Politburo and an ultraconservative.[16]

Mátyás Rákosi, "the most devoted Hungarian disciple of Stalin," was removed from power in 1956. He was held partly responsible for the outbreak of the 1956 crisis and was not permitted to return to Hungary. Living in Moscow, where he was quite active, he appeared from time to time in the Kremlin and would hand over long memoranda in which he criticized Kádár's "revisionist policy." Rákosi regularly visited János Boldócky, the Hungarian ambassador to Moscow. The ambassador, who had been Rákosi's foreign minister before 1956, remained faithful to his former master.

A kinsman of Rákosi, Colonel István Dékány, head of the Hungarian intelligence service in 1956, traveled between Moscow and Budapest on behalf of Rákosi with a Soviet passport. Kádár had precise information about Dékány's

missions and his meetings with the underground left, but could do little to
stop the colonel, who had the backing of the Soviet intelligence services.
With Ambassador Boldócky, however, the situation was different. The ambassadors in Moscow did not usually play an important role in Hungarian policy-making. Kádár relied exclusively on party channels for his communications
with the Kremlin and thus bypassed Boldócky entirely. To check Boldócky's
activities further, in 1959 he dispatched Minister Péter Kós, a career diplomat,
to the embassy, and in 1960 Boldócky was dismissed from the foreign service.

THE RÁKOSI PROBLEM

At the Twenty-second Congress Kádár's private discussions with the Soviet
leaders focused on the "Rákosi problem." Referring to the case of "the anti-party
group" and to "the Chinese danger," Kádár had no difficulty obtaining Soviet
consent to silence Rákosi permanently. Khrushchev agreed that the leading
Hungarian Stalinists should be expelled from the H.S.W.P. and promised that
Rákosi would not be permitted to stay in Moscow or to engage in any kind
of political activity. Finally, the Soviet leader accepted Kádár's view that persons
who had participated in Rákosi's reign of terror should be removed from the
party apparatus, as well as from the police.

This decision opened a new chapter in the history of the Kádár regime.
The party leadership shifted its general policy. In "the two-front battle" the
fight against dogmatism and Stalinism was now emphasized, and revisionism
became "the lesser danger." As in the U.S.S.R., those of the party elite who
had played to the left were safe only if they changed sides in time. Those
who did not understand that Kádár was determined to use the ideological support
of the Twenty-second Congress to eliminate the remaining forces of the Rákosi
era lost their position and influence, at least for as long as Khrushchev remained
in power.

The first sign of the new trend was seen at the Central Committee meeting
of the H.S.W.P. on 17 November 1961, at which Kádár reported on the Twenty-
second Congress of the C.P.S.U. At first the meeting seemed to be routine.
The members of the Central Committee had already read the public materials
of the Congress. They were aware that Kádár had fully endorsed Khrushchev's
new policy. But it was always interesting to listen to Kádár. He was not in
the habit of using high-sounding rhetoric, but expressed himself simply and
directly. When he departed from his prepared text, which he did often, his
words became more colorful and personal. This is what happened at the November
meeting. He pointed out that the Hungarian party must take advantage of the
experience of the Twenty-second Party Congress. Like the Soviet leadership,
the Hungarian party must also fight against conservatism and leftism and guard
against the dangers of the revival of the personality cult. At this point he referred
to Rákosi's personal responsibility for the political show trials and the illegal

proceedings of 1949-53, the period of the cult of personality. Underlining the need to terminate this chapter of the party's history, Kádár insisted on setting up a committee to investigate past misuse of power. Although the published part of the Central Committee's resolution made no mention of the forthcoming investigation, it foreshadowed de-Stalinization in Hungary.[17]

Following the Central Committee meeting, Kádár used all public occasions to intensify his attack on the left-wing opposition. The first secretary of the party declared before the workers of Csepel that the cult of personality had been suppressed in Hungary. There remained "people with dogmatic and sectarian views," however, and the party had to fight against them. Kádár made clear that he was not talking about those "who were sectarian eight years ago"—the party had forgiven them. But he threatened the left by saying, "we will burn them by slow fire if they continue to preach sectarian views."[18]

In a speech delivered at the end of the year before a rally of his supporters, the Congress of the Patriotic People's Front, Kádár made public his own formula: "He who is not against us is with us."[19] He thereby quietly revised the Stalinist doctrine (he who is not with us is against us) concerning the class struggle. Kádár later published an article in *Pravda*, in which, instead of writing about "the errors of the old Rákosi direction" (the customary language for referring to the abuses of Rákosi), he branded Rákosi a tyrant who, before 1956, had "undermined the forces of the Party and the regime by his dogmatic and sectarian policy."[20] This strong statement carried special weight, for it appeared in the central organ of the Soviet Communist Party, indicating that the Kremlin had approved the steps taken by Kádár. If Kádár had in any way considered the timing of his statements, he could not have chosen a more opportune moment. The majority of the Hungarian population, who remained practicing Christians, were celebrating Christmas. Kádár's new terminology seemed to presage a change, perhaps for the better. The condemnation of the Rákosi despotism and the repeated assurances that power would not be misused again gained wide public acclaim. The new policy was as popular in Hungary as was the anti-Stalinist drive in the Soviet Union.

In March 1962 Kádár went one step farther. He acknowledged that most Hungarians were not Marxists and that the party must constantly bear this in mind. He pointed out that most people in Hungary were peaceful and honest workers and were not to be treated as class enemies. "Whatever the class enemies may do," Kádár added, "they cannot do us as much harm as we can do to ourselves with our own mistakes." This led him to the conclusion that "the people demand human treatment and confidence."[21]

SOCIOECONOMIC REALIGNMENT

The conciliatory rhetoric was backed by controlled socioeconomic measures. The party launched an appeal for the placing of non-party members in administrative and managerial posts.[22] Old-line party and government officials, including six deputy ministers, were removed from key positions and were replaced by young technicians.[23] The regime encouraged the appointment of the rich farmers who had previously been considered class enemies to membership in and leadership of the cooperative farms. Children of the former upper and middle class were henceforth to be admitted to the universities.

The change in economic leadership created much animosity among the hard core of the party. They rightly sensed that their economic privileges and political influence were being threatened by Kádár's new policy. In defense of their vested interests, the old-liners spread rumors to the effect that Kádár intended to eliminate "the workers' cadres" from all leading posts, and that by doing so he was betraying "the workers' state" and the "dictatorship of the proletariat" to intellectual revisionists. They accused the party leadership of forgetting the services which the old guard had rendered in "the fight against the counterrevolution." The anti-Kádár propaganda was disseminated mainly among the rank and file of the middle and lower echelons of the party. It did not reach the workers, who were interested primarily in getting better wages. Moreover, the rising managerial class moved closer to the party leadership and offered support in the fight against the opposition from the left.

While this socioeconomic realignment was taking place, the special committee set up after the November 1961 Central Committee meeting was conducting a painstaking investigation of Rákosi's crimes. Kádár's old friend, Politburo member Béla Biszku, directed and supervised the task, which took more than six months. The official communiqué released after the investigation stated that "the search for the evidence and the hidden and scattered materials required a protracted effort."[24] The transcripts of interrogations at the A.V.H. headquarters had been destroyed during the fighting in 1956. Much of the pertinent material was in the hands of the Soviet secret police (better known as the K.G.B.) and not accessible to the committee. In the search for evidence the investigators had to comb through the archives of the Supreme Court, the Ministry of Justice, and the files of Party Headquarters. A great number of the police officials who had conducted the examinations of the "show" trials in the Rákosi era and had remained in the political police after 1956, had attempted during the course of the investigation to dispose of compromising evidence. Many of the chief witnesses from Rákosi's prison camps were still on the scene, however, though their roles were now substantially changed. Former defendants János Kádár, Gyula Kállai, György Marosán, and others now, unfortunately for Rákosi, occupied top positions. Even though the former chief accuser was living in exile in the Soviet Union, many of his henchmen, such as A.V.H. Chief Gábor Péter and his deputies, were readily available for questioning.

The committee conducted its investigation in great secrecy. In mid-summer Biszku summed up the evidence in a report presented to the Politburo. About the same time, two Central Committee members, Sándor Nográdi and György Aczél, were sent to the Soviet Union to speak with Rákosi. Though the mission was a formality, Kádár insisted on communicating the findings of the Biszku committee to Rákosi. Not only did party laws require a personal interview in such cases, but Kádár may also have wanted to let Rákosi know that any further hostile activity against the new regime would be useless.

In a stormy session with Rákosi, Nográdi and Aczél recited the charges. The ex-dictator flatly rejected the assertion that he had never possessed any legal powers to order mass arrests, deportations, and trials. In Rákosi's view his police actions were "the natural state of affairs of the revolution ... Socialist legality is nonsense, squaring the circle." He added, "Dammit, let them the Hungarian people feel the existence of the dictatorship of the proletariat."[25] Rákosi strongly criticized Kádár's "compromising spirit," "social democratism," as well as his favoritism toward the new managerial class and the intellectuals. The meeting ended with the two envoys explaining to Rákosi that the Central Committee would probably expel him from the party and that he would never be permitted to return to Hungary.

If Rákosi needed any confirmation of his impending fate, he did not have long to wait. On 19 August 1962 the official party newspaper *Népszabadság* carried the Central Committee's resolution "On Ending the Illegal Proceedings Brought Against the Members of the Labor Movement on Trumped-up Charges."[26] The investigation of the Biszku committee revealed, the Central Committee stated, that the political trials organized and directed by Rákosi had been rigged. The contrived trial of László Rajk in May 1949 had set off a chain reaction, resulting in the trials of former social democrats Árpád Szakasits, György Marosán, and Ödön Kisházi, as well as the trials of János Kádár, Gyula Kállai, and a great number of other communists.

These and many other facts enumerated in the resolution were already well known to the public both within and outside Hungary. Everyone who had followed the reign of terror in Eastern Europe during the early 1950s was aware of the heavy onus of responsibility resting on the shoulders of Rákosi and his henchmen. No party document in Hungary, however, had ever provided such a straightforward account of the crimes committed by the ex-dictator as the report of the committee. For obvious reasons, the part played by the real stage manager of the terror, Stalin's police chief in Hungary, M.V.D. General Fjédor Belkin, was not commented upon.[27] Even though all of the assembled evidence showed that Rákosi had been guilty of capital crimes, no leading party official suggested that there should be any prosecution. The Politburo and the Central Committee seemed to be satisfied with having smashed Rákosi's political career. Rákosi, Gerö, and several other leading Stalinists were simply purged from the party. Six persons were expelled on charges of "factionalism" in collusion with Rákosi, and fourteen former high officials of the old secret police (A.V.H.) were also ousted.

For its own protection the Kádár leadership insisted that no one who had taken part in the staging of the show trials would be permitted to continue working in the Ministry of the Interior, the Judiciary, or the Prosecutor's Office.

Even before the Central Committee decision had been made public, therefore, a great number of known or supposed enemies of Kádár had been discharged from the political police. By way of closing this tragic chapter in Hungarian history, the dead as well as the surviving victims of the Rákosi terror were rehabilitated. These were people who for the most part had belonged to the political elite of the regime. The official communiqué called them "leaders of the labor movement." But tens of thousands more, non-party members who had been executed or imprisoned or deported or who were simply not heard of again—these were never rehabilitated.[28] The reader may very well be led to wonder about the fate of those who disappeared in the long nights of Stalin's terror.

Along with this politically motivated rehabilitation process, Kádár's party apparatus provided new jobs for the dismissed persons. Many were transferred to cultural and commercial areas and some to the diplomatic service. Soviet assistance subsequently enabled some of these figures to return to important positions.[29] Even Rákosi was reportedly permitted to return to Hungary after fourteen years of exile in the Soviet Union.[30] The Soviet leadership was impressed by the way Kádár handled de-Stalinization in Hungary. In the eyes of Khrushchev, the purge of August 1962 was a great success because it had not only strengthened Kádár, his Hungarian ally, but in the process had indirectly strengthened Khrushchev himself in his fight against the dogmatist left within the Soviet Union.

THE MAROSÁN AFFAIR

Kádár's success was temporarily weakened, however, by the so-called Marosán affair. György Marosán, a former social democrat who had spent several years in prison under Rákosi, had played an important role in consolidating the Kádár regime. He had served as the second highest ranking functionary in the party hierarchy. As administrative secretary of the party he had been responsible for the ministries of Defense, Interior, and Justice, which included the armed forces, the police, and the intelligence apparatus. On 14 October 1962 the party newspaper *Népszabadság* announced out of a clear sky that Marosán had been expelled from the Central Committee and the Politburo. The strange defection of Marosán, as his case was spoken of in party circles, took place in the first days of September. Marosán had simply refused to go to his office at party headquarters. Instead, in a long explanatory memorandum to the Central Committee, he had accused Kádár and his close collaborators of failing to restore collective leadership in the party. The important decisions, he maintained, were not taken at the bi-weekly Politburo sessions, but during Kádár's hunting parties and his games of cards. Although Marosán supported the August purge in general and in particular the expulsion of Rákosi, Gerö, and the other leading figures of the dogmatist past, he objected to the shake-up in the police apparatus. In his view, no regime could afford to dismiss at the same time the head of the intelligence service and the head of counterintelligence and his deputy, as was done in the summer of 1962. He maintained that while those police officials had carried out Rákosi's orders, they had been useful also in suppressing Kádár's opposition. Without effective police support, Marosán had written to the Central Committee, no socialist country could exist.

The Marosán memorandum was never published. Some of his accusations were answered by the Central Committee. On 11 October Deputy Prime Minister Kállai reported the affair to an enlarged session of the Central Committee. Though Kállai himself had visited Marosán at his residence in an all-out effort to convince him to withdraw his memorandum and his resignation, all his efforts had been in vain, leaving Kádár with no choice but to expel Marosán from the Central Committee. This dismissal of the number two man of the Hungarian Party occasioned a good deal of speculation. Some said that the action had been provoked by Marosán's incompetence and taste for demagoguery, which Kádár had deemed excessive; and rumors circulated inside the party apparatus to the effect that high-ranking intelligence officers had influenced Marosán when he decided to challenge Kádár's power. Although the Marosán affair caused Kádár some inconvenience, it was soon forgotten. After the Eighth Hungarian Party Congress, Béla Biszku, former minister of the Interior, later deputy prime minister and member of the Politburo, assumed Marosán's functions in the party apparatus.[31]

In the final analysis the August 1962 purge of the leading Stalinists represented a substantial strengthening of Kádár's position. He had eliminated the left-wing opposition and he had obtained new support from the managerial class. Now, without competitors, he could afford to follow a more liberal, middle-of-the-road policy. But he was still haunted by the memories of 1956, and the continued presence of Soviet troops in Hungary remained a barrier between his regime and the people.

The austerity of communist rule relaxed. Although he did not tolerate political opposition, Kádár accepted the indifference of the masses as a fact of life. The population was not forced to attend meetings and rallies organized by the party, as it had in Rákosi's time. The Kádár leadership promised higher living standards and was ready to offer economic posts to non-party specialists to achieve this aim. While supporting the old concept of ''socialist realism'' in literature and art, Kádár promised greater intellectual liberty provided this was not turned against his regime. He liberalized the educational policy, but he defended the past practice of academic discrimination enforced previously by the communist party.

In many respects Kádár went farther on the road of liberalization than Khrushchev. Moscow voiced no objection to this trend as long as policy was controlled by the party and the Soviet leadership was consulted. What mattered to the Kremlin was only that Kádár should act in accordance with the general policy-line of the Twenty-second Congress of the C.P.S.U. and that the purge should not occasion undue disturbances in Hungarian society.

— 9 —

Diplomatic Thrust and Parry

While the domestic life of Hungary was gradually attaining a certain degree of stability, the Kádár regime, with Soviet support, was being compelled to exert great effort to break Hungary's isolation in the international arena. In 1959, following Premier Khrushchev's talks with President Eisenhower at Camp David, Maryland,[1] Soviet Deputy Foreign Minister Vasily V. Kuznetsov attempted to exploit the relaxed international atmosphere created there to reestablish Hungary's full membership at the United Nations. Using attack as the best possible tactic for defense, Kuznetsov made an impassioned speech before the Fourteenth Session of the United Nations in which he took the position that to debate the question of Hungary would seriously interfere with the relaxation of international tension and would be contrary to what he called "the spirit of Camp David." He emphasized that such a move would hinder any further improvement in international relations—an improvement initiated by Khrushchev during his recent visit.[2]

The Soviet argument, however, failed utterly to put an end to the annually recurring discussion of Soviet intervention in Hungary. Ambassador Henry Cabot Lodge, who had been present at all the meetings at Camp David, made it unmistakably clear in the forum of the world organization that nothing had been said in the talks between the two leaders that would justify overlooking or condoning the situation still existing in Hungary. He pointed out that the Camp David communiqué had announced very plainly that "all outstanding international questions should be settled not by application of force but by peaceful means through negotiation." In "the spirit of Camp David," he added sarcastically, the Soviet Union and Hungary should comply with the resolutions of the United Nations.[3]

The overwhelming majority of the members of the United Nations supported Lodge's viewpoint. Among others, the representatives of Brazil, the Netherlands, the United Kingdom, France, Canada, Pakistan, the Federation of Malaya, Nepal, Venezuela, and Uruguay recalled the terms of the previous General Assembly resolutions and urged the Soviets to withdraw their troops from Hungary. They expressed grave concern regarding evidence that reprisals against individuals who had participated in the 1956 revolution were still continuing despite repeated promises by Hungarian officials.

On 9 December the General Assembly adopted a 24-power resolution in which the United Nations once more "deplored the continued disregard by the Union of Soviet Socialist Republics and the present Hungarian regime of the General Assembly resolutions dealing with the situation in Hungary."[4] The renewed condemnation naturally thwarted Kuznetsov's plan and indicated conclusively that nothing less than a long and difficult series of diplomatic negotiations would be required to solve the Hungarian question. In order to secure for Hungary the same treatment as that accorded other Soviet-bloc countries, the Kádár government's diplomatic service first of all had to reestablish channels of communication with U.S. officials. Early in 1960 and continuing into 1961 a strange sort of dialogue had developed between the Hungarian legation in Washington and the State Department. Hungarian diplomats and State Department officials, who had avoided meeting one another for years, finally began to communicate. At receptions and cocktail parties the Hungarian chargé, Tibor Zádor, and the head of the East European Office of the State Department, Harold Vedeler, and his deputy, Robert McKisson, began in more or less tentative fashion to exchange views on the "Hungarian question." As a prelude they would chat about the weather, the percentage of humidity in the Washington air, and the meteorological forecast. These were the only points on which both the Americans and the Hungarians agreed. These matters once disposed of, the conversation would then become livelier, with Vedeler asking Zádor about the political climate in Budapest and about the possibility of creating an atmosphere for lessening the tension between the United States and Hungary. The Hungarian chargé would counter that his government had always desired better relations with the United States, and that the cause of the strained relations was the longstanding hostile American policy toward the Hungarian communist regime. In his opinion, this hostility had reached its peak in 1956, when the United States had "instigated and assisted the counterrevolution" in Hungary.

A long discussion would inevitably follow on how to characterize the Hungarian events—revolution or counterrevolution. Zádor would argue that the Hungarian government had incontestable evidence of American intervention. He would express the view that Radio Free Europe and the Voice of America broadcasts had directed the plot. This repetition of the official version of the Kádár government would not surprise Vedeler, who would merely note that the 200,000 Hungarians who had fled from their homeland in 1956 suggested a different explanation of the story. Arguments and counterarguments would be exchanged. Zádor would charge that the unfriendly attitude and bad intentions of the U.S. government toward his government epitomized American policy on the Hungarian question. Vedeler would reject this complaint by citing U.S. responsibilities toward the Hungarian people under the terms of the Peace Treaty and the Charter of the United Nations. The Hungarian diplomat would then charge the Americans with interference in the internal affairs of Hungary. These animated discussions and exchanges of views between the Americans and the Hungarians would produce no visible results, but the mere fact that the officials of both countries were now not only engaging in chitchat but were actually touching upon the delicate question of 1956 was in itself important.

A marked change occurred in the U.S. position when the Hungarian government announced in April 1960 the abolishment of political internment camps. To commemorate the fifteenth anniversary of the liberation of Hungary from Nazi Germany, the Kádár regime granted personal amnesty to certain categories of political prisoners. Among those released were the writers Tibor Déry and Gyula Háy, who had played prominent roles in the 1956 revolution. Mihály Farkas, the minister of defense under Mátyás Rákosi, and his son, Vladimir Farkas, a former colonel of the A.V.H. who had personally tortured Kádár, were also pardoned.[5] Vedeler and other State Department officials informed Zádor that to some degree the United States government considered the partial amnesty a positive sign. Vedeler stressed, however, that the normalization of bilateral relations required further steps toward the removal of all traces of 1956. He hinted delicately that the administration was hoping the Hungarian government would ease the friction between the two countries by releasing the remaining political prisoners of 1956.

Zádor rebuffed this new suggestion, branding it a renewed attempt to interfere in the internal affairs of Hungary. Reporting back to his Foreign Ministry, the Hungarian chargé pointed out that the State Department had taken an ultra-reactionary attitude vis-à-vis the Hungarian government, and that the new U.S. demand—the release of the counterrevolutionary element from prison—was a "dangerous imperialistic move to undermine the stability of the Kádár regime." In his report Zádor did not dare state that even now, in the year 1960, the crushing of the Hungarian revolution, the Russian occupation, and the repressive measures of the Kádár regime remained a cruel reality in the minds of the American people. Instead, he sent to Budapest a recommendation on how to counterbalance "the directed American propaganda apparatus" in order to influence public opinion in the United States and to improve the image of Hungary, especially among the American working class. In the face of readily available evidence to the contrary, one must assume that only a blind supporter, an indoctrinated disciple of the regime, or an overcautious diplomat could have sent such a misleading and ill-founded report. Although Zádor and his diplomatic staff, living in Washington as they did, could not have failed to be fully aware that public ill will toward the Hungarian regime was more than a matter of propaganda, the chargé evidently slanted his report to please the Foreign Ministry.

He was playing the game safely and wrote the report as Budapest would have wanted it. One possible explanation of his need for caution may be that the political and military intelligence services working inside the legation sent separate messages to Budapest, and he never knew the content of their communications.

Zádor's strategy was no doubt influenced also by other considerations. Along with other East European diplomats, he assumed that the Bay of Pigs invasion would eventually be followed by an all-out U.S. attack against Cuba. The Vienna meeting of Kennedy and Khrushchev, the Berlin crisis, and the Wall had made him view American foreign policy as the aggressive behavior of the strongest power of the capitalist world. He looked at international events from the communist point of view. He was indeed convinced (as he later told me on several occasions) that the United States was preparing to draw the East European socialist countries away from the Soviet Union. In Zádor's mind the cold war was a preparation for the hot war. The chargé's approach was by no means unique; it was, rather, the general conceptual and psychological outlook of communist diplomats, an outlook that was reflected in their personal assessments and official reports.

In the midst of this stalemated situation, an event occurred during the fall of 1961 that was both unusual and noteworthy. While Zádor was absent briefly from Washington, a senior diplomat from the Hungarian legation had a private conversation at a social gathering with State Department official Turner Shelton during which the American once again repeated his administration's position. Shelton explained that his government could do nothing to normalize relations if the Hungarian government did not at least make a formal declaration promising amnesty for the participants in the 1956 revolution who had been jailed. This was essential, he added, because, until the question of the political prisoners in Hungary was settled, the administration simply could not sell Congress and the American public on the idea of reconciliation with the Hungarian regime, nor could it vote to drop the Hungarian question from the agenda of the United Nations.

The Hungarian diplomat, in a surprising display of ineptitude, reported the actual American position to the Foreign Ministry. Furthermore, he went so far as to explain that the State Department's view made sense to him, for even years after the "counterrevolution" the American public was still hostile toward the Hungarian government. If his government was interested in a quick solution, the only way he saw to get rid of the Hungarian question in the United Nations was to declare a general amnesty. The report caused an uproar in the Foreign Ministry, as well as at party headquarters in Budapest, and resulted in the diplomat's being recalled. The legation was instructed to tell the State Department that Shelton's proposal was totally unacceptable and represented a gross insult and an interference in the internal affairs of Hungary. The State Department refuted this charge, pointing out that Shelton had not made any formal proposal. He had given only his private opinion, though his views corresponded in general with the administration's assessment of the situation. Both Vedeler and McKisson made it clear that the next step was up to the Hungarian government if it was interested at all in improving relations between the two countries.

A few months of inaction followed the Shelton episode, with neither side raising the question of normalization. Zádor, whose assignment in the United States was coming to an end anyway, and who wanted to avoid further complications, especially with his own Foreign Ministry, steered clear of further acrimonious tangles with the Americans. For its part, the U.S. State Department, since it did not consider the Hungarian question a major issue in East-West relations, was willing to wait.

— 10 —

The New Chargé's Contradictory Instructions

In March 1962 I was appointed chargé d'affaires to take over Zádor's Washington post, inheriting with it the six-year-old Hungarian question. Before leaving Budapest I had prepared for the assignment by studying all reports, memoranda, and notes relating to the matter and had come to the conclusion that no specific plan was available to chart my course. Interviewing competent officials at lower levels, including the director of the Department of the Western Division—or, as it was then called, the NATO Countries Division in the Hungarian Foreign Ministry—I found expressions of hatred and hostility mixed with fear and feelings of inferiority. These seemed to be compensated for by an attitude of belligerency and self-righteousness. The officials of the ministry considered the United States Public Enemy Number One of the Hungarian regime. They found it impossible to forgive America for its "intervention" in 1956 and seemed unwilling or unready for any kind of accommodation. Those colleagues of mine who had been sympathetic to Imre Nagy's policy during the revolution dared not challenge the accepted line. The only safe policy was to blame the Americans for everything. They seemed completely sincere and well-meaning when they advised in private: don't do anything; then you won't get into trouble.

At a higher level I found the same inflexibility. Deputy Foreign Minister Károly Szarka, who at that time was in charge of the Western Hemisphere, bluntly informed me that the Americans must be made to realize that they lost their battle in Hungary in 1956. Szarka maintained that Hungarian interest dictated a firm stand against the United States. Thus normalization of relations between the two countries could not be considered until the State Department was prepared to offer evidence of having given up its policy of hostility toward Hungary. He demanded that as a prior condition for improved relations the

Hungarian question must be removed from the U.N. agenda. In his opinion, a new approach toward Washington was possible only if the U.S. administration abandoned the Hungarian question as a cold war issue and approved the Hungarian credentials at the United Nations.

Being somewhat undecided as to the precise foreign policy to be pursued on the other side of the world, I found it difficult to agree with these views that appeared to be so prevalent in the Foreign Ministry. I assessed Hungarian-U.S. relations as a part of the Soviet-American world conflict and hoped that during a lull in the confrontations between the superpowers the Hungarian question at the United Nations could be solved and Hungary's isolation ended. I felt that the developing dialogue in Washington between U.S. and Hungarian diplomats could be seen as a step in the right direction. Although such discussions in the past had produced no specific results, at least the positions of the two sides were becoming somewhat clarified. It seemed encouraging too that the new Kennedy administration was represented in Budapest by Horace G. Torbert, a man of great diplomatic skill, who had already indicated to Hungarian officials his desire for a détente.

My hopes for improved relations were given a boost by certain new trends developing at the United Nations. At the Fifteenth Session of the General Assembly (20 September 1960 to 21 April 1961) most of the newly admitted African countries, anxious to enjoy the political friendship and economic assistance of both the United States and the Soviet Union, abstained when the delicate question of Hungary was proposed for inclusion on the agenda of the Assembly. This resulted in a sharp increase in the number of abstentions during the roll call vote.[1] Even more important for the Hungarian government, the president of the U.N. General Assembly, the Irish diplomat Frederick H. Boland, stated at the closing session on 21 April 1961 that subsidiary organs whose reports had not been considered because of the pressure of time were authorized to submit reports to the Assembly's Sixteenth Session. The Hungarian question was one of the issues not discussed.[2] Whether the Assembly really had had no time to discuss the Hungarian issue in substance or whether the State Department had arranged the postponement was uncertain. This could very well have been a U.S. gesture extended to Khrushchev, who attended the Fifteenth Session along with the East European leaders.

At the Sixteenth Session of the General Assembly a sixteen-power resolution "deplored" the U.S.S.R. and Hungarian governments' disregard for the General Assembly's resolutions concerning the situation in Hungary. This mild resolution was adopted by 49 votes in favor and 17 opposed, with 32 abstentions.[3] Of all the African states, only one—Dahomey—voted for the resolution; two voted against and the remainder abstained. Similarly, among the Asian nations, only Pakistan aligned itself with the West, while the other Asian governments abstained, considering the Hungarian question no longer relevant to world politics. Leftist Guinea and Mali voted against the resolution.

These new developments convinced me that the situation was indeed changing and that some sort of arrangement could be and should be worked out to end the Hungarian debate at the United Nations. Because I was very anxious to be as well prepared for my post in Washington as possible, I continued to explore the possibilities. Since my soundings at the lower diplomatic levels had proved more or less unproductive, I proceeded to seek guidance from the top. When I entered the office of Foreign Minister János Péter, therefore, I was determined to press for clear-cut answers, and felt fortunate in finding the minister in a good mood. Péter's office, on the second floor of the Hungarian Foreign Ministry Building, commanded a magnificent panoramic view of the Danube with its bridges, the Gothic Parliament, and the ultramodern party headquarters. For a moment I could not resist studying Péter's inscrutable countenance and wondering about his strange life story.

Born in 1910, Péter had been educated in Budapest, Paris, and Glasgow to become a priest in the Hungarian Reformed Church. There is some reason to believe that in the 1930s, and even in the early years of World War II, he had Nazi sympathies. In 1944, however, when he was chaplain of Budapest's Bethesda Hospital, he had helped to conceal Zoltán Tildy, one of the leaders of Hungary's bourgeois Smallholders' Party and also a clergyman. Two years later, after the war, when Tildy became president of Hungary, Péter was appointed to head his secretariat. At the same time, however, Péter was an undercover agent for the communist-controlled secret police. He guessed correctly that the communists would ultimately take over, as they in fact did in 1948. That summer Tildy's son-in-law, Victor Chornoky, was recalled from his post as minister to Cairo and arrested. Chornoky was accused of selling the Hungarian diplomatic code to the British and of smuggling valuable stamps. The following December he was hanged. This hopelessly compromised President Tildy, who resigned.

Before the trial Péter had gone abroad to try to persuade Chornoky's wife to return to Hungary. Although he failed, his effort was appreciated and he was given a seat in Parliament and the bishopric of the Trans-Tibiscan Synod in Debrecen, the center of Hungarian Protestantism. He visited the United States in 1954 to represent the Hungarian Reformed Church at the second assembly of the World Council of Churches held in Evanston, Illinois, where his fellow clergymen attacked him as a propagandist of the communist regime.

Driven out of his church office during the revolution of 1956, he was among the first to declare his support for the Kádár government. He became a member of the Presidential Council in 1957 and subsequently played an important role in preventing the Moscow-created World Peace Movement from falling apart. He traveled through Asia and the Arabic countries with Deputy Foreign Minister Szarka, trying to convince the leaders of the nonaligned countries that the 1956 revolution had been a counterrevolution plotted by imperialists. He was appointed chairman of the Institute of Cultural Relations, then first deputy foreign minister. His ultimate dream was fulfilled in 1961 when he became foreign minister. Only then, at a meeting which I attended, did he openly join the Communist Party. His readiness to cooperate with the political police as well as his close friendship with high officials in the Soviet Union was well known in the inner circles of the Foreign Ministry, and nobody was surprised when he was appointed a member of the Central Committee of the Hungarian Socialist Workers' Party.

At our meeting I launched almost at once into a series of questions. Could Péter give me any guidance with regard to Hungarian-American relations? Should I continue to carry out the present policy-line (that is, to wait and see), or was there anything else to do? Responding to the first question, Péter answered that I should study the American political and economic situation and report back to him, at which time he would decide upon an answer to the second question. His response was actually meaningless, for even on less important questions decisions were not made in the Foreign Ministry. The party headquarters was the center of decision making, and Péter would be invited there only as a guest or as an adviser.

My next query related to the Hungarian question. On the basis of Zádor's recent reports, I asked, should I take any initiative on this issue? Should I try to find out from the State Department officials the latest American position? What should be my position if the State Department should bring up the topic? No direct answer to any of these questions was forthcoming. Instead Péter spoke at length about the starting-point of the conflict. According to him, the "Americans' hatred of Hungary" dated back to 1947, when the Hungarian government had refused to participate in the Marshall Plan, and had reached its climax in 1956. He thought that the United States government had been too confident that it would win in 1956, certain that Hungary, by leaving the Warsaw Pact, would have become either an American military base or at least another Yugoslavia. However, the Soviet armed forces had shattered American dreams. The foreign minister then spoke of the "provocative" 1956 Security Council meeting where the Kádár regime had been condemned by the United Nations; Henry Cabot Lodge he dismissed as a madman, and Sir Leslie Munro as an American agent who was receiving extra pay from the U.S. government for his "anti-Hungarian services." He added that the U.S. delegation to the United Nations was deliberately using the Hungarian question not only as a cold war issue, but as a means of misleading Hungarian public opinion.

Finally he advised that the best thing to do under the present circumstances would be to wait and see. According to his calculations the Asians and the newly admitted African countries were not interested in the "Anglo-American cold war propaganda" over Hungary, and sooner or later their votes would make it impossible for the United States to gather enough strength to include the Hungarian question on the agenda of the United Nations. The last part of this explanation made sense to me, although I foresaw the possibility that the Americans would be able, at least for the next few years, to muster the necessary two-thirds majority.

As the interview drew to a close, the foreign minister offered a few general observations. He was convinced that the U.N. General Assembly would soon cease to play the role of an "imperialistic voting machine" and that at the United Nations the communist bloc would defeat the Americans with the assistance of the Third World nations. He emphasized that time was working for the Hungarian government, and for that very reason I would have to refrain from taking the initiative to normalize relations. This approach, in a sense, was a more direct answer to my questions. Though not agreeing with the foreign minister, I preferred not to oppose him directly. I was planning to follow through by seeing Kádár, and knew that Kádár did not always see eye-to-eye with his foreign minister.

My meeting with János Kádár fulfilled my expectations. The first secretary stated flatly at the outset that Hungary's international status would require sooner or later a settlement of the Hungarian question and of Hungary's outstanding problems with the United States. He pointed out that the two questions were closely related and that he could foresee no separate arrangement regarding them. He seemed confident and determined; his phrases were sharp and incisive, his sentences—in contrast to Péter's vague circumlocutions—quite uncomplicated.

Continuing, Kádár explained that relations between Hungary and the United States must not continue as tense as they had been during the past six years. The normalization could proceed rapidly if the U.S. government would only stop pressing him to release those who had been imprisoned in the wake of the 1956 events. As an example he cited the case of the writer Tibor Déry. The Writers International Pen Club had addressed telegrams, protest notes, and all kinds of messages to the Kádár government demanding an end to the writer's prison term. That was the worst thing they could have done for Déry, said Kádár, because the action made it virtually impossible to exercise clemency. Kádár had finally sent word to the Pen Club to stop its interference and pressure. The leaders of the club understood the message, gave up their liberate-Déry campaign, and a few months later Déry was released from prison. The same rule applied to the Americans, noted Kádár. Until the State Department officials stopped insisting on amnesty as a precondition for improvement, no amnesty would be granted.

Interestingly, Kádár recalled his 1960 New York visit, when he had attended the Fifteenth Session of the United Nations General Assembly. He considered ridiculous the Eisenhower administration's request that his movements in the United States be restricted to Manhattan Island.[4] He added that he had no intention of promoting revolution in the United States, although he did acknowledge that security arrangements were necessary because hostile émigré groups made too much noise around him. He had been disappointed that he could not see more of the United States, for he was especially interested in the organization and management of the American economy. He recalled that the ship *Baltica*, on which he had traveled, was towed into New York harbor by a little ship with only three or four men on board. He remarked that in Hungary this type of work would be performed by at least fifteen men. On the whole, he preferred not to speak much about his U.N. experiences. He was especially sensitive about the walkout of more than half the delegates present when he was called to the rostrum to deliver his speech before the General Assembly. Kádár could hardly have failed to notice the degree of isolation to which his regime was subject in the world organization; and these first-hand impressions, as I was later told, influenced him greatly in his later decisions.

Returning to political questions after this short digression, Kádár expressed partial agreement with Péter's views concerning the Hungarian question. He too thought that this issue would eventually fade away, but he knew that in the meantime the United States could continue to force inclusion of the item on the agenda, thereby prolonging an annoying situation for his government.

Kádár's final instructions to me were to establish as much high-level contact with American officials as possible because this might be useful in the future. He also wanted me to inform the State Department that it was useless to press for amnesty. The more they pressed, he said, the less likelihood would there be for positive results.

By this time it was becoming crystal-clear that Kádár was seeking a face-saving solution and was delivering to me the proxy for finding it. And I was aware, too, that I could disregard Péter's speculation on the voting record in the United Nations, for I knew well enough who had the last word.

— 11 —

Amnesty Before Normalization

My first conversations in Washington with State Department officials could be characterized as a game of diplomatic blindman's buff. In March 1962, when I met with Harold C. Vedeler, director of the Eastern European Department, and his deputy Robert McKisson, the Americans were naturally anxious to discover whether I had received new instructions for dealing with the problem of Hungarian-U.S. relations. Answering in general terms that my aim was to improve rapport between the two countries, I tried in turn to sound them out as to possible American reaction to ending the debate on the Hungarian question in the United Nations—a matter that had kept the Hungarian regime in the purgatorium of world opinion every year since the crushing of the 1956 Hungarian revolution. Vedeler's answer was similarly vague and evasive: the U.S. government's position had already been explained to my predecessor, Tibor Zádor, and had not changed in the meantime.

Though the two State Department officials were amiable and ready to discuss almost any political question, I realized that they were less interested than I in resolving the Hungarian question at the United Nations. I understood also from their discussion that the State Department was unlikely to agree to the normalization of relations until the Hungarian government should express its willingness to release the political prisoners of the ill-fated events of 1956. Following this first meeting I reported to Budapest that the Americans were as rigid as before vis-à-vis the Kádár regime, and that they still clung to the old "amnesty before normalization" formula.

On 4 April at a reception at the Hungarian Legation, I had a long, informal conversation with Director Vedeler and Deputy McKisson. In the warm, friendly atmosphere created by the excellent Hungarian wines and gourmet food, I told McKisson half in jest that because of the rigid policy of the State Department,

American tourists were being deprived of tasting the nectar of the Tokaj vines and of enjoying gypsy music on the banks of the Blue Danube. The deputy director replied that American tourists were simply afraid to go to Hungary. His office, he explained, received letters almost every day inquiring about the safety of Americans traveling to Budapest, and the State Department was forced to reply that visitors must proceed at their own risk; the State Department could neither give them adequate protection inside Hungary nor guarantee their personal safety. I pointed out in turn that many tourists from West Germany and other West European countries were coming to Hungary in a steady stream, and they were not afraid. Whenever the Hungarian Foreign Ministry was prepared to guarantee that American tourists could be properly protected by the American legation in Budapest, predicted McKisson, the flow of tourism would begin. He observed, however, that the memories of the 1956 revolution and its aftermath were still alive in America and that for this reason many American tourists would be likely to avoid Hungary. He added by way of general advice that the best means for boosting tourism would be a general amnesty. Of course I reminded McKisson that I myself was under strict instructions to reject officially any American attempt at interference in the internal affairs of Hungary and that his remarks had fallen into this category; but unofficially I advised McKisson not to press the issue of amnesty if the State Department was genuinely interested in witnessing a general clemency. Without showing any reaction to this last remark, McKisson praised the excellent quality of the Hungarian wines.

At a meeting I had a few weeks later with the two State Department East European specialists, the conversation began with discussion of the forthcoming 1962 Congressional elections. I speculated that the 1961 Bay of Pigs fiasco would strengthen the Republican Party's position, at least in Congress, and would influence the foreign policy line of the Kennedy administration. Vedeler appeared somewhat reluctant to go into details, but volunteered that he was not expecting any basic foreign policy change as a result of the Congressional elections.

The deputy's comment provided me with a good opening for easing into the Hungarian question. Complaining that the Democratic and Republican senators and congressmen alike had been demonstrating hostility toward the Hungarian regime, I warned that harsh words would not frighten the Hungarian government nor alter the faith of the Hungarian people. Animosity, I added, would only heap fuel on existing anti-American sentiment in Hungarian government circles and would make a settlement more difficult. Although both American officials agreed with me in principle, they pointed out that the State Department was powerless to influence Congress in this respect. Vedeler repeated once again the argument that American public opinion was still deeply affected by the repressive measures employed in the 1956 revolution, and that congressmen and senators—especially those from districts where there were many Hungarians,

Czechs, Poles, or other East Europeans—would naturally take into consideration the political opinions of their constituents. Being well aware of the anti-Kádár attitude of Hungarians living in Cleveland, Detroit, New York, Los Angeles, and other large cities, I could easily understand Vedeler's position. But wanting to avoid an embarrassing situation, I replied simply that in light of the American political system, foreign countries were indeed forced to anticipate and adjust to American elections.

At this point McKisson interrupted me with the suggestion that the Hungarian government could perhaps influence both Congress and public opinion if it were to declare a general amnesty in Hungary. Emphasizing that he was not "suggesting" such a course, and that the State Department did not want to "interfere" in the internal affairs of Hungary, he observed that he could foresee no changes in the general attitude toward Hungary on the part of Americans until those who had been sentenced for political reasons after the 1956 revolution were released. McKisson argued that because almost six years had elapsed since the outbreak of the uprising, the Hungarian government should feel secure enough to close all the cases connected with 1956.

With mixed feelings and with a desire to probe deeper into a minute crack, I asked McKisson what would happen if the Hungarian government were to declare amnesty. Vedeler answered the hypothetical question very directly: he was certain the U.S. government would exercise its influence to drop the Hungarian question from the U.N. agenda. *Pro forma*, I reminded him not to press too hard on the issue of amnesty but quickly emphasized that both sides, the American and the Hungarian, must strive for a more flexible, more suitable compromise solution. I felt that this was as far as I could go without exceeding my authority or misleading the U.S. negotiators.

The next step was to speak with George C. McGhee, the undersecretary for political affairs. For any other head of a foreign diplomatic mission in Washington, such a visit would have been routine. In the case of a Hungarian chargé, however, a visit at that level was unusual. Since 1956 no Hungarian diplomat had been received by high U.S. officials in the Department of State, nor were U.S. representatives in Budapest granted audiences by high Hungarian officials. I called the chief of protocol, Ambassador Angier Biddle Duke, telling him of my intention to pay a visit to the undersecretary, and within a week received word that McGhee would see me on 26 April.

Notifying Budapest of the forthcoming visit, I asked for instructions. A few hours before the scheduled meeting a cable arrived from the Foreign Ministry providing a general guideline. I was to tell the undersecretary that the Hungarian government hoped, as always, to eliminate its differences with the United States and to improve relations, but that the attitude of the U.S. government toward Hungary until now had made any progress in this direction impossible. The Hungarian Foreign Ministry, stated the telegram, would consider with interest any suggestions offered by Undersecretary McGhee and would like to know whether the United States was planning again to place the Hungarian question on the U.N. General Assembly agenda in the fall of 1962. Apart from this specific question, I was given a free hand to bring up any matter of general interest.

The conversation with McGhee began rather clumsily. After the initial exchange of greetings, I thanked him for agreeing to see me. Without saying a word, McGhee inclined his head and waited to hear what I had to say. On my part, I had half hoped he would make the first move. In an attempt to lighten the atmosphere, I tried to establish some degree of rapport by selecting at random the earth-shaking news that in preparation for this meeting I had looked up McGhee in *Who's Who* and had learned that the undersecretary had been the organizer of rescue operations for pilots shot down over the Pacific during World War II.

McGhee seemed taken aback at first, but then began slowly to recount his wartime experiences. He explained that the Japanese had been quite effective in the air war at the beginning of the military operations and were shooting down American planes one after another. Those pilots who survived the crash perished in the water. Something had to be done, he said, and he had been placed in charge of solving the problem. "We worked out a communications system between the Air Force and the Navy, and when a pilot was shot down, he was picked up by our submarines. That was more or less the entire operation," said McGhee modestly.

From this point the official part of the discussion flowed more easily. I explained that it was my intention to adhere to the mandate given me by the Hungarian government—to devote my efforts to the improvement of Hungarian-American relations. For this reason I was asking the undersecretary for suggestions as to how this might best be accomplished. Not surprisingly, McGhee replied that in order to be realistic he felt compelled to tell me that the State Department could take no steps in this direction until the Hungarian question had been debated at the United Nations. Therefore, he concluded, the Hungarian government should first straighten out its relations with the United Nations. Perhaps a voluntary act, he suggested almost parenthetically, an amnesty, might be the key to the solution.

Although the suggestion for a "voluntary act" sounded far more conciliatory than had earlier demands for amnesty, I could hardly agree with him openly and simply reviewed for him the official stand of the Hungarian government. I pointed out that Hungary had had no problem with the world organization and that a voluntary step was a purely internal affair. To strengthen my argument, I told him that conditions had greatly improved in Hungary, particularly in comparison with those existing during the Rákosi regime, and cited the slogan launched in one of Kádár's recent speeches: "He who is not against us is

with us.''[1] The undersecretary found Kádár's formulation interesting but did
not comment further. I told McGhee that he would be welcome in Hungary
if he were to visit the country to see the situation for himself.

As the meeting came to a close I returned once again to the Hungarian
question, asking whether the United States planned to propose that the issue
be placed on the agenda this year. McGhee answered briefly that he was unaware
of any definite plan but that he had heard of no change in the U.S. position.
Reminding me that the United States had assumed clear responsibilities toward
the Hungarian people under the international treaties following World War II,
he pointed out that the Hungarian government had not allowed representatives
of the United Nations to enter Hungary. Realizing that the issue would most
probably be debated again in 1962, I told him that the Hungarian government
could be ''very patient'' and could ''wait'' if necessary.

Back in my office, I composed a long report to the Foreign Ministry
pointing out that Undersecretary McGhee had presented the American insistence
upon amnesty in a slightly different formulation from that of Director Vedeler.
Instead of pressing the ''amnesty before normalization'' formula, he proposed
a ''voluntary step'' in ''exchange for improvement.'' I added that although
this sounded less aggressive, it still contained the basic element of interference
in the internal affairs of Hungary.

Aware of the necessity of slanting my report to the liking of Budapest,
I ventured the suggestion that the apparent change in the State Department's
attitude resulted from ''the Hungarian government's firmness in rebuffing the
constant American attempts at interference.'' I added, however, that the State
Department officials were probably correct in characterizing public opinion as
hostile to the Kádár regime. ''Naturally'' I attributed this state of affairs to
the inflammatory speeches of various congressmen and senators who used every
possible occasion to attack the Hungarian communist regime. In closing my
report, I mentioned that, on the basis of McGhee's remarks, the American
administration would most likely ''provoke'' another debate on the Hungarian
question in the United Nations. However, I added that I wanted to obtain
further proof and to solicit opinions from the White House and from the senators
with whom I was acquainted. I was, in fact, planning to contact Chester Bowles,
President Kennedy's special representative in the White House, as well as Senator
Claiborne Pell and Senator Allen Ellender.

In drafting my report, I had to take into consideration, as had my pre-
decessors, the fact that the intelligence agencies operating inside the Hungarian
legation would send separate reports on the same subject to their Budapest
headquarters. This parallel reporting took place not because the political and
military intelligence agencies wanted to present original points of view, but
basically because each was suspicious of the other and each hoped to gain
control over the other. The weakest element among these competitors was the
foreign service, because its reporting was literally controlled by the political

intelligence. For this reason, I wrapped my report in an ideological cover. Unwilling to commit political suicide, I did not propose that Hungary's best interests demanded the closing of debate on the Hungarian question at the United Nations, for which the prerequisite was general amnesty. If I had sent such counsel to the Foreign Ministry, I would without doubt have been labeled "soft" with the State Department.

While waiting for an answer, I wondered how Budapest would respond to the "voluntary step" formula offered by Undersecretary McGhee. Would Kádár and the other members of the Politburo accept it as a face-saving solution or reject it as a renewed attempt to interfere in the internal affairs of Hungary? Four weeks later came a brief answer to the report. The director of the Western Hemisphere Department, who signed the letter, agreed with me that the Hungarian government's "firm attitude had forced" the leaders of the State Department to change the "amnesty before normalization" formula to the "voluntary step" version. He wrote that Vedeler and the others "finally understood" the ineffectiveness of pressing the Hungarian government on the issue of amnesty. For that reason he considered my discussions with the State Department officials important. He added that no new decision had been taken regarding Hungarian-American relations, but that the Ministry planned to study it intensively in the coming months. Finally, he gave me permission to proceed with plans to visit Chester Bowles and the two senators.

Along with this letter, I received a so-called personal letter from the deputy foreign minister informing me that my report had been sent to party headquarters and had been presented to First Secretary Kádár. As a result of Kádár's reaction, the Foreign Ministry had been ordered to prepare for the Politburo a study containing a ten-year background history of Hungarian-American relations, including important issues and proposals for a reasonable solution. The last part of this study, he wrote, was the most difficult to compose because the leadership of the Foreign Ministry held that as long as the United States was forcing the Hungarian question to appear on the agenda of the United Nations, no meaningful discussion could be conducted with the State Department, and the Foreign Ministry could foresee no radical change in the American position. The letter sounded pessimistic and seemed to promise very little for the future.

On 13 June Chester Bowles invited me to lunch. Arriving promptly at noon at his fashionable Georgetown home, I was greeted by Bowles and his assistant, Andrew E. Rice. Once the weather and the Washington humidity had been disposed of, the ambassador asked me whether I had had the opportunity to meet people in the State Department and to exchange views frankly and openly. I summarized briefly my meetings with the East European specialists and with Undersecretary McGhee. I observed that unfortunately the Hungarian and American positions differed greatly on the most important issue, the question of Hungary at the United Nations.

Bowles interrupted at this point to explain that he was fully informed about the problem and that I should bear in mind some of the basic elements of the American political system. The ambassador explained that the White House and the State Department were formulating policy in accordance with the best interests of the country. While making foreign policy decisions, the administration had to take into account the opinions expressed in Congress. The division of power between the legislative, judiciary, and executive branches in the United States, he pointed out, was an essential element of democratic procedure. For that reason U.S. policy makers would have to convince first the congressional committees—the senators and congressmen—before the nature of Hungarian-American relations could in any way be altered. The ambassador assumed that I knew these facts, but his own experience in the Soviet capital had shown him that although the basic elements of American democracy were presented in many Soviet books, even persons in the higher echelons of the government did not understand how these principles were actually applied. Bowles went on to explain that in his view Soviet and East European diplomats, familiar with political systems where decisions are made exclusively by party leaders, find it difficult to realize that in the United States the president (or the administration) must try to maintain good working relations with Congressional bodies.

Of course I had to acknowledge the fact that it was difficult for a foreigner to grasp all the intricacies of the American system, in much the same way, I supposed, that Americans were puzzled as to how to deal with foreign governments. With regard to Bowles's explanation of the interrelation of the various decision-making bodies, however, I argued that by now it should be evident to all parties involved that conditions in Hungary had improved substantially and that the events of 1956 should no longer stand in the way of better relations. The ambassador agreed that the situation in Hungary was, indeed, more relaxed than it had been years before. He mentioned also that he was aware that further changes were currently under way. He felt, however, that more convincing evidence was required for international recognition of this improvement. It would therefore be wise for the Hungarian government, he said, to take some action in this direction. Thinking we had arrived at a crucial point in the conversation and hoping to anticipate the ambassador's comments, I emphasized that actions such as general or individual amnesty for political prisoners were an internal affair for the Hungarian government. I added that the United States government would certainly reject, for example, any suggestion from Kádár that convicted persons be released from Sing Sing. On this last remark Chester Bowles made no comment.

Then, hoping that my arguments would be carried to higher American government circles, I explained at length that Hungary, a small country, had been treated unjustly during the last half century by the great powers. This had been the case with the Trianon Peace Treaty after World War I and again with the Paris Treaty of 1946. Having paid endless reparations, it was a wonder,

I said, that ten million Hungarians had survived. I explained that not surprisingly Hungary was suffering from a kind of inferiority complex, and for that reason was particularly sensitive to interference from a big nation like the United States. While expressing hope that American policy makers would understand this situation, I added that 1956 had been a tragedy for the Hungarian people, the remnants of which must and would be eliminated by the Hungarians themselves.

Bowles looked at me with astonishment. He had probably never heard a diplomat from the other side speak in this way. He simply nodded acquiescence and promised that the U.S. government would follow closely the development of the situation in Hungary. He refrained from pointing out that it was the Soviet Union and not the United States that had invaded Hungary in 1956, and that in 1947 the United States had offered sweeping economic assistance to the whole of Europe, including Hungary. Perhaps he was being careful to preserve the friendly atmosphere and to avoid putting his guest in an uncomfortable position.

I told Bowles on parting that I would be returning to Budapest to report to my government and that I would be glad to convey to Kádár any opinions or suggestions concerning Hungarian-American relations. To this announcement Chester Bowles replied that the United States wished improved relations with Hungary but felt it necessary that the consequences of the 1956 revolution be erased.

I came away from the meeting with Ambassador Bowles fully convinced that on the specific foreign policy issue of Hungary little if any difference in position existed at different levels of the American administration. Both the special adviser to President Kennedy and the State Department officials firmly insisted that amnesty was a precondition for ending the debate on the question of Hungary at the United Nations and for improvement of U.S.-Hungarian relations.

— 12 —

The Roles of Senator Ellender
and Senator Pell

As I had mentioned in my report to Budapest, I hoped to follow up my conversation with Chester Bowles by discussing the Hungarian issue with Senator Allen J. Ellender of Louisiana and Senator Claiborne Pell of Rhode Island. My purpose in meeting with these senators was twofold. In the first place I had become convinced that some type of contact with the legislative branch of the U.S. government was essential to my task, and I hoped from these meetings to get some feel for the attitude of the Senate toward Hungary. Because both these men had visited Hungary in recent years, they seemed obvious choices.

Senator Ellender was the first U.S. senator to visit Hungary after the revolution. While spending two days in Budapest in October 1957, he had met with Prime Minister János Kádár, Foreign Trade Minister Jenö Incze, and Deputy Foreign Minister Károly Szarka. The senator had an unusually frank conversation with Kádár.[1] In discussing the 1956 Hungarian events, Ellender concentrated on the key questions of the Hungarian revolution by asking who had issued the order for the Russian soldiers to intervene. To this Kádár answered quite candidly that the Soviet Union was in mortal fear that Hungary would fall into the hands of the West and would then be used by the West as a base to attack Russia. Whenever the senator pressed for further details, Kádár returned to the position that it was not in the best interest of Hungary to turn her back on the Soviet Union, that Hungary must not fall to the West and be used as a base to attack the U.S.S.R.

Senator Ellender returned to Hungary and Eastern Europe on a fact-finding tour in July 1960. Again he received the red carpet treatment from the Hungarian government. As chairman of the Senate Agricultural Committee he showed great interest in Hungarian agricultural development. He met with the Hungarian minister of agriculture, Pál Losonczi, and his deputy, and with the deputy minister of foreign trade in charge of Hungarian agricultural matters, János Mulató. The most important feature of his visit, however, was his political discussions with Hungarian leaders. He met Ferenc Münnich, president of the Council of Ministers, and Dr. Endre Sik, the foreign minister. With Münnich he explored a number of current international topics: the Congo question, the German problem, and the cold war in general. Münnich expressed hope that the cold war would end soon and that as a result an improvement in Hungarian-American relations could be realized in the near future.

Foreign Minister Sik used the occasion to put out a feeler through the senator to the U.S. government expressing Hungary's desire to normalize relations between the two countries. Although he recognized many points of conflict between the two governments, he expressed certainty that a genuine effort made by both sides would lead to an eventual improvement of relations.

Probably impressed with both Münnich's and Sik's remarks, and concerned by the fact that no communication existed between U.S. diplomats and Hungarian officials, Ellender wrote in his report to the Senate in 1960: "Efforts should be made to either open and normalize relations with Hungary or withdraw our representation. It is my belief that it would be better for us to resume diplomatic relations with Hungary."[2]

I realized that although Senator Ellender's report exhibited a realistic approach in dealing with Hungarian-U.S. relations, he had condemned the 1956 Soviet intervention and the execution of Imre Nagy. I learned from the report that Ellender held the view that communism could not be defeated by being ignored, and for that reason he advocated the restoration of full diplomatic relations with Hungary. He was the first public figure in the United States to propose East-West cooperation, for he felt that foreign trade between the Soviet bloc and the West would lessen international tension. He entertained no illusions, however, that any of the East European countries he had visited in 1960 (Poland, Czechoslovakia, and Hungary) would assume a foreign policy position independent from that of the Soviet Union. He took a pragmatic approach to the postwar East European situation; he felt that Russia was fearful of the consequences of losing Eastern Europe, its buffer zone between itself and Western Europe.

At my conference with the senator in Washington, my first question concerned Ellender's reaction to his reception by high officials in Hungary during his recent trip. The senator gave a favorable account of his experiences and explained that he had been free to call on prominent figures and to visit places of special interest to him. The Hungarian Foreign Ministry, he said, had placed at his disposal a young diplomatic officer by the name of István Varga, who had arranged his transportation and appointments quickly and efficiently. (Varga was, in fact, an officer of the Hungarian intelligence service who had not only given Ellender police protection but had transmitted to intelligence headquarters [not to the Foreign Ministry] his every word. During the conference with the senator, of course, my official position prevented my revealing Varga's real identity.)

In Budapest Ellender had observed what he considered an out-and-out absurdity: while most Western diplomats in the Hungarian capital maintained at least a working relationship with Hungarian officials, U.S. and Hungarian personnel were not even on speaking terms.

I mentioned to Ellender that U.S. Chargé Garret G. Ackerson, whom the senator had cited in his report as having no contact with Hungarian officials, had been recalled and that Horace G. Torbert had been sent to replace him. Attempting to offer some explanation for Ackerson's difficulties, I told the senator that the former chargé had served in Hungary before the war and that unfortunately for himself he had retained his old friendships with opponents of the present regime. Understandably, he had taken a very negative approach to dealing with officials of the Kádár government. (It appears in retrospect that Ackerson's difficulties were not entirely of his own making. The Hungarian authorities in Budapest, using simple but effective police methods, had done everything in their power to isolate him and the personnel of the American legation.[3] For example, Hungarian citizens who visited the American legation or who communicated in any way with American diplomats had been thoroughly investigated and threatened with arrest if they did not sever their ties with the "number one enemy of the regime.")

In the course of my conversation with the senator I asked him whether his report had influenced the change of personnel. Attributing Ackerson's replacement to routine diplomatic rotation, Ellender replied that his document had not been published until after the change had been made and that he could therefore claim no credit. I explained to Ellender that I had met Torbert, the new American chargé, several times while I myself was serving as chief of protocol in Budapest. As a matter of fact, Torbert had made his first call on me in February 1961. Because I shared Senator Ellender's concern about the communications gap between U.S. and Hungarian diplomats, I had tried my best to establish contact for Torbert with high Hungarian officials. Unlike his predecessor, Torbert had displayed a real interest in the problems at issue between the two countries and had been perfectly amenable to attending social functions sponsored by the Hungarian government. Later, at the New Year's reception in January 1962, Torbert was the first American diplomat to meet Kádár socially. Kádár found Torbert a serious and pleasant man and hoped that Torbert would be more realistic than his predecessor, Ackerson, in reporting to Washington. Kádár was convinced that Ackerson's hostility toward communism and the Kádár regime in particular had greatly influenced "the State Department's negative attitude vis-à-vis Hungary."

Senator Ellender, though expressing pleasure with the change in personnel, proved reluctant to discuss in detail any other aspects of Hungarian-U.S. relations. My most persistent attempts to elicit his opinion on the Hungarian question at the United Nations met with no success. In contrast to the official State Department insistence upon amnesty as a prerequisite to the normalization of relations, Ellender suggested as a possible first step the expansion of trade between Hungary and the United States. He remarked that during his entire senatorial career he had felt it his duty to approach domestic and foreign issues objectively. Even on such controversial matters as the Hungarian situation, he had always attempted to present a very frank opinion. At this point I asked Ellender very directly how the Senate had received his report on Hungary and whether any senators were prepared to change their attitude on the Hungarian issues. The senator replied that his report had aroused interest among the senators, but that few of them had altered their opinions substantially; the events of 1956 had produced an emotional response that was too deep-seated to be changed quickly.

The meeting with Senator Ellender left me disappointed and pessimistic. Although the senator on his own part continued to show concern for the improvement of relations between the two countries, he was obviously not prepared to use his efforts to lobby among his colleagues in behalf of the cause, not even to the extent of trying to create an atmosphere conducive to normalization. Furthermore, his interest in Hungary did not seem to embrace the fate of the Hungarian question at the United Nations, an issue that I considered to rate top priority.

My first meeting with Senator Claiborne Pell took place in November 1961 at the U.S. legation in Budapest, when I was serving as chief of protocol of the Hungarian Foreign Ministry. The occasion was a dinner party given by Chargé Torbert in honor of the visiting senator. It was a memorable event, since Hungarian Deputy Minister Szarka and the chief of protocol representing the Foreign Ministry were the first Hungarian officials to be invited as dinner guests to the U.S. legation since the 1956 revolution. (I learned much later that it was Senator Pell himself who had insisted that the Hungarian officials be invited, for he was convinced that the time had come for a resumption of communications between the Americans and the Hungarians in Budapest. Torbert too appeared pleased with the opportunity the occasion presented for Hungarian Foreign Ministry officials to get from an independent-thinking U.S. senator a straightforward expression of some of the ideas he was trying to put across.)

At the time of the party the Hungarian Foreign Ministry had no file on Senator Pell or any information concerning his background. Consequently the Hungarians attended the dinner party unaware of the fact that Senator Pell had been on the Hungarian border during the revolution, and afterward had served as vice-president of the International Rescue Committee. He had spent the following year in Vienna organizing the American program for Hungarian refugees. Had the Foreign Ministry known of Senator Pell's 1956 activities, it never would have permitted its officials to sit at the same table with a "dangerous imperialist; an obvious enemy of the Hungarian communist regime."

Once arrived at the dinner party, Szarka and I attempted to keep well in mind our instructions to remain cool and aloof toward the Americans. The atmosphere in the spacious salon of the chargé's residence was tense. Torbert, in an effort to put his guests at ease, offered the Hungarians American whiskey and complimented them on the beauty of the Hungarian capital. Coming to his assistance, Senator Pell joined the conversation. He explained to Szarka that his interest in Hungary had originated before World War II. He added that his father had been the American minister in Budapest at the outbreak of the war and had been faced with the unpleasant duty of declaring war on Hungary, not only on behalf of the United States but also on behalf of the British Commonwealth countries because there was no British representative in Budapest at the time. As Senator Pell recalled, his father, in attempting to fulfill his mission, had found himself in a rather bizarre situation: it was on a Sunday, and he could find no one in the Royal Hungarian Foreign Ministry to whom he could deliver the declaration of war.

In response I told Pell that I had, in a way, been on his father's side. Belonging to an anti-fascist guerrila group, I too had fought the Nazis. I added, however, that during the war, when the famous American B-24 "Liberators" had flown over Budapest and I had heard the nearby whistling of their bombs, I had not known whether to be happy or sad. When the senator asked me whether I had been in the army at all during the war and if so, what rank I had attained, I was compelled to confess that my highest rank had been that of a deserter. For the first time in the evening everybody smiled. Senator Pell followed up with his personal history, recounting that he had been the first postwar American consul general in Bratislava, the site of the old Hungarian Diet, and that he had made many trips to Hungary after the conclusion of the Paris Peace Treaty.

The discussion now became more animated and more charged with emotion as Senator Pell remarked that although he had seen some bullet holes on the outside of buildings, physical traces of the 1956 revolution seemed scarce. Aghast, Szarka corrected the senator, asserting flatly that the 1956 events had not been a revolution but a counterrevolution fomented by American imperialists and Hungarian fascists. The atmosphere became increasingly uncomfortable as the conversation continued and the tension and the volume rose. Senator Pell inquired whether the workers and the intellectuals who had led and participated in the "revolution" had all been fascists. He had found, when speaking with Hungarian refugees who had escaped in 1956, that many of them had been motivated by a genuine desire to build a democratic, humanistic socialist society in Hungary. None of them, so far as he could tell, wanted to restore the prewar fascist regime.

Ignoring Senator Pell's remarks, Szarka repeated that 1956 had been a counterrevolution and that the Foreign Ministry had concrete evidence of American complicity. As an example, he mentioned that Radio Free Europe had instigated the uprising and had broadcast instructions to the armed bands for fighting Soviet and Hungarian troops. American and West German light weapons had allegedly been found and confiscated by Hungarian authorities. Warming to his subject, Szarka charged that the American public had been gravely misled by Western press coverage of the counterrevolution. Obviously irritated, Senator Pell said that he only wished the Hungarians had access to as much information on world events as the Americans. He remarked that in every American home one could find at least two or three radios and that on the street newspapers of all political persuasions were available. Szarka, of course, was ready with a response. He told the senator that he had been stationed in the United States and had traveled widely in the country, and that although there were radios in most homes they could pick up only local stations carrying only local news. And with that, Szarka changed the subject.

He pointed out that his government had made a number of unilateral concessions to improve relations between Hungary and the United States. A great number of American businessmen and scientists were being permitted to visit Hungary. Efforts had been made to extend trade relations between the two countries. But, according to Szarka, the State Department had taken no such initiatives. Instead, the United States, misusing its influence as a great power, kept forcing the so-called question of Hungary on the United Nations General Assembly agenda. With a grim look the deputy foreign minister warned that the Americans need not be surprised if the Hungarian attitude should become less and less friendly toward Washington. While rejecting the charges, Senator Pell expressed the hope that the Kádár government might work out some way for reasonable cooperation with the United Nations and find a solution for the Hungarian question.

Torbert tried to save the situation by changing the subject again. He said that he found Budapest a very interesting city, and mentioned that he particularly enjoyed the museums and art galleries. Recounting some of his excursions to the countryside, he described the old chapels and historical sites he had visited. Meanwhile Szarka began to calm down and eventually interposed the hope that the senator too would have the opportunity to travel in Hungary and observe things as they really were. Careful not to resume discussion of 1956 nor of the current political situation in Hungary, Senator Pell merely regretted that he had very little time to spend in Hungary.

As the guests began to leave the dinner party, Senator Pell remarked that although a definite difference of interpretation did exist between Hungarian and American officials, he felt that the evening's conversation had been a step in establishing the contact that was so vitally necessary. He added that if Szarka or the protocol chief were ever in the United States, he would enjoy seeing them and continuing their conversation. Little did I guess then that within a few months, in the spring of 1962, I would actually visit Senator Pell in Washington in the capacity of Hungarian chargé d'affaires.

As I waited for the senator to leave the Senate floor, I could not help recalling the dinner party and wondering whether the senator's attitude toward the Kádár regime still remained as harsh. I learned soon enough. Almost the first words Pell uttered on greeting me were to ask about the barbed wire along Hungary's western border. Taken aback, I replied that the barbed wire merely served to keep infiltrators out of Hungary, to which Pell countered with some asperity that on the contrary it served to keep the Hungarians in. But almost at once he apologized profusely for his intemperate outburst and became as amiable as he had been unfriendly a moment before. He asked what had been taking place in Hungary and was told that conditions had improved considerably. The shops were full of merchandise, more and more tourists were visiting from the West, and the wounds of the 1956 events were gradually healing.

Coming rather quickly to the point, I explained that my mission in the United States was to attempt to improve Hungarian-American relations, and I hoped that Senator Pell, as a friend of Hungary, would help to promote a better attitude toward Hungary in the Senate. Just as had Senator Ellender and so many of the officials with whom I had spoken in the State Department, Senator Pell stated that the memory of the 1956 Russian intervention was still fresh. It was therefore hard to envisage an American-Hungarian reconciliation in the near future. He added, however, that if amnesty were to be granted to those imprisoned during the aftermath of 1956, the political atmosphere would greatly improve. Voicing his personal opposition to the cold war and to the rift between East and West, he assured me that he would do his utmost to bring the two camps closer together. However, the Hungarians must also exhibit a willingness to move in this direction. As we parted, the senator reassured me of his long-standing interest in Hungary and of his readiness to talk with me again.[4]

Following my visits with Senators Pell and Ellender, as well as those with American government officials, my view of the future of Hungarian-American relations finally began to clarify. The special adviser to the White House, Chester Bowles, and the State Department officials insisted that amnesty was the precondition for improvement of relations. Congressional spokesmen took the same position. Although the Americans acknowledged that as of 1962 the general situation in Hungary was certainly more relaxed than it had been in previous years, they repeated time and again that vivid memories of the Russian military intervention and the repression of the 1956 revolution were still a source of animosity toward the Kádár regime. This was a fact of life that had to be reckoned with; it commanded far greater importance than certain legal rights which the United States, as one of the victorious powers in World War II, was asserting with regard to Hungary.

If the Kádár government was genuinely interested in ending the debate in the United Nations on the question of Hungary and in improving Hungarian-American relations, its only option was amnesty. There was no question, I felt, but that such a solution embodied the best interest of Hungary, for it would bring to an end her international isolation and would lead to further internal liberalization. I realized, however, that formulating these ideas in my own mind was one thing, but that selling them to Budapest was quite another. Much depended on the internal situation in Hungary. Although Kádár enjoyed the support of the party in general, the dogmatic left seemed strong enough to oppose the release of the two to three thousand political prisoners. György Marosán, the administrative secretary of the party, the number two man of the regime, opposed relaxation. The Ministry of the Interior and a group of high-ranking officers in the Ministry of Defense supported his position. On the other hand, Politburo members Ferenc Münnich, Gyula Kállai, Lajos Fehér and, above all, János Kádár wanted to extend the influence of the party and to gain popular support through conciliation.

Despite the divergence of views inside the leadership, the final response to the U.S. position—amnesty before normalization—depended on the decision makers in the Kremlin. Would the Soviets agree to an amnesty leading to improvement of Hungarian-American relations? Would such a move fit into their general policy aim? In preparation for my next meeting with the party leadership, I began to wonder how I would present my conclusions.

— 13 —

Another Shift in Hungarian Foreign Policy

The 1962 liberalization in domestic affairs was the main factor responsible for softening the rigid foreign policy line of the Kádár regime. The change was particularly apparent in the position of the Hungarian party leadership vis-à-vis the United States. The first secretary of the party, János Kádár, and other high-ranking Politburo officials began to demonstrate unexpected flexibility in handling the delicate matter of Hungarian-American relations. As a result, the prospect of working out a compromise solution for the six-year-old Hungarian question at the United Nations improved considerably. Such were my general observations after meetings with Party Chief Kádár, Deputy Prime Minister Gyula Kállai, and Politburo member Dezsö Nemes in the summer of 1962. I was pleased to find that the Kádár leadership was approaching the question of amnesty realistically. On the other hand, I was surprised to learn that at Party Headquarters the generally held opinion was that the basic issue of Hungarian-American relations revolved around the problem of Cardinal Mindszenty rather than the question of amnesty.

My first important meeting that summer was with Kádár. Without being too explicit, Kádár explained that he was interested in seeing a gradual normalization of relations between Hungary and the United States. He was well aware of the fact that the State Department connected the question of normalization with amnesty. He remarked in passing that the American pressure for pardoning political prisoners constituted an interference in Hungary's internal affairs, but that in spite of this the Politburo was studying the possible impact of a general amnesty. The party chief granted that the release of the political prisoners would no longer create a special internal problem for his regime.

When at this point I interposed my observation that Kádár's new slogan, "He who is not against us is with us," had created a positive response in the United States, the first secretary replied somewhat sharply that politicians in the West were apt to delude themselves. They supposed that the new slogan meant the abandonment of "socialist principles." The slogan, added Kádár, had nothing to do with the theories of Marxism-Leninism; it was put forth simply as a practical statement and would result in further stabilization of the internal situation.[1] He explained briefly that a recent re-reading of the Stalinist formula, "He who is not with us is against us," had prompted him to turn the slogan around.

I had no reason to question Kádár's sincerity on this point. I had known him long enough to understand that the first secretary's centrist position in practical matters in no way contradicted his firm stand on ideological questions. The fundamental rule for Kádár was that the Communist Party should maintain a monopolistic control of the political life of the country and should exercise a dominant role in the society as a whole.

The meeting with Kádár had been significant in that it had given me a general understanding that the regime, in the view of its leader, could afford an amnesty. I now proceeded to sound out other members of the Politburo to see how far I might venture in future negotiations with the Americans. Deputy Prime Minister Gyula Kállai for one, the Politburo member who coordinated Hungary's international activities inside the government, doubted whether Undersecretary McGhee and other American officials were serious in suggesting normalization in return for amnesty. He was certain that the U.S. government wanted to settle the problem of Mindszenty first, and he added that the Americans must remove the cardinal from their legation before any meaningful negotiation could start.[2] Not sharing Kállai's opinion I argued that none of the American officials with whom I had been in contact had ever brought up the Mindszenty question. The deputy prime minister rejected this reasoning out of hand. He referred to his 12 December 1961 press conference, where he had been asked by the Reuters correspondent—in Kállai's opinion, on behalf of the State Department—whether the Hungarian government had any intention of starting negotiations with the United States about the future of Cardinal Mindszenty. At that time Kállai told the thirty Western journalists present that Mindszenty presented no particular problem to the Hungarian government. He said:

> What presents a factual problem to us is how to improve relations between Hungary and the United States. . . . Should the United States government raise the Mindszenty problem within the framework of settling this larger issue, we can also negotiate about the Mindszenty problem.[3]

That, according to the deputy prime minister, was and would remain the position of the Hungarian government.

Politburo member Dezsö Nemes, an experienced old *apparatchik* and the "gray eminence" of Hungary's international relations, held the same belief as Kállai.[4] He mentioned that even though an amnesty could be announced at the Eighth Party Congress in November 1962 or at the beginning of 1963, he felt that the Americans were not primarily interested in an amnesty. What the Catholic president of the United States and the Vatican really wanted was to restore Cardinal Mindszenty's ecclesiastic position and thus to reestablish the cardinal's political influence. Nemes added that the Hungarian government would permit Mindszenty to leave the country, but that neither the State Department nor the Vatican was interested in solving the Mindszenty problem that way.

I was unable to learn the basis for this erroneous assumption, for neither Kállai nor Nemes indicated whether he had been influenced by intelligence reports or by some expert in the Foreign Ministry. It is altogether likely that the misjudgment resulted from a misunderstanding of American and Vatican intentions.

The views of Kállai and Nemes concerning the Mindszenty matter differed substantially from those of the first secretary. There flashed through my mind at this time the recollection of an unpublicized meeting between János Kádár and Special Ambassador João Portella Ribeiro Dantas of Brazil. Dantas, a wealthy Brazilian newspaper publisher, while on a tour of the Soviet Union and Eastern Europe as a special representative of the president of Brazil, had conducted negotiations in Budapest to establish diplomatic relations and promote cultural and economic agreements with Hungary.[5] Dantas met Kádár in mid-May 1961 while I was chief of protocol, and I had served as interpreter between the Brazilian envoy and the Hungarian party chief.

Stimulated by the success of the diplomatic and economic talks, Dantas unexpectedly asked Kádár's permission to bring up a delicate question. To this Kádár replied that he did not know of any delicate questions and encouraged the ambassador to speak freely. Dantas then told Kádár that in Brazil, the largest Catholic country in Latin America, there was considerable concern for the fate of Cardinal Mindszenty. The Brazilian government would therefore gladly offer refuge to the cardinal should the Hungarian government grant him safe conduct out of the country. Kádár was polite and seemed quite open. He asked Dantas first whether he had seen Mindszenty, to which Dantas replied that the American chargé had refused to give him permission to do so. Kádár explained in a matter-of-fact way that the Mindszenty problem was indeed most complex, in that it involved three governments and a stubborn old man. Any solution would have to satisfy the American and Hungarian governments as well as the Vatican. The Hungarian government was completely aware that this question would have to be settled sooner or later; it would be extremely awkward for all of the interested parties if Mindszenty were to die at the American legation in Budapest. So far as the Hungarian government was concerned, the sole condition for Mindszenty's release was a Vatican guarantee that Mindszenty would not engage in anti-communist activities abroad. When the time was right, Kádár added, the Vatican would give some indication. He expected preliminary talks between the Vatican and Hungarian authorities. According to Kádár, the

Americans were simply victims of circumstance because the cardinal had chosen their building for refuge. For all these reasons Kádár discouraged Ambassador Dantas from getting involved in and thereby further complicating an already intricate situation.

On the occasion of my second meeting with Politburo member Dezsö Nemes, we again reviewed Hungarian-American relations. As was to be expected, Nemes still refused to accept my suggestion that a general amnesty would cause the Hungarian question to be struck from the U.N. agenda. Nemes maintained that, in the first place, the Americans wanted the release of Mindszenty and not the amnesty. With the proviso that the Mindszenty problem could not be the subject of official negotiations but might be the topic of private conversations, Nemes offered no objection to the continuation of the Hungarian-American diplomatic dialogue.

Nemes instructed me to go no farther than the merest hint that an amnesty might follow should the United States take action in the United Nations to remove the Hungarian question from the agenda and express its readiness to restore normal relations with the Hungarian government. On the whole, Nemes remained skeptical and was quite reluctant to believe that the Americans were seriously interested in détente. When I proposed getting from the Americans some sort of written confirmation of their intentions, the party secretary refused to consider that such a possibility existed. I was not altogether sure myself that I could secure such confirmation, but I felt that nothing was to be lost by trying and the prize was surely worth the effort.

Although I had had several meetings in the Foreign Ministry with Péter and with other high officials, the discussions had been limited to routine matters. All political questions had been taken up only in Nemes's office.

The three meetings I have mentioned—with Kádár, with Kállai, and with Nemes—took place a few weeks before the memorable August 1962 Central Committee meeting at which Kádár removed from positions of power the Hungarian Stalinists (the dogmatist left opposition) and consolidated his middle-of-the-road policy in internal and external affairs. At the time that I was meeting with the three leaders, I was unaware that the purges were to take place in August; but I could sense that something was in the air. I noticed nervousness among the party *apparatchiki*, who feared that they might lose their jobs because of the direction of Kádár's managerial reform. There were also rumors in the party of an impending shake-up in the Ministry of the Interior and the political police.

The talks with the three leaders during the weeks preceding the Central Committee meeting indicated clearly that there was no longer any real obstacle to an amnesty, and that I would have a good opportunity of working out some compromise after my return to Washington. Acting as a go-between is likely to be an uncertain and a thankless task, but the prospects for success then seemed fairly bright. The only unknown factors were what initiatives the Kremlin might take in the international arena during the months ahead, and how these actions might affect the Hungarian question at the United Nations.

In August 1962, before returning to Washington, I had an opportunity to renew acquaintance with H. G. Torbert, my American counterpart, who represented the United States in Budapest for almost two years. The occasion was a dinner party, where the two of us found ample opportunity to talk over our parallel roles as intermediaries. This led naturally enough to a consideration of the prospects for rapprochement. On my part I indicated a greater degree of optimism than my American colleague. I predicted some change in Hungarian policy, or at least a changing attitude toward the United States, within the next six months or so. On the basis of previous briefings, I suggested that the Eighth Congress of the Hungarian Socialist Workers' Party in November would offer concrete evidence of a change in policy, but I was concerned lest the Hungarian question would already have been raised at the forthcoming U.N. session, thereby diminishing the prospects for improving relations between our two countries. Torbert thought that the Hungarian question was likely to be raised unless some specific prior development permitted the question to be settled. Obviously the specific development that Torbert looked for was the amnesty. Since I considered it premature to disclose the Hungarian government's plans for the amnesty, I was not in a position to offer this information to Torbert, and was not surprised, therefore, that Torbert felt that any improvement in relations would take place only slowly over an extended period of time.

Having in mind Nemes's concern for the Mindszenty problem, I mentioned in the course of the discussion that it was essential to solve the problem of the cardinal in order to restore normal relations between the two countries. Torbert was obviously taken completely by surprise, for this was the first time since 1956 that a Hungarian diplomat had raised this question with an American. He agreed that it was highly desirable to dispose of this matter, but he expressed the opinion that the Mindszenty problem was not quite as basic as I had implied. Torbert added that in any event the Mindszenty affair was not subject to purely bilateral negotiation. This gave me all the reassurance I needed that it was indeed the amnesty that was the chief problem; and I then and there decided to refrain from bringing up the Mindszenty issue at all on my return to Washington.

— 14 —

The "Piece of Paper"

The fall of 1962 was a busy time for me. I divided my days between New York, where I was a newly appointed member of the Hungarian delegation to the United Nations, and Washington, where I continued to carry on as chargé d'affaires. I could not help feeling some concern, for it seemed to me that the American attitude toward the Hungarian question had not changed perceptibly. Torbert's prediction that the question would be brought up again had proved only too true.

On 17 August Adlai Stevenson, U.S. permanent representative to the United Nations, wrote a letter to Acting Secretary-General U Thant pointing out that the problem of Hungary remained an outstanding issue. Ambassador Stevenson noted that "the governments of the Soviet Union and of Hungary have failed thus far to cooperate with the United Nations and its appointed representatives as requested by pertinent decisions of the organization." Stevenson concluded that in the view of his government the Hungarian question merited further discussion and should be put on the agenda of the Seventeenth Session of the General Assembly.[1]

I thereupon made arrangements for a luncheon meeting on 7 September 1962 at the Mayflower Hotel in Washington with Richard Davis, deputy assistant secretary of state for European affairs, and Harold Vedeler, director for Eastern Europe. I reported on this occasion that in the course of my two months' visit to Budapest during the summer I had met with all the key officials there, including Kádár. I mentioned that I had seen Torbert also and had had a pleasant discussion with him. The two Americans were naturally eager to hear about my experiences and accomplishments in Budapest, especially insofar as they might have resulted in my bringing back any new instructions. At that time I was still not free to reveal any details of my meetings with Kádár. But I did mention that in July, when I had left the first secretary's office, I had been more optimistic

115

than I was after reading Ambassador Stevenson's letter of 17 August to the U.N. secretary-general. I had not known that the U.S. State Department would persist in having the Hungarian question entered on the U.N. agenda. To this statement Davis replied sharply that the Hungarian government had not shown any readiness to cooperate with the United Nations.

My response was that the time had come to break out of this vicious circle. I told Davis that I had known beforehand that he would repeat the old argument that the State Department could do nothing to end the debate on the Hungarian question at the United Nations unless the Hungarian government granted amnesty to political prisoners. And I would be compelled to reject this proposal as an interference in Hungary's internal affairs. At this point I judged the moment opportune to persuade the Americans that some solution could surely be found to the long-standing issue at the United Nations, and that Hungarian-American relations could certainly be improved. Consequently I suggested that Hungary might declare a general amnesty, I continued, if she could be assured that the U.S. government would take concrete measures to drop the Hungarian question from the agenda.

The State Department officials were noncommittal, observing only that it would be difficult to explain to the American public why the question had been shelved so abruptly. Vedeler pointedly asked how many people convicted for their participation in the 1956 uprising were still in prison, to which I replied that there were not many.

Toward the close of the discussion I repeated the suggestion that the Hungarian Presidential Council might pardon the political prisoners. I hoped, however, that such a move would be accompanied by appropriate action on the part of the United States. Realizing that my suggestion indicated a new approach to the issue, Davis and Vedeler promised to give it careful consideration.

Now came the most delicate part of the discussion. I asked Davis for a State Department reply in written form. I argued that only such a reply would demonstrate to Budapest the seriousness of U.S. intentions. The form of the reply itself was deliberately left open. All three of the seasoned diplomats present realized that such a piece of paper would entail some risk. There was no guarantee that the Hungarian communist regime might not use a document of this nature for propaganda purposes at the United Nations or elsewhere. Most probably for this reason, Davis made no definite commitment, but neither did he dismiss the possibility of some form of written reply. It was not until 20 October that I heard anything further on this matter from either Davis or Vedeler.

In the meantime I attended the U.N. General Assembly sessions in New York, where I spent most of my time in the Third Committee listening to debates on women's marriage rights. In addition I cast Hungary's vote on numerous draft resolutions. This occupation was pleasant: it did not require too much diplomatic work nor did it contain hidden complexities. The chief Hungarian delegate, Foreign Minister János Péter, simply instructed me to observe the representative of the Soviet Union on the Committee and to vote as he did. I attended the General Assembly only when the Hungarian question was to be debated.

On 24 September the Assembly decided by a vote of 43 to 34 with 19 abstentions to include the Hungarian question on the agenda. The following day the U.N. special representative on Hungary, Sir Leslie Munro, submitted his third yearly report to the Assembly. It contained nothing new. In Sir Leslie's opinion the core of the problem was still the issue of the withdrawal of Soviet armed forces from Hungary, for which the Assembly had repeatedly called. He reported to the General Assembly also that neither the U.S.S.R. nor the Hungarian government had complied with the Assembly's resolutions on the matter of the world organization.[2]

As usual, Ambassador Károly Csatordai, the permanent representative of Hungary to the United Nations, protested the distribution of Munro's report. In the ambassador's view the report presented a distorted picture of the situation in Hungary and was a product of cold-war policy. The Soviet troops in Hungary, he insisted, had nothing to do with the internal situation in his country. These troops were there in accordance with the Warsaw Treaty.[3] After six years of annual debate on the subject, by the year 1962 the Hungarian question was generating little excitement among the U.N. delegates. The Assembly followed its by now accustomed procedure of referring the question to the Special Political Committee, whose heavy schedule was likely to hold off consideration of the matter until the middle of December.

Even Hungarian Foreign Minister János Péter's address to the General Assembly failed to stir any degree of interest either for or against the Hungarian question. Like all the other East European speakers, Péter supported without reservation Soviet Foreign Minister Gromyko's position on key international issues. Speaking about Hungarian-U.S. relations, Péter referred obliquely to the delicate negotiations going on in Washington and Budapest, but fortunately did not reveal any details prematurely. On the contrary, he condemned the United States for placing the Hungarian question on the agenda. In addition he questioned the credibility of the United States, branding its attitude toward Hungary "two-faced." He warned the United States that his government would not enter discussions under pressure or meet unjustified preconditions. The walk-out of the entire U.S. delegation during Péter's speech furnished evidence of the degree of deterioration in the relations between the two countries and reflected the general atmosphere prevailing in the world organization.

It was becoming quite clear that in the absence of some unexpected development either in the international arena, at the United Nations, or between Budapest and Washington, Hungary and the Soviet Union would again be condemned by the General Assembly as they had been in previous years. The U.S. delegation to the United Nations had simply to renew the previous year's draft resolution, which deplored "the continued disregard by the Union of Soviet

Socialist Republics and the present Hungarian regime of the General Assembly resolutions concerning the situation in Hungary.''[4] It could be assumed that the United States and its allies in the United Nations would continue to maintain that the debate over Hungary was essentially a question of the repression of the right of self-determination. For the representatives of the U.S.S.R., this would be a ''cold war'' issue. While the Hungarian representative would continue to charge the United States with having originated the events of 1956, he would certainly maintain that it was purely an internal affair. Moreover the permanent Hungarian representative and his staff would be active among the representatives of the newly admitted African states, as well as among the Arab and Asian delegations, seeking to convince them not to vote with the Americans on the Hungarian question in the Special Political Committee or in the General Assembly. So far there was nothing in the picture to suggest any variation from the established pattern.

Back in Washington it was not until 20 October, as I have mentioned, that I again met with Richard Davis, this time in the secretary's office at the State Department, with Deputy Director of the Eastern European Department Robert McKisson present. It became readily apparent from the serious manner of the Americans that they had something important to communicate.

With almost no preliminaries Davis took from his desk a sheet of paper and proceeded to read from it. He summarized the American position concerning Hungarian-American relations. First, he read that it was hoped the Hungarian government would either take convincing public steps, or would issue an authoritative statement, to give assurance that the consequences of the 1956 events would be erased. Without explicitly linking this point with the next he continued reading, to the effect that the government of the United States would exercise its influence at the United Nations to end the debate on the Hungarian question and to get the Hungarian credentials recognized. As for Hungarian-U.S. relations, the State Department would be ready to discuss all outstanding matters relating to bilateral relations, such as travel restrictions and restrictions on diplomatic and administrative personnel employed by the diplomatic missions of the two countries. The assistant secretary mentioned also that pending financial claims as well as expansion of trade between the two countries might be discussed. The United States was prepared further to conclude a cultural exchange program. One of the last points on Davis's list referred to the desirability of resolving the problem of Cardinal Mindszenty but in no way was this to be regarded as a condition for normalization. Davis concluded his statement by emphasizing that the State Department was ready to accept any suggestion of the Hungarian Foreign Ministry to supplement the proposed plan.

Without waiting for my reaction, Davis made it clear that his verbal statement was written on a sheet of paper that was not to be regarded as an official document—a memorandum or a *note verbale*—but simply as a memo of his verbal statement. As he handed over the sheet of paper, he cautioned me once more not to regard it as an official document. He expressed the hope that this would be the proof of American good faith that I had sought at our 7 September meeting.

Alluding to János Péter's speech to the U.N. General Assembly accusing the United States of interference in Hungary's internal affairs, Davis assured me with a certain delicate irony that since I had specifically asked for the paper, it did not constitute any such meddling. I acknowledged receipt of the paper with great satisfaction and promised to forward the contents of Davis's statement to Budapest. I took pains to assure the assistant secretary that I would consider the memo not an official document but merely a "piece of paper."

In the course of the discussion I took occasion to indicate that many steps had already been taken, and that others would be taken, toward normalizing the situation inside Hungary. However, I went on to explain, I was not in a position at this particular moment to say when an authoritative statement might be issued. Many internal developments, such as the coming Eighth Party Congress in November 1962, the elections for the National Assembly in February 1963, and other preoccupations might make it impossible for the Hungarian government to take any action before December, the time when the Hungarian issue would be coming up for debate at the United Nations. The Hungarian government, however, would like to see the issue finally disposed of at this General Assembly session. I called to the secretary's attention the voting record on the Hungarian question during the current session, which showed that among the member states there was hardly any real interest in the matter. I hoped that the State Department would take into consideration both the internal situation of Hungary and the U.N. voting record, and would keep in mind that it would probably be impossible to get a two-thirds majority vote for another resolution condemning Hungary. I wished it might be possible to find some alternative solution. If the item could not be dropped, for instance, perhaps there could be a postponement. Davis listened politely and responded that the next move was up to the Hungarians.

In my report to Budapest I used the "wrapping technique" commonly practiced in the Hungarian diplomatic service. So far as the description of the meeting itself was concerned, I was factual and precise. I reported accurately what Assistant Secretary Davis had told me. I attached to my report the memorandum or, as it was called, the "piece of paper." This factual picture, however, had to be balanced by a sugar-coated presentation. For this reason I characterized the American initiative as being in accordance with Deputy Prime Minister Gyula Kállai's "condition" put forward at his 1961 press conference. Because I was aware that they did not have too much faith in American intentions, I "speculated" that the latest voting record in the United Nations must have influenced the State Department to offer the package deal in writing. The Hungarian question was too sensitive, and the relations between the governments of Hungary and the United States were too controversial, for me to go so far as to suggest what type of answer, if any, should be given to the State Department.

The Hungarian government never did in fact reply officially to the memorandum. Yet in itself it represented a diplomatic step of major importance. The document or, as the American officials always called it, the "piece of paper" formed the basis of a tacit understanding between Budapest and Washington. But the task of successfully transforming into reality the proposals contained in this piece of paper hinged on the outcome of that most dangerous confrontation of the two superpowers—the Cuban missile crisis.

— 15 —

The Cuban Crisis and the Hungarian Question

In the summer of 1962 neither the Hungarian Politburo nor the leadership of any other East European socialist country was aware that the Soviet merchant vessels *Omsk* and *Poltava* were quietly transporting to Cuba carefully packed medium-range ballistic missiles, related electronic equipment, and atomic warheads. Only the parties directly involved—the Cubans, the Russians, and the Americans, plus the Chinese—had any knowledge of the situation that was to lead eventually to the most dangerous confrontation of the superpowers, the well-known Cuban missile crisis. In late October 1962 this event brought about a sharp departure from the prevailing pattern of cold war diplomacy and ultimately resulted in a partial détente.

A few days before returning to Washington from my stay in the Hungarian capital in the summer of 1962, I had met with State Minister Ferenc Münnich. Although our discussion had centered on Hungarian-American relations, Münnich had expressed interest in learning the opinions of U.S. officials concerning Cuba. He had wondered whether the United States would put further pressure on Castro, and whether the Kennedy administration was preparing a direct assault against Cuba or a combination attack using anti-Castro refugees in conjunction with U.S. and Central American troops. Although I was unable to provide any well-based evidence, I did know at that time that rumors were circulating around Washington to the effect that American military personnel were training Cuban refugees in special camps in the United States and in South America. Münnich listened attentively, lit up a long Havana cigar, and then pointed out that according to information he had received from Moscow the Russians were building up Castro's defenses at great speed. By sending anti-aircraft batteries, new types of aircraft, and all sorts of military equipment, they planned to make Cuba a real fortress. The next invasion of Cuba, he prophesied, would result in more bloodshed than had the unsuccessful attempt at the Bay of Pigs in April 1961.

Münnich discounted the possibility of an uprising in Cuba. In his estimation Castro had the internal situation well under control and enjoyed popular support. The minister added that the Czechs had taken charge of the reorganization and modernization of the Cuban police and security forces. Furthermore, the Cuban intelligence service had effectively infiltrated the Cuban refugees. The Hungarian state minister did express concern, however, over Castro's low ideological standards. He explained that Fidel and his closest collaborators had never studied Marxism, had never read Lenin's basic revolutionary works, and thus did not understand communism. Taking issue with this statement, I told Münnich that, according to my best knowledge, Castro and his closest collaborators had organized a study group where they were analyzing Marx's *Das Kapital*. Münnich sneered, and replied that the latest report out of Moscow indicated constant fricton between Castroites and the old guard communists. Münnich ended the conversation with a rather surprising statement. While emphasizing that Khrushchev probably knew what he was doing in Cuba, the Hungarian state minister offered his opinion that Moscow would be well advised to observe more caution about whom it supported.

My discussion with Münnich about the Cuban situation was followed by a long conversation with First Secretary Kádár on the same subject. The first secretary wanted to know what the Americans thought about Fidel. I had to confess that the mere mention of the Cuban leader's name to an American official or to the man on the street was like waving a red flag in front of a bull. Kádár confirmed the fact that the Soviet Union was giving Castro substantial military aid. He recalled Castro's trip to the U.N. General Assembly in 1960 and mentioned that Khrushchev had at that time given Castro firm assurances that the Soviet Union would defend his regime under any circumstances. Kádár explained that the 1960 Soviet-Cuban discussions had begun at the Teresa Hotel in Harlem, where Khrushchev had visited Castro, and had continued in the garden of Soviet headquarters at Glen Cove, Long Island. According to Kádár, Khrushchev was deeply impressed with Castro and his entourage, and eventually promised him not only substantial economic aid but also military assistance, including missile support. Kádár was probably referring to Khrushchev's statement warning that "in case of need, Soviet artillerymen could support the Cuban people with their rocket power if the aggressive forces in the Pentagon dared to launch an intervention against Cuba." Khrushchev himself labeled this statement a "warning to those who would like to settle international issues by force and not by reason."[1]

Kádár speculated that perhaps the Americans had known about this arrangement and had attempted to overthrow Castro with the Bay of Pigs invasion before intensive Soviet military aid could reach Cuba. He argued that Soviet missile threats had helped to halt British and French aggression against the Suez in 1956 and expressed the belief that an intercontinental ballistic missile system based in Russia might also be effective if another American invasion of Cuba should be attempted.

In September and October 1962 secret Soviet-Cuban negotiations in furtherance of the Khrushchev-Castro 1960 basic agreement resulted in missile deployment in Cuba. After the 2 September visit to the Kremlin of Ernesto "Che" Guevara, Castro's minister of industry, the Hungarian Foreign Ministry requested its Washington legation to supply a routine report on the State Department reaction to the joint Soviet-Cuban communiqué in which the Soviet Union announced arms shipments and the dispatch of specialists to Cuba.[2] Drawing upon information received from diplomats and Washington correspondents, I wrote that the American administration was, as usual, overreacting when Cuba came into the news. I reported that President Kennedy, under heavy pressure from the Pentagon, had asked on 7 September for Congressional authorization to call up 150,000 reserve troops. He had warned the Soviet Union and Cuba that introduction into Cuba of offensive ground-to-ground missiles would have serious consequences. I remarked that a statement made by President Kennedy on 3 September and his subsequent press conference not only reaffirmed the Monroe Doctrine but also served as part of the Democratic Party's congressional election campaign.

Before sending my report to Budapest, I asked high-ranking Soviet diplomats in Washington for their assessment of the Kennedy statement. They replied that the whole uproar was part of the pre-election campaign and should not be taken too seriously. They did not mention that Ambassador Anatoli Dobrynin had met with Attorney General Robert Kennedy and had assured him that the Soviet Union would not introduce ground-to-ground missiles in Cuba, nor would Khrushchev do anything to upset Soviet-American relations during the pre-election period.[3]

In contrast with my report, the Hungarian intelligence chief in Washington (the first secretary of the legation) dispatched alarming cables to his headquarters. He reported that the CIA had recently intensified its training of Cuban refugees in camps located in Central America and in Puerto Rico. Noting that he had "concrete evidence" that President Kennedy would act before the election in order to bury the issue of the Bay of Pigs, he predicted that the United States would soon attempt a second invasion of Cuba. The Hungarian military attaché, Colonel Lajos Varga, was more cautious. Observing the Cuban question strictly from a military point of view, he felt that the calling up of 150,000 reserves did not necessarily signify an American invasion.

In accordance with customary procedure, the legation received copies of the dispatches sent by other Hungarian missions abroad. One interesting communication came from the Hungarian embassy in Havana, in which Hungarian Ambassador János Beck, a highly intelligent man and a great admirer of the Cuban revolution, described his meeting with Castro's brother Raúl. In his capacity as defense minister, Raúl had told Beck that Fidel and the Cuban leadership had established an excellent working relationship with the Soviet leaders. He explained that the Soviets understood that Aníbal Escalante and many of the other old bolsheviks in Cuba were adventurist dogmatists who wanted to seize power for their own benefit and that Fidel had had to take measures against them.[4]

Speaking of military matters, Raúl had explained to the ambassador that although the 1961 Bay of Pigs affair had been a great victory for Cuba, it had depended mainly on the enthusiasm which Fidel had generated among his troops. The invaders, he said, had been badly organized, had had no air support, and had been greatly confused; hence, their defeat had been relatively easy. Raúl summed up the affair by observing that the enemy had learned a lesson and so had Fidel. He had worked in by way of conclusion the idea that in his estimation Cuba was stronger and more united behind Fidel Castro than ever.

In the same report the Hungarian ambassador made it a point to discount information he had received from the Chinese embassy in Havana as being provocatively anti-Soviet. The Chinese ambassador had apparently told him that according to information he had received from private sources the Soviet Union was delivering surface-to-surface ballistic missiles to Cuba and that Soviet military advisers had come to Cuba not as instructors but as members of Soviet special rocket force units to operate these missiles. Ambassador Beck remarked that his Chinese friend had complained of Soviet unwillingness to disclose any details and had asked Beck whether he knew anything more about the whole affair. Beck argued that the story of the deployment of ground-to-ground missiles had been launched by "American warmongers" and observed that neither the Soviet ambassador in Havana nor high-ranking Cuban officials had mentioned anything to him about the missile build-up. (In fact it appears that Ambassador Beck was so sure that nothing would happen in Cuba during the coming months that in September he left Havana for New York to join the Hungarian U.N. delegation there. His wife, a doctor, remained in Cuba and continued to work as a volunteer in one of the hospitals near Havana.)

During the ensuing weeks, despite frequent visits to New York my knowledge of the Cuban situation increased very litte. In New York I discussed the matter at some length with the permanent Hungarian representative to the United Nations, Károly Csatordai, who made no attempt to hide his extremist political views nor his sympathy for Peking. His contributions on the Cuban situation amounted to nothing more than worn, tired phrases and propaganda. Although he appeared convinced that the Americans were plotting against Cuba, Csatordai felt that this was nothing to be feared—the Cuban people under the leadership of Fidel Castro were strong enough to cope with American aggression.

When I asked the representative whether he thought there were any Soviet medium-range missiles deployed in Cuba, his answer was a categorical no.

He added that the Americans were using "such fairy tales" to arouse anti-Castro sentiment in the United States. To prove his point he cited New York Republican Senator Kenneth Keating's statement on 10 October which charged that six intermediate-range missile sites were currently under construction in Cuba.[5] Csatordai accused the senator and the CIA of working together to build up a case for a new intervention. I thought at first of mentioning to Csatordai that the U.S. administration had categorically denied the allegations in Keating's report and that former Presidential Assistant for National Security Affairs McGeorge Bundy, in a television interview on 11 October, had expressed doubt about the presence of Soviet intermediate-range missiles in Cuba. But feeling that any further talk with a man blinded by such hatred would only be wasted time, I decided to say nothing.

Meanwhile a curious sequence of events had taken place in mid-September. All military attachés stationed in Washington, including Hungary's Colonel Lajos Varga, were invited by the Pentagon on a tour of military bases in Florida. Such an invitation was a customary courtesy among military persons. It could very well be that the Pentagon, hoping to be shown some military bases in the Soviet world, was extending the invitation to the military attachés of the Warsaw Pact countries in Washington. This, at least, was the explanation that Varga gave when he showed me the invitation from the Pentagon's liaison office.

After receiving permisson to accept the invitation, Colonel Varga went about procuring the latest camera equipment and studying the map of Florida furiously in preparation for the trip. On the other hand, I myself completely forgot about the whole Florida business until the morning of 16 October, when Colonel Varga rushed into my office excitedly with the announcement that the Pentagon had abruptly cancelled the excursion without any explanation.

Speculating on the reasons for the cancellation, both of us came to the conclusion that something unusual was taking place at the Florida military bases, something that could not have been hidden from the expert eyes of visiting military attachés. Naturally enough, both the colonel and I guessed that the cancellation might very well be related to the Cuban situation. The Czechoslovak, Polish, and Bulgarian military missions in Washington had meanwhile arrived at the same conclusion. All immediately began to reconstruct recent American troop movements and the activity of the Marines and the Air Force in the neighborhood of Key West; and they had come up with a fairly good picture of the strength of the American armed forces facing Cuba.

None of them, however, could agree on the motivation behind the American military movement. Was it simply a military maneuver or preparation for an invasion of Cuba? At this time, the communist countries' intelligence officers, including the Soviet military attaché, General Vladimir A. Dubovik, were probably unaware of the ground-to-ground missile deployment in Cuba and of the fact that Air Force Major Rudolf Anderson, Jr., and Richard S. Heyser, in

U-2 planes, had flown over the Cuban town of San Cristobal and had brought back the first pictures taken of the construction sites of the medium-range ballistic missiles.

On the evening of 18 October the ambassadors of the communist countries in Washington held their regular monthly dinner party at the Czechoslovakian embassy. These dinners provided an opportunity for consultation and exchange of information. Half an hour after the party had begun Anatoli Dobrynin, the Soviet ambassador, made his appearance. Although he looked tired, he was, as usual, friendly and cheerful. He explained that he had been extremely busy writing a report of the Kennedy-Gromyko conversation at the White House the day before. Everyone at the embassy party was naturally anxious to learn the details of Gromyko's meeting with Kennedy, and all wanted Dobrynin to fill them in on the contents of his report. He insisted with a smile that official business could hold until he had had a drink and his dinner.

Following dinner, the guests moved into the salon for coffee and brandy. Then with Dr. Miloslav Růžek, their Czechoslovakian host, presiding, the ambassadors gathered around a large table to discuss the issues of the day. Polish Ambassador Edward Drozniak, who had been president of the Polish National Bank before becoming ambassador, preferred to speak about economic and fiscal matters. Explaining that in securing credit he had experienced more difficulty with the Kennedy administration than with Eisenhower's, Drozniak charged that Kennedy was only toying with the idea of liberalizing trade relations between the United States and Eastern Europe. He explained that Kennedy was influenced to a great extent and in a "negative way" by the opinions of American labor leaders, particularly George Meany.

Růžek followed Drozniak with an account of his study of the applications of IBM computer systems in use around the United States and of his plans to recommend to his government the adoption of similar programs. Computerization of everyday life, he felt, would aid substantially in the modernization of his country. When my turn came I spoke at length about Hungarian-American relations. I mentioned that I was scheduled to meet Assistant Secretary of State Richard Davis on 20 October. I said I was hopeful that my current discussions with the State Department would result in the normalization of Hungarian-American relations. My remarks produced hardly a ripple.

The Rumanian ambassador, Petre Bălăceanu, switched the subject to more immediate political issues, explaining that he was seriously concerned about the developing Cuban situation. Quoting newspaper reports of 18 October, he noted that the U.S. Department of Defense had apparently initiated an intensive military build-up in the southeastern states close to Cuba. He added that his anxiety had grown when he learned that the Pentagon considered this deployment of troops and concentration of air power "routine" in light of the rapidly increasing Soviet aid to Cuba. Turning to Dobrynin, he asked the Soviet ambassador for his opinion of the Cuban situation. Dobrynin felt that the importance of the Cuban issue had been exaggerated by American politicians, particularly by the Republicans, because of the upcoming elections in November, and assured his audience that recent reports of Soviet ground-to-ground missiles in Cuba were completely without foundation. During the past few weeks, Dobrynin explained, he had met with high U.S. officials who had also raised the question of Soviet missiles in Cuba. In response he had insisted that the Soviet Union had no intention of deploying missiles anywhere outside the U.S.S.R. (One of the high officials alluded to was Attorney General Robert Kennedy. As early as 4 September he and Dobrynin had discussed the Cuban military build-up, and the Soviet ambassador had transmitted Khrushchev's assurance that no ground-to-ground missiles would be deployed in Cuba.)

Continuing, Dobrynin launched into the subject his hearers had been patiently waiting for: an account of the Gromyko-Kennedy conversation of 17 October. He stressed at the outset that the ambassadors would be able to draw very little information from his report because nothing extraordinary had happened at the meeting. Gromyko had attended the yearly General Assembly session of the United Nations as usual and had taken this opportunity to visit his embassy in Washington and also to pay a visit to President Kennedy. The appointment with the president, Dobrynin noted, had been arranged long before and was more a courtesy call than an official meeting. The two statesmen had discussed the German situation at length, but had found no new basis for agreement. While Gromyko had emphasized the need for a peace treaty between the two Germanies and the Allies of World War II, Kennedy remained opposed to any recognition of the German Democratic Republic. Mentioning to the guests that Kennedy and Gromyko had also discussed disarmament, Dobrynin ended his remarks with no further reference to the Cuban question. Of course on my part I was not surprised when I learned later that President Kennedy had indeed expressed to Gromyko his anxiety over the Soviet military build-up in Cuba. Such omissions were standard procedure when the Soviet leadership was in the process of making important policy decisions or when these decisions were being implemented.

The record of the Kennedy-Gromyko meeting is now available from various reliable sources.[6] It reveals the fact that Gromyko, following instructions from Khrushchev, assured the president that the only assistance furnished Cuba was designed to improve Cuban agriculture and land development. According to Gromyko the Soviet arms sent to Cuba were purely defensive in nature. As the record shows, President Kennedy had known of the presence of Soviet missiles in Cuba since 16 October but had decided not to reveal this fact to Gromyko. In response to Gromyko's claim, Kennedy read his 3 September statement in which he had spelled out the consequences that might arise if the Soviets were to place missiles in Cuba. Gromyko assured the president that his country entertained no such plans and asked for the president's assistance in lessening the tension surrounding the Cuban question.

Although many experts are now speculating that probably neither Gromyko
nor Dobrynin had any knowledge of actual Soviet plans, it seems highly unlikely
to me that Gromyko, the Soviet foreign minister, had not been privy to the
Kremlin discussions that eventually resulted in the decision to send intermediate-
range missiles to Cuba. However, since the secrecy of the operation required
that as few people as possible should know about it, it is altogether possible
that Dobrynin may not have been informed.

On 22 October the American president appeared on nationwide television
to tell the world of the Cuban missile crisis and of U.S. plans to "quarantine"
the island. An hour before Kennedy's speech, Dobrynin had been asked to
meet with Secretary of State Dean Rusk and had been presented with a copy
of the president's speech. The Kennedy broadcast took the whole world by
surprise—the East European countries no less than any other part of the globe.
The Politburo of the Hungarian Socialist Workers' Party and its leader, János
Kádár, had no prior information at all of Soviet-Cuban plans to transform the
island into a base for Soviet medium-range ballistic missiles. Indeed, Kádár
had been so ignorant of blow-by-blow developments in the situation that he
had been spending hours at wire service headquarters attempting to find out
what was going on. Not until Tuesday the 23rd was I able, from Washington,
to supply my government with specific details concerning the developing crisis.
That morning, Dobrynin's secretary had unexpectedly appeared in my office
and had informed me that the ambassador would like to meet with the representatives of the socialist countries at noon. I guessed immediately that the
meeting would concern the Cuban crisis.

Appearing unusually serious at this conference, Dobrynin told the assembled
ambassadors of his talk with Rusk immediately preceding the Kennedy speech.
He showed us the most important excerpts from the copy given him by Rusk
and explained that the secretary of state had provided him with no additional
information. Dobrynin's reply to Rusk had apparently been limited to his saying
that he would forward the text to Moscow. Dobrynin then went on to explain
that he had called the socialist ambassadors together to collect information and
to solicit opinions on the Cuban situation. As he himself assessed the affair,
Dobrynin characterized it as serious, and offered two reasons for his concern.
First of all, he foresaw a possible American attack on Cuba that would almost
surely result in the death of some Soviet military personnel who had been
sent to handle the sophisticated new weapons. Thus by implication the Soviet
ambassador was admitting the presence in Cuba of Soviet medium-range missiles.
Secondly, he feared that when Soviet ships reached the announced quarantine
line a confrontation was inevitable.

Reaffirming his earlier position that the Americans were exaggerating the
importance of Soviet arms in Cuba, Dobrynin explained that any defensive
weapon could be labeled offensive as well and dismissed American concern
over a threat from Cuba. The Pearl Harbor attack, he suggested, might have

been responsible for this unwarranted paranoia. Everyone agreed that the situation was serious and that the possibility of an American invasion of Cuba could not be discounted.

I mentioned to Dobrynin that the Hungarian military attaché had already received information concerning the strength of the U.S. build-up against Cuba. Colonel Varga had estimated that a force of 250,000 to 300,000 men from the U.S. Army, 100,000 Marines, and substantial air power had been massed in Florida and Puerto Rico. Varga had learned also from his sources that the United States Strategic Air Command's activity had been intensified. Růžek, the Czechoslovak ambassador, added that according to refugee sources, newly organized refugee commandos had also been put on alert. Officially representing Cuban interests in the United States, Ambassador Růžek speculated that Castro might soon announce general mobilization of Cuba. Bălăceanu, the Rumanian ambassador, a reserved yet highly nervous person, asked Dobrynin whether a new German crisis might result from a further aggravation of the Cuban situation. Apparently he had overheard Western officials voicing concern over such a development. Dobrynin could only reply that he had received no information from Moscow substantiating such reports and that he himself felt that the likelihood of another German crisis at this point was minimal.[7]

Some of the ambassadors then asked Dobrynin how the Soviet Union planned to deal with the quarantine. Dobrynin was forced again to reply that he simply had no information about Soviet strategy and in turn requested the East European representatives to pass on to him any news that came their way. The general mood was one of gloom and uncertainty. Most of those in the room felt that the world situation had never before been so hopelessly and dangerously confused.

On the evening of 23 October, the day after President Kennedy's Cuban-missile broadcast, I returned to the Soviet embassy to attend the Soviet military attaché's party. Circulating among the guests were the usual figures from most of the diplomatic units. However, from the State Department and the Pentagon the number was noticeably smaller than normal. During the course of the evening the Russian diplomats argued with American newsmen over the actual presence of Soviet medium-range ballistic missiles in Cuba. I chatted at some length with Bernard Gwertzman, a reporter for the *Washington Star*, who wanted to know precisely why the Soviets had put the missiles in Cuba and whether Soviet ships would challenge the blockade. According to news service reports, Gwertzman added, the first ship to reach the quarantine line would be the Soviet cargo boat *Poltava*. Not knowing the answers myself, I simply told the reporter that I was not in a position to offer any explanation. Gwertzman and I were soon joined by Marcello Spacarelli, an Italian correspondent, who also wanted to know about Soviet plans and motivations. Offering only my own opinion, I responded that I doubted that the Soviet ship would turn back. Soviet prestige, I speculated, would not permit them to bow so easily to defeat.

In the meantime, General Vladimir Dubovik, the Soviet military attaché, was also surrounded by reporters. His reply to their questions, however, was far more specific than mine. He informed the press that the captains of the ships heading toward Cuba were under orders to defy the blockade. "I have fought in three wars already," he boasted, "and I am looking forward to fighting in the next. We are ready to defend ourselves against all acts of aggression—against ourselves or against any of our allies."[8]

Later in the evening, when the party was already well under way, Dobrynin entered, calm and self-possessed. The newsmen immediately gathered round him, asking for confirmation of Dubovik's statement. Disclaiming any inside information, Dobrynin told them that he was not a military man and that Dubovik, as military attache, knew more about navy plans.

Shortly after Dobrynin's statement, I came upon Deputy Undersecretary of State Richard Davis. Finding him unwilling to volunteer his personal opinion of the Cuban situation, I asked him whether the Americans would fire on Soviet ships if they tried to run the blockade. Davis avoided a direct answer, indicating only that this information could be found in President Kennedy's speech.

Toward the end of the evening I asked Dobrynin whether he had received any new information from Moscow or had had any new run-ins with American officials. Dobrynin explained gravely that the situation was even more confused and unstable than it had been earlier and that he had received no new information from Moscow concerning the planned Soviet response to the blockade. He neglected to mention, however, that just before coming to the party he had had an unpleasant discussion with Robert Kennedy in his own office. According to Kennedy's subsequent account of the meeting, the attorney general had continued to press home the point to Dobrynin that the Soviets had gravely misled the U.S. government and had deceived the president. The main reason for the attorney general's visit, however, was to ask Dobrynin whether the Soviet ships were going to go through to Cuba. Dobrynin had replied that those had been the instructions and that he knew of no change. When I learned the details of this discussion sometime later, it occurred to me that Kennedy's inquiry about the Soviet response may have been unwise, for Soviet analysts might easily have interpreted it as evidence of American fear and hesitancy.

The events of 25, 26, and 27 October represented the peak of the crisis and the height of confusion over Soviet intentions. On the 25th, after all the armed forces of the Soviet Union had been alerted in Eastern Europe, the Warsaw Pact armed forces were also put on alert. In Washington, on the other hand, Walter Lippmann wrote a column in which he appealed to President Kennedy not to press the Russians for the removal of the missiles from Cuba. Proposing a face-saving solution, Lippmann suggested that perhaps the Soviet Union might agree to dismantle its bases in Cuba if the United States were to promise to withdraw its Jupiter missiles from Turkey. The Soviet embassy apparently considered the Lippmann article a trial balloon, launched by the

U.S. administration to seek out a suitable solution. On 26 October, when the East European ambassadors met again at the Soviet Embassy, Dobrynin sought their opinion as to whether they thought the Lippmann article should be regarded as an indirect suggestion on the part of the White House. The Rumanian ambassador announced that he had learned from a reliable source that the administration had communicated to Lippmann the idea for his compromise solution. Since, according to most authoritative accounts of the Cuban missile crisis that appeared later, the Lippmann article was not inspired by the administration, the Rumanian ambassador's "reliable source" must be considered a little less than completely reliable.

At the meeting on 26 October I took the opportunity to repeat to Dobrynin the question I had put to him on the 23rd: was the Soviet Union heading toward a major confrontation with the United States, and would Soviet ships turn back or run the blockade? Dobrynin replied once again that he still had no information. I told him that according to my information the American build-up for an invasion of Cuba was nearly completed and that American missile bases had aimed all their missiles toward targets on the island. Only a go-ahead signal from the president was needed. The Soviet ambassador concurred with my analysis, adding that the Soviet Union found itself in a difficult position in Cuba because its supply lines were too long and the American blockade could be very effective. Růžek remarked grimly that if the Americans invaded, it would definitely trigger a nuclear war. At this point I lost self-control and asked whether it was not the same to die from an American missile attack as from a Soviet one. Dobrynin attempted to assure me that the situation had not reached such proportions and that a solution would no doubt be found. Although his remark was completely unsubstantiated, it was nonetheless somewhat comforting.

Dobrynin naturally did not mention the fact that on 26 October Khrushchev had sent President Kennedy a secret letter in which the Soviet leader apparently proposed that if the president offered assurance that Cuba would not be invaded, the Soviet Union would remove its missiles from Cuba. Similarly, Dobrynin refrained from revealing that his counselor, Alexander Fomin, was at that very moment at the Occidental Restaurant discussing with ABC Washington correspondent John Scali peace plans for solving the crisis. Fomin probably based his peace proposal on the contents of Khrushchev's secret letter.[9] Finally, Dobrynin did not refer to the fact that he remained in constant contact with high American officials, specifically Robert Kennedy and Dean Rusk.

At the close of the meeting, any last remaining ray of hope I may have had for a peaceful solution was abruptly shattered. Dobrynin now announced that the Soviet embassy was at this very moment burning its archives. Shocked at this news I inquired of Dobrynin whether he planned to evacuate the families of Soviet diplomatic personnel. Dobrynin replied in the negative.

Back once again at the Hungarian legation I rushed off to Budapest a long summary of my latest meeting with Dobrynin, and informed the Foreign Ministry that Dobrynin had confirmed the information that the Americans were militarily prepared to invade Cuba. I emphasized that unless a quick political solution were found within the next few days, the United States would proceed with the invasion and nothing short of a miracle could save the world from nuclear war.

Within two hours I received a troubled inquiry from Budapest asking whether I could possibly be aware of the implications of my words. I insisted that I would take full responsibility for every word in my report.

On the same day, 26 October, I visited Afghan Ambassador Mohammed Hashim Maiwandwal,[10] a good friend whom I considered very wise. Like everyone else during those crucial days, the envoy was deeply disturbed. The conversation revolved around the Soviet ships approaching the American blockade. To Maiwandwal's question as to whether I had received any information about Soviet plans, I replied that I had seen the Soviet ambassador a few hours earlier but had learned nothing. We agreed that the Pentagon announcement of 25 October indicating that a dozen of the Soviet vessels had turned back, was a hopeful but not entirely reassuring sign. There was still the possibility that those ships which continued to approach the blockade or the Soviet submarines dispatched to the area might somehow become involved in a confrontation. Contemplating the situation, I expressed the hope that both Khrushchev and Kennedy could and did appreciate the fact that the advent of the atomic age had changed the nature of international behavior and that what might have represented a loss of face yesterday could be considered a compromise today. Ambassador Maiwandwal agreed, adding that there must be more than one solution to a question as complex and potentially explosive as the present one. Both of us deplored the fact that little countries could not avoid the repercussions of a nuclear confrontation. I observed that at least Afghanistan was in a better position geographically and politically than Hungary, which was after all a member of the Warsaw Pact.

On 27 October, Radio Moscow broadcast a long letter from Khrushchev addressed to President Kennedy. Combining threat with a willingness to compromise, Khrushchev stated:

> We agree to remove those weapons from Cuba which you regard as offensive weapons. We agree to do this and to state this commitment in the United Nations. Your representative will make a statement to the effect that the United States, on its part, bearing in mind the anxiety and concern of the Soviet state, will evacuate its analogous weapons from Turkey.

In the remainder of the letter Khrushchev solicited a pledge from the United States that it would neither invade Cuba nor make its territory available as a *place d'armes* for a future attack.

Although Khrushchev's letter contained certain positive elements and indicated some willingness to compromise, I feared that while the Russians were attempting to bargain over the Turkish missile bases the time for diplomacy would pass and American military action would begin. Listening to the radio all that night, I remained tense and worried about the prospects of war.

On 28 October Dobrynin's secretary telephoned to suggest that I turn on the radio at once. I was just in time to hear Khrushchev's latest letter addressed to President Kennedy being broadcast over Radio Moscow:

> In order to eliminate as rapidly as possible the conflict which endangers the cause of peace ...the Soviet government has given a new order to dismantle the arms which you described as offensive, and to crate and return them to the Soviet Union.

Khrushchev apparently was gravely concerned about the time element, for he had been informed by Dobrynin that the Americans would attack in forty-eight hours. Under these circumstances a Soviet message to Kennedy had to be transmitted by the quickest possible means—a radio broadcast. In a similar announcement over the Voice of America and in a message conveyed through Ambassador Dobrynin, President Kennedy informed the Soviet Union that the United States welcomed Khrushchev's "statesmanlike" decision and expressed the hope that with a solution of the Cuban crisis the governments of the world could turn their attention toward "ending the arms race and reducing world tensions."

This American-Soviet confrontation over Cuba had many far-reaching effects. Observers in the United Nations detected almost at once a cooling relationship between Cuban and Soviet delegates and recorded criticism on the part of radical African representatives who spoke of "cowardly Russian behavior" in Cuba. These Africans faulted the Russians for having yielded too quickly to American pressure, and for failing to fulfill their commitment to Cuba. They voiced the opinion that Africa should therefore regard with suspicion any future political promise given by the Kremlin. Although this criticism was expressed for the most part in private, it caused considerable concern and trouble for the Russians. Time and again the veteran Soviet delegate Platon Dmitrievich Morozov attempted to explain to Ghana's Alex Quaison Sakey, who was president of the Assembly that year, and to members of the Guinean and Mali delegations that the Soviet government had done nothing less than save the world from nuclear holocaust and, at the same time, had defended Cuba's independence. The Africans, however, remained unconvinced.

Madame Jeanne Martine, a native Guinean married to a Frenchman, had been a *militante* in the French Communist Party before Guinea achieved independence. In 1962 she was a member of the Guinean U.N. delegation. In the U.N. delegates' lounge she told me quite openly that she was deeply shocked

by the "Russian treason" in Cuba and that from now on Moscow should not
expect trust from independent, free African governments. She added very seriously that East Europeans should regard Soviet policy more realistically, particularly
in light of the Cuban missile crisis. Of course I could not reveal the fact that
similar discussions were taking place within the Hungarian U.N. mission and
that the Peking-oriented members of the mission, including Hungarian Ambassador Csatordai, agreed with her completely. I simply told her instead that
I was glad the world had avoided an all-out war, the third and possibly the
last world war. With this, Madame Martine branded me a satellite of the Soviet
Union and turned on her heel. The nonaligned Asian countries and the Europeans
in the United Nations generally felt a huge sense of relief after 28 October.
As for the Arab group, they were as always too preoccupied with their own
problems in the Middle East to be much concerned with Cuba.

After the danger of direct confrontation between the superpowers had been
averted, it was Castro who presented the most serious complications for the
Soviet government. During the crisis Khrushchev had apparently been unable
or unwilling to consult in approved diplomatic fashion with his Caribbean ally.
When the Soviet leader informed President Kennedy in his 28 October letter
that he was prepared to reach an agreement that would allow U.N. representatives
to verify the dismantling of the missile sites, he did so without the prior consent
of Castro. Not surprisingly, the angry Cuban laid down his own terms for
the solution of the crisis. Shortly after Khrushchev's peace proposal was heard
over Radio Moscow, Radio Havana transmitted the Cuban conditions. Ignoring
the Soviet agreement to withdraw the ground-to-ground missiles under U.N.
inspection, the Cuban government categorically demanded that the United States
(1) end the blockade and all economic pressure on Cuba, (2) end all harassment
by Cuban exiles, (3) stop the raids by exile commando groups, (4) stop the
overflights of Cuban territory, and (5) withdraw from its naval base at Guan-
tanamo Bay.

Although Castro's five points were clearly unrealistic, the communist bloc
pounced on them for propaganda purposes, representing them in the forum
of the United Nations and elsewhere as just demands. But the line between
propaganda and realpolitik is a sharp one. The same Russian military technicians
who, in great secrecy, had built the missile sites dismantled them without the
permission or the consent of Castro. In this situation the only option Castro
had was to oppose U.N. inspection. He stated firmly that whoever wanted
to come to inspect Cuba must come in battle array. On 30 October in Havana,
he bitterly told Secretary General U Thant that he considered the matter of
inspection to be one more attempt to humiliate Cuba and for that reason he
did not accept it.

On the other side of the globe, inside the walls of the Kremlin, the Soviet
Presidium was having its own share of problems. The elementary question
was what to do with Castro, how to convince him of the necessity of an inspection
under U.N. auspices. Since the Soviet leaders had consistently refused during

the disarmament negotiations to agree to on-site inspection on Soviet territory, how could they now press the Cubans to accept similar conditions on their territory? Khrushchev, apparently feeling that perhaps Anastas Mikoyan, the U.S.S.R.'s best troubleshooter, could sell the idea, dispatched him to Cuba on 2 November. At the same time Khrushchev sent Deputy Foreign Minister Kuznetsov to New York to work out final arrangements with U Thant and U.S negotiators Adlai Stevenson and John McCloy for the inspection of the removal of the missiles and the Il-28 bombers.

Mikoyan spent three weeks in Cuba, the first fruitless argument with Castro. During the next ten days Castro completely ignored his illustrious guest, who was reduced to passing his time visiting sugar plantations. It was only when Mikoyan threatened to fly back to Moscow and to cut off Soviet oil supply to Cuba that Castro consented to resume discussions.

On his way home Mikoyan stopped in Washington to see President Kennedy. At the invitation of Ambassador Dobrynin the ambassadors of the communist countries in Washington attended a dinner at the Soviet embassy on 30 November to meet Mikoyan. The Russian diplomat looked extremely tired and depressed. His wife had died in Moscow while he was in Havana and he had missed the funeral, reason enough in itself for anyone to be gloomy. In addition, his difficult discussions with Fidel must have increased his distress. He is reported to have said that Castro was like a mule, hard to convince and hard to deal with.

Despite all these difficulties Mikoyan displayed great willingness to recount his Cuban experiences in detail. Speaking Russian in a low voice, with a heavy Armenian accent, he politely characterized his meetings with Castro as "confrontations of opposite views." The Cuban doctor (the term by which he referred to Castro) had been almost out of his mind when their first discussion opened. He tended to blame everything on the Soviet Union. He complained that the general mobilization which he had been compelled to put into effect after the United States declared the blockade had almost ruined Cuba's economy. This aspect of the problem was easily solved, however, by the offer of a new long-term loan from Mikoyan.

On the question of the withdrawal of the missiles it was more difficult for the Moscow troubleshooter to placate Castro. Mikoyan noted that Castro had behaved more like a guerrilla leader than a statesman. Wild and flamboyant, he smoked one cigar after another; and when he spoke, he gesticulated with both hands, ran up and down the room, and then, sitting down, put his feet on the table. Mikoyan is said to have feared that in the heat of the discussions Castro might put a revolver under his nose. It required long days of patient argument just to calm the Cuban leader to the point where he was ready to discuss matters quietly.

Castro bitterly reproached Mikoyan for dismantling the ground-to-ground missiles because he felt the very security of his island depended on the presence of these devices. To Castro's way of thinking, Americans respected only hard deterrent force, that is, nuclear missiles; and although the Cuban army was ready to fight to the last man, without Soviet missiles Cuba could not resist a direct American attack longer than two or three months.

Mikoyan attempted to explain to Fidel that the Soviet Union was still guaranteeing Cuba's independence and sovereignty by military and political means, and tried to convince him that he should allow the U.N. inspection team to supervise the dismantling process. As Mikoyan had expected, Castro adamantly refused. Realizing that the presence of an international team could have an undesirable political effect on the Cuban population, he did not press Castro too hard on the inspection issue. He proposed to Moscow instead that the Americans observe the evacuation of the missiles from the air and, if necessary, might inspect Soviet ships on the high seas. On the basis of Mikoyan's report, Soviet Deputy Foreign Minister Kuznetsov finally succeeded in convincing McCloy at the United Nations that this was a suitable substitute for on-site inspection.

Plans for the actual evacuation of the Il-28 bombers from the island were painful, said the old Armenian politician, for the Soviet government had delivered these planes to Cuba as Soviet military aid and had handed them over to the Cuban Air Force. It was only after several trying sessions with Castro that Mikoyan was able to arrange the removal of these bombers, and even then he accomplished this by convincing Castro that Kennedy would withhold any public non-invasion pledge until after the removal had been completed.

While Mikoyan cabled word of Castro's assent to the Kremlin, Dobrynin, on 20 November, informed Robert Kennedy of the agreement. That same day President Kennedy announced at his press conference:

> . . . if all offensive weapons are removed from Cuba and kept out of the hemisphere in the future, under adequate verification and safeguards, and if Cuba is not used for the export of aggressive communist purposes, there will be peace in the Caribbean. And as I said in September, we shall neither initiate nor permit aggression in this hemisphere.

After dinner, Mikoyan continued his briefing by explaining that the Cuban situation had been complicated by the continual advice which Castro had received from the Chinese. Peking, according to Mikoyan, had sent tons of propaganda material, and Mao Tse-tung had transmitted to Havana one message after another assuring the Cubans that the eight hundred million Chinese stood firmly behind them and that the Americans were paper tigers. Mikoyan reported that while the Chinese had done nothing to help defend Castro, they had refrained from shelling Quemoy and Matsu during the days of the crisis.[11] Mikoyan noted ironically that they might easily have stepped up pressure against Taiwan, which—with the Americans involved in the Caribbean—could have changed the whole situation. Instead they did not move. And after the crisis was over the Chinese heaped bitter reproaches upon the Soviet Union, charging that to deploy missiles in Cuba was "adventurism," but to take them out was "capitulationism."[12]

In defense against the Chinese charges Mikoyan offered two explanations for the Soviet action. The missile deployment in the Caribbean, he said, was aimed at defending Castro on the one hand and, on the other, at achieving a definite shift in the power relationship between the socialist and the capitalist worlds. After evaluating the strong American reaction during the crisis, however, the Presidium had decided against risking the security of the Soviet Union and its allies for the sake of Cuba.

Almost in a flash I grasped for the first time the ultimate goal of the Soviet Union. In light of Mikoyan's remark, I realized that the purpose of the extremely dangerous Soviet missile deployment was to upset the balance of power. Nor could I fail to understand Castro's angry reaction, for the Cuban leader had been left completely abandoned in the midst of a deadly power struggle with nothing but verbal guarantees.

Before getting down to his 29 November meeting with President Kennedy, Mikoyan spoke again about Castro. He explained that Castro's chief deficiencies were his youth and his inexperience. He was as yet a man who did not understand politics and who did not know how to retreat when the international communist movement required it. He was a revolutionary idealist rather than a Marxist. Although Castro insisted that he knew the Americans better than Khrushchev did, he had in fact completely misjudged the situation. Mikoyan pointed out that Castro refused to cooperate with the great powers at any point. He remained aloof even after the Kremlin had received firm guarantees on the part of President Kennedy that the United States would honor Cuban independence in return for the Soviet decision to dismantle the missiles.

It had been far easier, said Mikoyan, to reach an understanding with Kennedy than with Castro. During his visit to the White House, the Kremlin's envoy once again received the pledge that the United States would not launch an invasion against Cuba. According to Mikoyan, Kennedy was anxious to know when all the Soviet troops would leave the island. Mikoyan assured him that they would be withdrawn gradually, and added that under the Soviet-Cuban agreement Soviet artillerymen had been handling the anti-aircraft missiles in Cuba until the Cubans could learn the job. Mikoyan jokingly commented that the Americans should pray that this arrangement continued, implying that the Cubans entertained fewer reservations about shooting down American U-2s than did Moscow.

Mikoyan had apparently discussed other important issues with the president on this occasion. According to his account, Kennedy had given him a firm guarantee that the U.S. Jupiter bases in Turkey would soon be dismantled and had expressed the hope that the United States and the Soviet Union could work toward a nuclear test ban treaty.[13] Mikoyan neglected to mention, however, that President Kennedy had reminded him that the missile crisis had developed as a result of a high-level, calculated attempt to deceive him.[14] Nevertheless, the president recognized that the Soviet Union was probably now more prepared than at any time before for serious negotiation. The next time I saw Mikoyan was in the autumn of 1963, when he came to Washington to represent the Soviet Union at the funeral of President Kennedy. Following the funeral cere- mony, the newly sworn-in president, Lyndon B. Johnson, invited the foreign guests to a reception at the State Department. I chanced to be standing with Mikoyan when President de Gaulle entered the room. The French president joined us, and before long Mikoyan and de Gaulle were deeply engrossed in conversation. De Gaulle asked the aging Soviet emissary whether he felt that closer collaboration between France and the Soviet Union might not be timely. Do you think, he asked Mikoyan, alluding to the poor relations which then existed between their two countries, that everything France is doing is against the interest of the Soviet Union? Would it not be better to work more closely in Europe, to have a European Europe from La Manche to the Urals? Mikoyan expressed interest in the Frenchman's views and promised to relay his remarks to Khrushchev on his return to Moscow.

A few minutes later Mikoyan was asked to see President Johnson and Secretary of State Rusk. Both assured him that the new administration would follow President Kennedy's foreign policy line and that they desired improved relations with the Soviet Union. To Mikoyan's question as to whether this assurance applied also to Cuba, President Johnson replied in the affirmative.

— 16 —

The Compromise Solution

The U.S.-Soviet "gentleman's agreement" over Cuba led to a stand-off in the Caribbean. Succeeding American administrations have kept President Kennedy's pledge not to invade Castro's island, and the successors of Premier Khrushchev have refrained from introducing offensive missiles there.

Without doubt it was Soviet national interest rather than ideological considerations that dictated Soviet action in the 1962 Cuban crisis. In the light of subsequent developments to which we have alluded briefly, the Soviet missile deployment, a risky and expensive operation, was aimed at upsetting the balance of power. Although the move ended in a well-advised but humiliating retreat, it apparently opened the eyes of Soviet leaders to their limitations. The Americans on their part became more determined than ever to stay out of the Soviet sphere in Eastern Europe.

LOSS OF SOVIET PRESTIGE

The Soviet Union paid a heavy price for its serious miscalculation in the Cuban missile crisis. Soviet supremacy within the communist world was shattered. The rift between China and the U.S.S.R. deepened. Inside the already polycentric communist camp, further polarization took place. Castro's Cuba on one side of the globe and North Korea on the other became prime examples of independent-minded nationalist communist regimes, each accepting military and economic assistance equally from both the Soviet Union and China, neither willing to take sides in the Sino-Soviet power struggle. Radicals all over the world ceased to look to Russian-style communism for support in the revolutionary movement. This change of attitude became especially relevant in Latin America, where the Kremlin, reading the handwriting on the wall, abandoned militant tactics and returned to traditional power politics by broadening trade and expanding cultural infiltration. As the Soviet revolutionary image faded, Castro's Cuba and Mao Tse-tung's China emerged as the ideological centers of the "peoples' liberation" movements.

Eastern Europe, shocked and panic-stricken by the fiasco of the bold missile adventure, breathed more easily after the Cuban compromise. However, the fear of becoming involved in a worldwide nuclear confrontation automatically and involuntarily did not subside completely. On the contrary, it became the prime concern of East European communist leaders. They began to ask the Soviet Union for more guarantees of security against nuclear attack and for a greater voice in the planning of Warsaw Pact nuclear strategy. Following the crisis, the Soviet Union and its allies endeavored to coordinate their policies more closely and to synchronize their propaganda.

János Kádár was the last of the East European-bloc leaders to hurry to Moscow in the wake of the Cuban crisis. On 7 November 1962 he conferred with Khrushchev, Brezhnev, and Kozlov. At a luncheon in his honor in the Kremlin he met with the rest of the Soviet leadership.[1] Western news agencies reported that in addition to the Cuban missile crisis Khrushchev and Kádár probably discussed the Sino-Indian border war, the Berlin question, and the economic troubles that the communist regimes in Eastern Europe were facing.[2] Although nothing official was disclosed in the communique issued after the meeting, subsequent events lent substance to this report. The communiqué simply stated that on all debated matters the discussions had demonstrated the complete identity of views of the Soviet and Hungarian leaders. Those around the Hungarian party secretary knew, however, that the main topic of conversation had been the final preparation for the Hungarian Eighth Party Congress, which was due to open on 20 November. The two leaders discussed also how to deal with the Sino-Soviet controversy over Albania. They agreed that pressure on Albania should be intensified and that the Hungarian party would sharply condemn the "deviationist" Albanian party chief, Enver Hoxha. This step seemed necessary after Peking and Tirana had stepped up their attack on Khrushchev for his "appeasement policy" during the Cuban crisis.[3] Thus, Khrushchev and Kádár coordinated their approach to the propaganda aspect of the Cuban missile crisis.

THE KHRUSHCHEV-KÁDÁR APPROACH TO AMNESTY

When it came to discussing the general situation, Khrushchev informed Kádár that the Soviet leadership felt it was in the interest of the socialist "commonwealth" to work for a temporary relaxation of international tensions. Without mentioning any deadline, Khrushchev indicated that in order to achieve this goal the Soviet Union would adopt a more flexible position in the ongoing nuclear test-ban talks with the Americans. This shift in Soviet foreign policy was of great help to Kádár in international diplomacy. He seized upon this opportunity to raise the question of Hungarian-American relations. Summarizing the results of the extended dialogue and the secret negotiations between the Hungarian and the U.S. diplomats, the Hungarian party chief told Khrushchev that the Americans held fast to their formula of amnesty as the price for normalization of Hungarian-U.S. relations and for the removal of the Hungarian question from the United Nations agenda. He explained that the Hungarian Politburo had studied the question of amnesty independently of the American "offer" and had found that the internal security of the country would certainly not be endangered by such a move at this stage. Referring to the "piece of paper" handed over to the Hungarian chargé in Washington, Kádár argued that this time the American intention to achieve a compromise solution appeared far more serious than it had been on previous occasions.

The fact that he introduced the Hungarian question into his conversation with Khrushchev made it clear that Kádár was eager to reach some sort of accommodation with the U.S. government. His main concern was not so much to improve Hungarian-U.S. relations (which he considered a matter of secondary importance) as to avoid the embarrassment caused to his government and the Soviet Union by the annual General Assembly censure, which he was finding more and more intolerable. In addition, the fact that the Credentials Committee of the United Nations, as a result of American insistence, did not accept his delegation's credentials lowered Hungary's status and resulted in its diplomatic isolation in the world organization. Some sort of compromise between the two countries would help to relax tension and would break Kádár's international isolation. Finally, the resolution of the whole question would represent little if any difficulty for Kádár at home because his regime was preparing a general amnesty in any case. What he could not bring himself to admit either to himself or to Khrushchev was that his government would be acting under the pressure of the American condition to trade "amnesty for normalization."

Kádár's motives, whatever they may have been, happened to coincide with Khrushchev's interests. Both men decided, therefore, that as a test of American sincerity, Kádár should announce at the Hungarian Party Congress on 20 November that more than ninety-five percent of the persons sentenced for "counterrevolutionary crimes" had been released, and that further amnesty would follow if the Hungarian question were dropped from the U.N. General Assembly agenda.

On 20 November 1962, less than a month after the Cuban crisis, and in the midst of the sharpening ideological battle between Moscow and Peking, the Eighth Congress of the Hungarian Socialist Workers' Party opened. Premier János Kádár, first secretary of the party, delivered a four-hour opening report in which he detailed his party's stand on every important international issue.

He stated, as he himself firmly believed, that the Soviet Union was "in the vanguard of the development of the socialist countries,"[4] and that "Soviet-Hungarian friendship forms our country's strongest support." He repeated the Soviet theme of peaceful coexistence and stressed that "the struggle between the capitalist and socialist systems must be decided peacefully in peaceful competition." Nobody was astonished when he voiced the common propaganda line of the communist parties of Eastern Europe: "Mankind can be grateful to Comrade Khrushchev" for having averted "the American imperialist provocations" and having safeguarded peace and "the sovereignty of Cuba."

A true internationalist in the Moscow sense, Kádár pledged that his party would strive to strengthen "our ideological and political unity, as well as our economic ties" with the U.S.S.R., China, and all socialist countries in Europe and in Asia. Kádár felt that the best way of "strengthening the unity" was to condemn "the dogmatic stand of Enver Hoxha," the Albanian Workers' Party chief, and "similar symptoms in other communist parties." Otto Kuusinen, the veteran Bolshevik and representative of the Soviet party, was well pleased with Kádár's remarks on Albania; they prepared the way for the Soviet attack planned for the next day. Kuusinen branded the Albanians "traitors" to the communist cause and to world peace, for they had criticized Premier Khrushchev's Cuban compromise policy, although "in practice they were incapable of giving the slightest support in the struggle against imperialism." The Chinese party's delegate, Wu Hsiu-chuan, believed with good reason that Kádár, Kuusinen, and the others were attacking China through Albania, and in his turn struck back at the "revisionism" of the "Tito clique," and defended the Albanians.

The confrontation aroused no special interest among the delegates at the Congress, who, aware of the growing Sino-Soviet controversy, had expected the skirmish. Western observers, however, noted that Kádár's criticism of the Albanian (that is, Maoist) position was the strongest ever publicly delivered by an East European leader. The conflict between the Russian and Chinese positions became even sharper when Kádár warmly echoed the Kremlin's new policy of friendship with Yugoslavia, a regime subject to vehement Chinese attack at that time, and called for closer "state and economic relations" with Tito "in spite of the ideological difference of opinion existing between us concerning the most important questions of the international labor movement."[5]

To the great displeasure of Peking, Kádár followed the Kremlin's lead in taking a neutral position on the Sino-Indian border dispute. He wished to see the frontier problems between fraternal China and friendly India settled peacefully, through negotiations.[6] The audience listened with moderate interest when Kádár restated his well-known position on the U.N. Hungarian question. For the last six years, he explained, the U.S. delegation in the United Nations had forced the world organization to include the issue on the agenda; yet the whole question was rooted not in the United Nations but in the unsettled relations between Hungary and the United States. Kádár insisted that the Hungarian government sincerely wished to normalize its relations with the United States. In his view all that was needed to this end was that Washington cease interfering in Hungary's internal affairs. He mentioned that "the United States had tried to interfere in the administration of justice of the Hungarian People's Republic."[7]

Then, out of a clear sky, the first secretary remarked:

> As is well known, in the cases of persons sentenced for counterrevolutionary crimes, the Presidential Council has repeatedly and broadly made use of its right to grant amnesty. More than 95 percent of the people sentenced for such crimes have...been released and have become integrated into normal life.

Kádár went farther, giving assurance that

> this is the situation in this sphere, and our state intends to apply the principles it has adhered to so far in the future also.[8]

Returning to the issue of Hungarian-American relations, he emphasized that no real differences existed between the peoples of the United States and Hungary. "On the contrary, the interest of both nations lies...in the normalization of relations between the two states." In what appeared to be a call for some kind of response from Washington, the Hungarian party leader added that "controversial questions between the two governments could be resolved, provided they are raised with goodwill and with the intention of settling them."

The announcement of the release of the great majority of political prisoners surprised the Eighth Party Congress. Few people in the audience understood the connection between these two questions; few were informed as to the delicate negotiations that had recently been taking place between Budapest and Moscow, as well as between Budapest and Washington.

Once Kádár's announcement had been made public, the solution to the Hungarian question was well on its way. A few days after the close of the Eighth Hungarian Party Congress, on 4 December 1962, I paid another visit to Assistant Secretary of State Richard Davis. This time the conversation took place in a relaxed, friendly atmosphere. Both of us felt we were in comfortable positions, for not only did we know in advance what the topic of our discussion would be, but each was able to predict with almost complete certainty exactly how he would hold up his own end.

Naturally, I took occasion to draw the assistant secretary's attention to Kádár's speech at the opening of the Party Congress. Without any reference to the American "piece of paper," I repeated the part of the text in which Kádár had unexpectedly told his audience that ninety-five percent of the persons arrested and tried in connection with the 1956 uprising had been freed. The point that, according to Kádár's speech, the release of the remaining political prisoners would continue came in for special emphasis. Of course Davis on his part tried to learn in as much detail as possible the future plans of the Hungarian government. All I was free to reveal at this time was that the Hungarian government's position would become easier if the Hungarian question were dropped from the agenda of the U.N. General Assembly.

Davis acknowledged that Kádár's announcement (concerning the release of political prisoners) was accepted by State Department officials as an authoritative statement. He was not sure, however, whether Congress or American public opinion would interpret Kádár's move in the same way. In any event, he assured me that the State Department would exert its influence in the United Nations to end debate on the question of Hungary. After the meeting with Davis I somehow felt convinced that since Kádár had found a face-saving formula with regard to the political prisoners, the U.S. government would certainly fulfill its end of the bargain. I had no doubt whatever that the specialists in the State Department or at the American U.N. mission in New York would find the means of disposing of the question of Hungary once and for all.

On the same day, Péter Mód, the Hungarian deputy foreign minister, called on U Thant. In the secretary-general's office at U.N. headquarters, the two went into the subject of Hungary's relationship to the United Nations. It was the first time in many years that high-ranking U.N. and Hungarian officials had discussed political matters with one another. During this brief but important meeting the Hungarian deputy foreign minister called the attention of U Thant to Kádár's announcement concerning the release of the political prisoners. Péter Mód was more open with the neutral U Thant, however, than I had permitted myself to be in Washington. To the secretary-general's question about the future plans of the Hungarian government, Mód revealed candidly that an amnesty was at that very moment in preparation. Furthermore, he filled in U Thant on the Hungarian-U.S. diplomatic negotiations and expressed the hope that the whole business would soon be shelved. Mód indicated also that he would like nothing better than to have U Thant relay to Washington, as discreetly as possible of course, the salient points of the report Mód had just given him.

From this point Mód moved quickly to the principal purpose of his meeting with U Thant. He extended an official invitation to the secretary-general to visit Hungary. U Thant, in accepting the invitation in principle, indicated that he could probably come to Hungary the following summer, when he would be attending the session of the Economic Council for Europe in Geneva. The news of the Hungarian invitation was reported in the *New York Times*.[9] The Hungarian step was regarded as significant in view of Hungary's previous refusal to admit U.N. representatives to investigate the aftermath of the 1956 revolution. Following the usual propaganda pattern, and for the sake of appearance, the spokesman for the Hungarian mission to the United Nations minimized the importance of the invitation. He pointed out that his government had simply renewed an invitation extended previously to the secretary-general of the world organization.

This indirect diplomacy, with its insistence on saving face, served a useful purpose and worked out to the advantage of all concerned. On 18 December 1962 the U.N. Special Political Committee spent almost the whole day discussing the endless problem of the Palestine refugees in the Middle East. Late in the afternoon (5 p.m.) Leopoldo Benites, chairman of the committee, wishing to dispose of the last issue of the year, proposed the continuation of the session and opened the debate on Agenda Item 85—the question of Hungary.

FINAL U.N. ACTION ON THE QUESTION OF HUNGARY

The delegates of the member states represented in the Special Committee were acquainted with the latest U.S. draft resolution, submitted the day before. In it the American delegation to the United Nations (1) requested the secretary-general to take any initiative he deemed helpful in relation to the Hungarian question, and (2) considered that under the circumstances the post of Sir Leslie Munro, the U.N. representative on Hungary, need no longer be continued.[10]

The new draft resolution indicated a complete shift in the U.S. position. The U.S. Government, the promoter of the question of Hungary in the United Nations, was ready to call a halt to Munro's investigation. The well-trained diplomats and newspaper correspondents who knew the rules of the world organization and were familiar with the six-year history of the Hungarian question did not expect much of a debate on dropping "Item 85."

Without once alluding to the tacit understanding between the parties directly involved, the Americans, the Hungarians, and the Soviets conducted themselves strictly in accordance with the principles of secret diplomacy. In the meantime, they made full use of the United Nations as a rostrum for propaganda. The Americans made some effort to explain to the public at home and abroad the reason for their changed attitude. The Hungarian and Russian representatives simply repeated their six-year-old arguments. All three used harsh words, as had become standard procedure in the Special Political Committee. The most vitriolic of the three was the representative of Hungary, whose position was the weakest.

In the course of the final debate Carl T. Rowan, the representative of the United States, reviewed the events of the 1956 emergency session of the Security Council.[11] He recalled the hopes, the sorrows, and the profound indignation felt by his delegation concerning the Hungarian tragedy. He reminded the committee that the General Assembly had adopted more than a dozen resolutions and had appointed special committees and representatives to investigate the unfortunate and tragic situation in Hungary. The Soviet and Hungarian authorities, however, had refused to cooperate with the United Nations.

Switching from the past to the present, Rowan granted that conditions in Hungary had undergone some improvement and that his government now felt the need for a "fresh approach" to this problem. He argued that this new approach incorporated in the American Draft Resolution proposed to improve the situation of the Hungarian people through the most effective practical means. The request made to the secretary-general "to take any initiative that he deemed helpful" reflected, according to Rowan, the legitimate concern of the United Nations for the welfare of the Hungarian people. However, the "legitimate concern" gave no authority to the secretary-general to continue direct or indirect investigation, nor did it compel him to report success or failure. The "fresh approach" was only an elegant way of ending the debate on the whole issue.

The leading NATO powers and other close allies of the United States had probably been informed by American diplomats about some of the aspects of the American-Hungarian tacit understanding. Morozov, the Soviet representative, was completely informed. The "normal bureaucratic procedure" of the United Nations, however, required a formal debate in which the Hungarian and Soviet representatives were supposed to reject ex officio the American Draft Resolution.

As was to be expected, Ambassador Károly Csatordai, the permanent representative of the Hungarian delegation to the United Nations, repeated the six-year-old charges of the Kádár regime. He stated that the inclusion of the so-called question of Hungary was an American-instigated attempt to intervene in "questions which were exclusively the concern of the Hungarian people."[12] In his view, this was a violation of the fundamental principles of the United Nations Charter derived from the clear-cut wish to bring a cold-war atmosphere into the United Nations. For this reason Csatordai protested the United States Draft Resolution and demanded that the question of Hungary be deleted from the U.N. agenda once and for all.

Soviet representative Morozov opposed the American Draft Resolution on the grounds that it would complicate the position of the secretary-general. Without spelling out in what way U Thant's position would be made more difficult, the Soviet delegate stressed that the sooner the necessity of considering the so-called question of Hungary was ended the better would world peace be served.

The Yugoslav representative argued that the secretary-general should not be burdened with a "nonexistent" question. Austria, France, Denmark, Colombia, Italy, and Peru supported the American Draft Resolution. Though nonaligned countries such as Cambodia, Syria, and Iraq regarded the question of Hungary as a cold-war issue, they abstained when the Draft Resolution was put to the vote.

Sir Leslie Munro, the U.N. representative on Hungary, was the last speaker. Before the meeting the veteran Australian diplomat, the "watchdog" of the Assembly on the question of Hungary since December 1958, who had been accused by the communist bloc of being an American stooge, had had a heated discussion with members of the U.S. delegation. Apparently he had not been informed in advance about the intention to end his mission. It was not surprising, therefore, that Munro's statement was filled with sharp remarks and bitter recriminations. He maintained that the situation in Hungary was unchanged. Hungary remained a police state under alien domination. Though he noted that it was for the General Assembly to decide how the question of Hungary should be dealt with, he reminded the representatives of the member states that neither the Soviet Union nor the Hungarian authorities had shown any willingness in the past to comply with the Assembly's resolutions.

Finally, the chairman announced that the list of speakers was exhausted; the committee would proceed to vote on the Draft Resolution presented by the American U.N. delegation to the committee. Some delegates asked that the different paragraphs be voted upon separately, but the Draft Resolution, as a whole, was adopted by a roll call vote of 43 to 14, with 32 abstentions. Thus, after less than three hours of debate this vote wrote finis to the question of Hungary, which had been on the agenda for six long years. For once, the interest of the various parties in this settlement coincided.

Two days later the General Assembly met to deal for the last time with the question of Hungary. Péter Mód, the Hungarian chief delegate, was satisfied to see that "the Resolution constitutes, in practice at any rate, recognition of the fact that this question...should finally be struck from our agenda." *Pro forma*, of course, Mód noted also that the form and general tenor of the draft resolution now before the Assembly were unacceptable to his delegation.[13]

The two superpowers, the Soviet Union and the United States, took the floor only after the Draft Resolution as a whole had been adopted by 50 votes to 13, with 43 abstentions. In explaining his vote, the representative of the U.S.S.R., Valerian Zorin, complained that the resolution contained "unfounded accusations directed against the Soviet Union and Hungary."[14] Referring to the Hungarian representative's remark, American delegate Carl Rowan noted that the Assembly's action was far from "liquidating" the question of Hungary.[15] Rowan did not elaborate on his remarks; nor did Adlai Stevenson, the permanent representative of the United States, at his annual press conference the following day, when he limited himself to restating the optimistic view that the new approach "will be of benefit to the Hungarian people."[16]

THE LAST BATTLE OVER HUNGARIAN CREDENTIALS

Although the Hungarian question had to all intents and purposes been resolved, one last problem, also a product of the events of 1956, yet remained. Ever since 1957 the General Assembly's Credentials Committee, at the insistence of the United States, had taken the position of neither accepting nor rejecting credentials of the Hungarian delegates themselves. It was simply the representative character of the Hungarian government that was in question. The failure to take action on the Hungarian credentials expressed disapproval also of the attitude of the Hungarian government vis-à-vis the United Nations. Thereafter the problem of the credentials had become an integral part of the wider question of Hungary and was discussed as such. The Hungarians resolutely maintained that their delegation's credentials had been issued in accordance with the rules of procedure of the General Assembly, and were formally and in substance in order. Hence the Credentials Committee's recommendation, based on the U.S. motions, was contrary to the United Nations Charter and to international law. Furthermore, this recommendation was inconsistent with the principle of the sovereign equality of the U.N. member states and the principle of noninterference.

Naturally the U.S.S.R. regarded the affair as a political campaign directed against its Hungarian ally and indirectly against itself. Thus, speaking in support of the Hungarian credentials, Soviet diplomats in the United Nations consistently defended their regime's interventionist policy in Eastern Europe.

The formula of nonaction on the Hungarian credentials (as the American motion was informally referred to) had played an important part, however, in the negotiations between the Hungarian and the U.S. governments. This innocuous device (which had evolved quite by chance, only to become later an effective stratagem) had made it difficult for the Hungarian government to break out of its embarrassing international isolation. In addition, the technique had served the Americans as a means of exerting moral pressure against the Kádár regime. This tactic was supported by the insistence of the State Department that there was a close connection between the recognition of the Hungarian credentials and the amnesty.[17] As Carl T. Rowan, U.S. representative to the General Assembly, stated: "until this assembly and the world are convinced that the situation of the Hungarian people has sufficiently improved no decision should be taken on the credentials of the Hungarian delegation." The allies of the United States in the United Nations—the NATO countries and the Latin American bloc—supported the American stand. The French representative was the most explicit. He reminded the world organization that human rights and fundamental freedoms were far from being restored in Hungary and that a full amnesty had not yet been granted.[18]

For the last time the Soviet and Hungarian representatives naturally did their utmost to have the Hungarian credentials accepted. Their intensive lobbying among the African and Asian nations, however, had limited effect. Algeria, Burma, Iraq, Nepal, Somalia, Syria, and a few others, though recognizing the validity of the Hungarian U.N. delegation's credentials, abstained from voting. Nor was the outcome of the 1962 General Assembly's decision altered by the forceful intervention of Hungarian representative Endre Ustor or by the blasts of Soviet Ambassador Zorin. The General Assembly finally decided to take no action at all on the Hungarian credentials. The formula of nonaction worked just as its proponents had expected.[19] The question of credentials flared up anew; then, as we shall show, in 1963 it was to fade away.

Inside the Hungarian U.N. mission, meanwhile, Ambassador Csatordai was busy composing his report to the Foreign Ministry on the proceedings of the General Assembly. He described the details of the debates; he offered comparative charts of the different voting records concerning the American Draft Resolution in the Special Political Committee as well as in the Assembly. He also presented an "analytic account" of the termination of the question of Hungary. He attributed the American new approach not to the tacit understanding between the American and Hungarian governments, but rather to the changed atmosphere in the United Nations. He indicated that on the basis of his personal information the leaders of the American mission, especially Adlai Stevenson and Charles W. Yost, had finally come to realize that the majority of the Asian and newly independent African countries considered the question of Hungary a cold-war issue. Allegedly the Americans had encountered serious difficulty in buying their "abstentions." For that very reason, he continued, the Americans had dissociated themselves from Sir Leslie Munro and had submitted a draft resolution which practically ended the so-called Hungarian question. He added to these obviously unwarranted and misleading statements the argument that the Seventeenth Assembly Session of the world organization had demonstrated once more that the Hungarian Communist Party had been justified in refusing to accept American interference in the internal affairs of Hungary and had thereby defeated American imperialist designs.

In January 1963, at the request of the Hungarian U.N. mission in New York, U Thant issued an executive order that the United Nations was not to beam radio broadcasts to Hungary from its Geneva station.[20] This order was issued without publicity. In reality, it did not represent a vital concession because very few people in Hungary had been aware of the existence of the U.N. radio programs in the first place. However, the action was taken as a conciliatory gesture on the part of the secretary-general toward the Kádár regime.

The next step taken by the Hungarians was more important. On 21 March 1963 the long-awaited and long-promised general amnesty was declared. It was announced by János Kádár in an address delivered to the National Assembly. On this occasion he made no mention of placing blame on the United States for interference in the internal affairs of Hungary as he had done at the Eighth Party Congress. On the contrary, he wished to "normalize and improve" relations with all states, including the United States:

> We are of the opinion that there is not one disputed question on which agreement could not be reached on the basis of respecting mutual interest.[21]

Switching from international to internal problems, he praised the stability and the accomplishments of his regime which had made possible the announcement of an amnesty on a broad scale. Amnesty had been granted to war criminals; it was also extended to the few Stalinist criminals who still remained in prison. The majority of the released prisoners were old communist and progressive left politicains, such as Sándor Kopácsi, the deputy commander of the National Guard during the uprising, and the politician Istvan Bibó, who had served as minister of state in Imre Nagy's cabinet. Amnesty was granted also to those who had fled Hungary after the 1956 Soviet invasion.

The amnesty did not however, cover persons guilty of espionage and high treason, murder, or arson. Cardinal Joseph Mindszenty, Hungary's Roman Catholic Primate, who had been convicted of treason on trumped-up charges in 1949, was automatically excluded from the general amnesty. He stood a good chance, however, of receiving personal clemency from the Presidential Council. But those familiar with the cardinal's strong character and bitter resistance against communism were almost sure that he would not ask for it.

The amnesty was well received in the West, especially in the United States. The State Department considered it the fulfillment of its main condition for normalization. It represented proof of the changing situation in Hungary. "The amnesty appeared to apply to most, if not all, of the political prisoners," the State Department informed the House and Senate Foreign Affairs Committees.[22] The report of the State Department laid special stress on the fact that the Kádár government had carried out an extensive de-Stalinization program and had curbed arbitrary police power. The conciliatory slogan of Kádár, "he who is not against us is with us," had indeed resulted in a policy shift in Hungary. The State Department soberly concluded that the foregoing developments in Hungary should be viewed "objectively and in proper perspective." By Western standards the changes probably appeared to represent a limited concession to the Hungarian people, and Hungary certainly remained a Soviet-bloc country. But conditions showed a decided improvement over those that had prevailed during the Rákosi era or in the early aftermath of the 1956 revolution.

The publication of the State Department report was both useful and timely. It outlined the changing situation in Hungary and it offered an explanation of why the American administration was considering the restoration of normal relations with the communist regime of Hungary. By issuing the report, the State Department took into account also the possibility that there might not be enough votes in the United Nations in 1963 to withhold approval of the Hungarian credentials.[23] Shortly after the publication of the report of the State Department, the U.N. Credentials Committee unanimously adopted a report to the General Assembly finding the credentials of all delegations, including those of Hungary, in order.[24]

U THANT'S VISIT TO BUDAPEST

Three weeks before the provisional agenda of the next (Eighteenth) session of the U.N. General Assembly was scheduled to be set up (in July 1963), Secretary-General U Thant arrived in Budapest, where he was welcomed with the highest honors. The Budapest Airport was decorated with United Nations and Hungarian flags. A high-level government delegation waited for him when his plane landed. The only detail lacking in the protocol reception was the "21-gun salute" accorded heads of state. U Thant was lodged in the same government guest house where Khrushchev had stayed when he visited Hungary. The secretary-general's limousine was escorted by a presidential-type motorcycle police honor guard, and security measures throughout were extremely strict. István Dobi, the president of the Presidential Council (the nominal head of state) received him. The government gave a brilliant reception in his honor where half of the Hungarian Politburo, party and government dignitaries, and the diplomatic corps greeted him.[25] He met intellectuals of the regime at the Academy of Science and visited the Csepel Steel Works—the largest industrial complex in Hungary.

The highlight of U Thant's visit, however, was his round of discussions with Kádár. In these he received all ᴜne information he needed to act in accordance with the General Assembly's resolution of 20 December 1962. Kádár revealed to U Thant the number of people freed through amnesty and assured him that, as of the time of his visit, no one remained imprisoned in Hungary for political offenses. Kádár had only one request: that the number of people freed as a result of the amnesty should not be released to the press. Apparently he wanted to avoid any appearance that the secretary-general had the right—in accordance with the decision of the United Nations—to conduct an inquiry in Hungary. In return for Kádár's "cooperation," U Thant stated that while he had particular functions in accordance with the Assembly's resolution, the main object of his visit had been to ease tension, to bring about better understanding, and to see how far the Hungarian government had liberalized its attitudes and concepts.[26]

U Thant's three-day visit to Hungary formally marked the end of a seven-year period of tension between the world organization and the Kádár regime. From this time onward the secretary-general considered his mission on Hungary closed. The United States observed the tacit understanding worked out directly with Hungary and indirectly with the U.S.S.R., and the question of Hungary simply ceased to exist.

Room To Maneuver:
A Guiding Principle For Eastern Europe

Time and again over the centuries the states of Central and Eastern Europe have been caught between contending empires. In order to maintain their national identity, if not their freedom, they have often been driven to seek protection from one large power by siding with another. Large or small, they have invariably been impelled to play this dangerous game without regard to their own form of government or their own ideology. In the nineteenth century, as the threat of pan-Slavism grew, Germany and the Austro-Hungarian monarchy seemed to offer shelter to nations in the area. A century later, National Socialism was pitted against Bolshevism; and many East European regimes looked still farther to the West for allies, this time to France and England and even beyond—to the United States.

After the Second World War this long-established pattern changed radically. Germany was defeated and divided. Western Europe was too depleted to stem the rising tide of Soviet influence in the East. The United States, with its strength pretty much intact, had no vital interests to protect against Soviet domination in Eastern Europe. The rapid division of the postwar world into antagonistic blocs and the deepening distrust characteristic of the prolonged cold war turned wartime allies into all but irreconcilable foes. In this atmosphere Stalin stepped up his pressure for undisputed control of Central and Eastern Europe. By 1948 the Kremlin was in a position to use East European "people's democracies" both as a buffer zone to shield the Soviet Union against attack from any direction and as an advance base for possible operations against Western Europe. The Soviet Union feared the West. Moscow considered any move toward neutralism in Eastern Europe a challenge to the doctrine of Soviet supremacy and an assault on Soviet national security. Hence in 1956 and in 1968 Hungarian and Czechoslovak reformers who disregarded their country's importance in the strategy planning of the Soviet Union were viewed as a threat.

The secret anti-Stalin speech of Khrushchev at the Twentieth Congress of the C.P.S.U. in February 1956 and the ensuing power struggle weakened the Soviet leadership at a critical moment. It was a time when nationalist aspirations were making themselves felt in one way or another in many parts of the world. In Eastern Europe these impulses found expression in a movement toward national communism. This was a factional struggle within the communist party, and the exposure of Stalin's crimes understandably lent strength to this reform movement wherever local Stalinist leaders had most abused their power. By the time the divided Soviet leadership had come to realize that it might not be able to control these forces, it was almost too late: the story of the Sorcerer's Apprentice had repeated itself. In Hungary, under the spiritual leadership of Imre Nagy, the movement had spread like wildfire and had transformed itself into both an anti-communist and an anti-Soviet revolution. For one historic moment Soviet influence in Hungary had vanished and the communist party had ceased to exist.

The Chinese communists adopted what seems to have been an inconsistent position concerning the 1956 Hungarian events. On the one hand, they insisted that the Soviet Union should treat the smaller communist countries as equals. (To press home this point they used the ideological term "great-power chauvinism," by which they meant "Soviet imperialism.") On the other hand, because they regarded Peking as the guardian of pure Marxism, they felt justified in demanding that the Soviet Union smash the Hungarian rebellion relentlessly. It appears in retrospect that the tactics adopted by Mao Tse-tung during the Hungarian crisis might have allowed him a greater say in East European politics. This could have helped to pave the way for his eventually stepping into the shoes of the late Stalin.

The decision of the Eisenhower administration not to become involved militarily in the Hungarian crisis followed from a fundamental rule of nuclear diplomacy: either superpower would avoid a direct confrontation with the other so long as its vital interests were not directly threatened. The Kremlin viewed the U.S. decision, however, as an indication that Washington had written off Hungary. The Soviet belief that in spite of verbal attacks the United States regarded Eastern Europe as essentially a part of the Soviet sphere was confirmed. The American posture thus helped the diehards in Moscow by showing that no global risk was involved in their opting for the suppression of the Hungarian revolution by force of arms.

The "diplomatic fireworks," a phrase used by representatives of the East European countries when discussing the problem of Hungary at the United Nations among themselves, were set off much too late. The United States, France, and Great Britain, far more concerned at the moment with the Suez crisis, delayed their response to Hungarian pleas to the United Nations for protection. When the Western powers recognized the urgency of dealing with the situation, it was too late to alter the course of events. By then neither

U.S. resolve, nor censure by the overwhelming majority of the member states of the United Nations, nor any power on earth or in heaven could have stopped the Soviet military intervention in Hungary.

The Soviet leadership was aware that the United Nations could take no collective action against one of the two superpowers unless the other was ready to move to the brink of war. They thus paid little attention to the appeals of the world organization. However, Moscow did miscalculate the odds at several points. Surely she had not expected the question of Hungary to keep coming up in the United Nations year after year. Nor had she imagined that the United States and its allies would continue to remind the world over six long years of the Hungarian happenings of 1956. Moreover, the Kremlin had taken it very much for granted that the credentials of the Kádár government would be accepted at the United Nations as a matter of course. As a result of American insistence, however, the Credentials Committee of the General Assembly withheld recognition of the credentials as long as the question of Hungary was being debated on the floor of the world organization. Although the U.S. motion in the U.N. Credentials Committee went largely unnoticed at the time, it forced Hungarian policy makers into adopting a course that finally led to the compromise solution. The unprecedented line of action in the United Nations, applied specifically in the case of the Hungarian representatives, was a purely political move, and was not in any sense based on the norms of international law.

The compromise solution was more than a routine drama of contemporary history for which rehearsals had taken place in Budapest, in Moscow, and in Washington, with the last-act curtain going up on the stage of the United Nations. As is not at all uncommon in dealings among nations, practical considerations were permitted to transcend principles of morality. Yet the diplomatic move eased the lot of the Hungarian people while also contributing in some measure to an East-West détente. At the same time the compromise pointed up the tactical changes in Soviet relations with the East European states introduced during the post-Stalin period. These changes had resulted mainly from Khrushchev's de-Stalinization drive, from the new push toward polycentrism in the international communist movement, and from the rising nationalism in Eastern Europe.

It was Soviet tanks that had prevented Hungary from achieving independence and the much-desired neutrality between East and West; and Soviet troops had remained on Hungarian soil to make the Kremlin's decision stick. The expression of popular discontent, or open rebellion, was suppressed; but long-range resistance against Soviet rule continued in one form or another. And the example of Hungary offered convincing evidence that the defeated revolution of 1956 did in the long run win a limited degree of freedom for Hungarians and helped to improve conditions within the country. As fate would have it, it was the "New Course," the economic program of the executed Imre Nagy, the leader of the revolution, that became the model for Kádár's economic reform, the so-called New Economic Mechanism. It is significant that the same Soviet leaders who reacted in 1968 with military might against the Czechoslovak reform—which was sparked by abuses and inequities substantially similar to those that triggered the Hungarian uprising—voiced no open criticism against the New Economic Mechanism. Moscow seems to have deemed it wiser to consider this a controlled economic reorganization rather than a basic reform that might undermine Soviet political and economic influence in Hungary. Moreover, what really mattered most to Soviet policy makers was that the Hungarian party leadership should maintain control, should follow the Moscow line in interparty matters, should make sure that Hungary remained a dependable member of the Warsaw Treaty Organization, and should participate fully in the Council for Mutual Economic Assistance, the Kremlin's top economic organization. The Hungarian party leadership, on its part, sought to treat the reforms as being without ideological or political overtones. From here on in, only time will tell whether the transformation is to be limited to economic reorganization or will result in a more fundamental sociopolitical change.

At this stage there still appears to be some lack of understanding in the United States of what makes the lesser communist countries tick. An important aspect of this mechanism is the degree of maneuverability enjoyed by these countries within the Soviet sphere. To argue that East European communist leaders have no room at all for political maneuvering would be misleading. In international relations, however, the communist regimes have been able to achieve freedom of action only to the extent that such freedom serves, or at any rate does not subvert, the national interests of the Soviet Union (as defined by Soviet leaders). This power relationship reduces to a minimum the ability of East European leaders to make independent decisions on major policy issues—regardless of whether or not these decisions may vitally affect their own national interests. What is more, the extent of their subservience has been greatly enlarged with emplacement in Eastern Europe of special Soviet rockets, equipped with missiles, carrying nuclear warheads. Since 1965, when the deployment of these weapons systems began, East European territories have been a logical target of NATO striking forces. Simultaneously the leaders of the bloc countries are compelled to reckon with the awesome possibility of their involuntary but automatic involvement in a worldwide nuclear confrontation.

On the other hand, it must be borne in mind that the East European communist leaders have never sought unlimited freedom of action—certainly not according to Western concepts of this term— and that whatever their waverings within the socialist sphere they are not on the point of repudiating the communist system. There are good grounds to argue that because their very survival depends on Moscow's support, they are as a rule not only willing but even eager to follow the Kremlin's lead in international affairs. (The case of Rumania, whose foreign policy sights in recent years have been set on the one primary objective of maintaining the country's autonomy in international affairs, is the exception that proves the rule.)

When U.S. decision makers speak of room for maneuvering in Eastern Europe, they know perfectly well that the Soviet leadership is determined to keep the East European "Commonwealth" intact. To all intents and purposes, Washington seems to accept the status quo in Eastern Europe as a fact of life, and the nations of Eastern Europe in turn are well aware of the American position.

The complex interplay between the undeclared intention in international affairs and the scope for maneuvering has come to occupy a place of far greater importance with the emergence of China as a force to be reckoned with on the East European political scene. Contrary to their 1956 position (when the Chinese leadership urged Moscow to crush the anticommunist uprising in Hungary), the Chinese in 1968 condemned out of hand the Soviet-led invasion of Czechoslovakia. According to Peking, the intrusion of Soviet "revisionist" tanks into Prague was not an indication of Soviet strength. On the contrary, the Chinese communists viewed the move as another milestone in the collapse of the Soviet colonial empire and regarded Eastern Europe as a powder keg, ready to blow up without notice. For all their harsh rhetoric, the Chinese refrained from taking concrete action. But their attitude did demonstrate that Peking had come to regard Moscow as its most dangerous enemy and that it was ready to back any government in any area that rejected superpower supremacy. Besides, China was rapidly becoming a full-fledged member of the nuclear club and was openly promising assistance to all those determined to "withstand foreign pressure." It is not surprising, then, that Rumania and Yugoslavia, both under what must be regarded as a permanent threat from the Soviet Union, sought to increase their political flexibility by appearing to align their policies more closely with those of China. The uncertainty of Chinese intentions is indeed likely to act as a restraining influence on Soviet moves vis-à-vis Eastern Europe; and this influence may be interpreted as a new dimension for giving Eastern Europe additional maneuvering space. Any present links with China thus should be seen primarily in terms of power politics rather than of ideology.

The postwar position of the small nations in Eastern Europe may be represented by a triangle whose three sides are the Soviet Union, the United States, and China, with Hungary or any other East European nation in the middle. This triangle is not a static figure. Its dimensions and its configuration may change with the shifting interrelationships of the three superpowers. At the same time this geometric form illustrates how a state like Hungary, exposed to external pressures, is limited in its freedom of action, and how the nature of such freedom as it does enjoy is subject to constant flux.

During the past quarter of a century we have lived through one crisis after another. We have seen more confrontations than compromise solutions.

We have watched the superpowers reduce world tension only to turn détente into even greater tension. We have learned that the precarious balance of power is maintained by the shaky balance of terror and is likely to continue so. On this crude fact of our times there is agreement between East and West, between the superpowers and the small nations. How Soviet decision makers will react in case of another East European crisis it is difficult to predict. But the ever-present threat of a nuclear holocaust is altering the formerly accepted norms of international behavior. If, in the future, skillful and imaginative diplomacy on the part of the other major powers can keep Moscow guessing as to their likely response, and if a firm stance is taken in the face of Soviet threats, then the small nations of Eastern Europe must feel reassured about their own room to maneuver.

Notes

CHAPTER 1: THE HUNGARIAN UPRISING AND EMERGENCY DIPLOMACY

1. Robert Murphy offers an exciting description of his experiences in connection with the Hungarian Revolution and the Suez crisis in his book *Diplomat among Warriors* (New York, 1964), pp. 476-81.

2. Alexis de Tocqueville, *Oeuvres complètes*, Vol. 12: *Souvenirs*, ed. by Luc Monnier (Paris, 1964), p. 87.

3. After the collapse of the 1919 Hungarian Soviet, the Communist Party was outlawed.

4. For further details see *The Truth about the Nagy Affair* (facts, documents, comments), with a preface by Albert Camus. Publ. for the Congress for Cultural Freedom (London and New York, 1959), pp. 120-22.

5. See text of Imre Nagy's speech "The New Course," delivered at the Hungarian National Assembly on 4 July 1953; see also *Hungarian Bulletin*, No. 8 (Budapest, 1963), pp. 1-5.

6. János Bojti is currently Hungarian ambassador in Sofia.

7. The biographical sketch of Kádár is here reconstructed on the basis of his official biography publ. in János Kádár, *On the Road to Socialism*, a collection of various speeches and interviews (Budapest, 1965), pp. 7-8, as well as on my own recollection.

8. For details, see Tibor Méray, *Thirteen Days That Shook the Kremlin* (New York, 1959), pp. 17-61.

9. See text of Khrushchev's speech at a closed session of the Twentieth Party Congress in Robert V. Daniels, ed., *A Documentary History of Communism*, Vol. 2 (New York, 1960), pp. 224-31.

10. Those Hungarian communists who had been living in exile in Moscow between the two world wars and who had returned to Hungary with the Red Army in 1945 were generally known as Muscovites. For details on Rákosi's ouster, see Tamás Aczél and Tibor Méray, *The Revolt of the Mind* (New York, 1959), pp. 412-19.

11. For a documentary history of the revolution, see "Report of the Special Committee on the Problems of Hungary," United Nations General Assembly, *Official Records*, 11th Session, Supplement no. 18 (A/3592). For a comprehensive scholarly presentation of events in Hungary, see Miklós Molnár, *Victoire d'une défaite: Budapest 1956* (Paris, 1968).

12. The meeting of Undersecretary Murphy and Zádor has been reconstructed on the basis of Zádor's personal account to the author and of the State Department transcript published in U.S. Dept. of State, "Conversation between Mr. Murphy and Mr. Zádor," *Department of State Bulletin*, 35, no. 906 (1956), p. 701. (The U.S. Dept. of State, *Department of State Bulletin*, is hereafter cited simply as *Department of State Bulletin*.)

13. *Department of State Bulletin*, 35 (1956), p. 701.

14. "Letter dated 27 October 1956 from the representatives of France, the United Kingdom of Great Britain and Northern Ireland and the United States of America to the President of the Security Council, 27 October 1956," United Nations Security Council, *Official Records*, 11th year, Supplement for October-December 1956, S/3690, 27 October 1956, p. 400.

15. "Letter dated 28 October 1956 from the representative of Hungary to the Secretary General, transmitting a declaration of the Government of the Hungarian People's Republic, 28 October 1956," United Nations Security Council, *Official Records*, 11th year, Supplement for October-December 1956, S/3691, 28 October 1956, pp. 100-01.

16. For the transcript of Sobolev's speech before the Security Council, see United Nations Security Council, *Official Records*, 11th year, 746th meeting, 28 October 1956, pp. 4-5.

17. Statement by Ambassador H.C. Lodge, 28 October 1956, U.S./U.N. press release 2480, *Department of State Bulletin*, 35, no. 907 (1956), pp. 758-63.

18. For further details of Imre Nagy's proclamation, see Paul E. Zinner, *Revolution in Hungary* (New York and London, 1962), pp. 274-76.

19. United Nations Security Council, *Official Records*, 11th year, 746 meeting, 28 October 1956, p. 34.

20. United Nations Security Council, *Official Records*, 11th year, 748th meeting, 30 October 1956, p. 2.

21. United Nations Security Council, *Official Records*, 11th year, 749th meeting, 30 October 1956, pp. 3-4.

22. "United States of America: draft resolution," United Nations Security Council, *Official Records*, 11th year, Supplement for October-December 1956, S/3710, 30 October 1956, p. 110. The draft resolution failed of adoption by the Security Council owing to the negative votes of two permanent members of the Council, the United Kingdom and France.

23. For a comprehensive study of the Suez crisis, see Kennett Love, *Suez: The Twice-Fought War* (New York and Toronto, 1969).

24. Information received from Dr. György Heltai, then first deputy foreign minister of the Imre Nagy government, at present chairman of the History Department at the College of Charleston, South Carolina.

25. President Eisenhower pointed out in his memoirs that he decided to warn the communists, especially the Soviet Union, that either a reasonable armistice would be promptly achieved in Korea, or else the United States would no longer be bound "by formerly understood limits regarding types of weapons." See Dwight D. Eisenhower, *Waging Peace 1956-1961* (Garden City, N. Y., 1965), p. 369.

26. *Ibid.*, p. 67.

27. "Secretary of State Dulles' news conference in Canberra on 13 March," *Department of State Bulletin*, 36, no. 927 (1957), p. 533.

28. Eisenhower, *Waging Peace*, p. 68.

29. John Foster Dulles, "The Task of Waging Peace," *Department of State Bulletin*, 35, no. 906 (1956), p. 697.

30. *Ibid.*, p. 758.

31. Eisenhower, *Waging Peace*, p. 71.

32. The Chinese position was revealed in the article "The Origin and Development of the Differences Between the Leadership of the C.P.S.U. and Ourselves," *Peking Review*, no. 37 (1963), pp. 9-10.

33. See Méray, *Thirteen Days*, pp. 164-65; also *Igazság* [Truth], newspaper of the youth and the Hungarian revolutionary armed forces, 1 November 1956, p. 1.

34. For further details see speech of János Kádár at the Hungarian Socialist Workers' Party's Conference in *Minutes of the National Conference of the Hungarian Socialist Workers' Party*, 27-29 June 1957, Budapest, 1957, pp. 23-27; also Ferenc A. Váli, *Rift and Revolt in Hungary* (Cambridge, Mass.), 1961, pp. 369-73.

35. "Deklaratsiia Pravitel'stva Soiuza SSR ob osnovakh razvitiia i dal'-neishego ukrepleniia druzhby i sotrudnichestva mezhdu Sovetskim Soiuzom i drugimi sotsialisticheskimi gosudarstvami," *Pravda*, 31 October 1956, p. 1.

36. "Deklaratsiia Pravitel'stva Soiuza SSR."

37. "Cablegram dated 1 November 1956 from the President of the Council of Ministers of the Hungarian People's Republic, addressed to the Secretary-General," United Nations General Assembly, First Emergency Special Session (1-10 November 1956), A/3251, 1 November 1956.

38. "Note dated 2 November 1956 from the permanent mission of the Hungarian People's Republic to the United Nations, transmitting a letter dated 2 November 1956 from the President of the Council of Ministers and Acting Minister for Foreign Affairs of the Hungarian People's Republic addressed to the Secretary General, 2 November 1956," United Nations Security Council, *Official Records*, 11th year, Supplement for October-December 1956, S/3726, 2 November 1956, pp. 119-20.

39. "United States of America: revised draft resolution," United Nations Security Council, *Official Records*, 11th year, Supplement for October-December 1956, S/3730 and S/3730/Rev. 1, 4 November 1956, pp. 125-26.

40. Dr. Péter Kós, whose real name was Leo Konduktorov, had been recalled on 29 October 1956, and Imre Nagy had appointed Dr. Szabó in his place ("Report by the Secretary-General to the President of the Security Council concerning the Credentials of the Representative of Hungary to the Security Council, 3 November 1956," United Nations Security Council, *Official Records*, 11th year, Supplement for October-December 1956, S/3729, 3 November 1956, p. 125.

41. United Nations Security Council, *Official Records*, 11th year, 753rd meeting, 3 November 1956, p. 3.

42. United Nations Security Council, *Official Records*, 11th year, 753rd meeting, 3 November 1956, p. 9.

43. Sir Anthony Eden, *Full Circle* (London, 1960), p. 545.

44. United Nations Security Council, *Official Records*, 11th year, 754th meeting, 4 November 1956, p. 12.

45. United Nations General Assembly, *Official Records*, Fifth Session, 302nd meeting, 3 November 1950, pp. 10-12.

46. The vote was 9 to 1, with the U.S.S.R. casting the negative vote and with Yugoslavia abstaining ("United States of America: revised draft resolution," United Nations Security Council, *Official Records*, 11th year, Supplement for October-December 1956, S/3730 and S/3730/Rev. 1, 4 November 1956, pp. 125-26).

47. United Nations General Assembly, *Official Records*, 2nd Emergency Special Session (4-10 November 1956), 564th meeting, 4 November 1956, p. 2.

48. See Stephen D. Kertész, ed., *East Central Europe and the World: Developments in the Post-Stalin Era* (Notre Dame, Ind., 1962), p. 148.

49. "Statement by Ambassador Lodge, November 4," *Department of State Bulletin*, 35, no. 908 (1956), pp. 800-03.

50. United Nations General Assembly, *Official Records*, 2nd Emergency Special Session (4-10 November 1956), 568th meeting, 8 November 1956, p. 21.

51. *Ibid.*, p. 23.

52. United Nations General Assembly, *Official Records*, 2nd Emergency Special Session (4-10 November 1956), 570th meeting, 9 November 1956, p. 56.

53. United Nations General Assembly, *Official Records*, 2nd Emergency Special Session (4-10 November 1956), 571st meeting, 9 November 1956, p. 81.

54. *Ibid.*

55. "Report of the Credentials Committee," United Nations General Assembly, *Official Records*, 11th Session, Annexes, Agenda item 3, A/3536, 3 February 1957.

56. "Note verbale dated 26 March 1957 from the Permanent Representative of Hungary to the United Nations, addressed to the Secretary-General, 26 March 1957," United Nations General Assembly, A/3573, 1 April 1957, p. 2.

57. "Report of the Credentials Committee," United Nations General Assembly, *Official Records*, 12th Session, Annexes, Agenda item 3, A/3773, 9 December 1957.

58. For further details, see U.N. Resolutions: 1006 (ES-11), 1007 (ES-11), 1129 (XI); Report of the Secretary-General A/3403; Statement by Deputy High Commissioner for Refugees at the 690th meeting of the Third Committee; and "Hungarian Questions"; cited in *Yearbook of the United Nations 1956* (New York, 1957), pp. 94-96. See also *First Aid for Hungary*, a special collection of correspondence of Herbert Hoover with President Eisenhower, Vice-President Nixon, and others in connection with the Hungarian refugees of 1956 (Hoover Institution).

59. A. G. Mezerik, ed., "Hungary and the United Nations," in *International Review Service*, 4, no. 40 (March 1958), p. 11.

60. For further details, see *Yearbook of the United Nations 1957* (New York, 1958), p. 80.

61. "Note by the Secretary-General, 7 December 1956," United Nations General Assembly, 11th Session, A/3435, 7 December 1956 and "Note verbale dated 12 December 1956 from the Permanent Mission of Hungary to the United Nations, addressed to the Secretary-General," United Nations General Assembly, 11th Session, A/3435/Add. 6, 12 December 1956, p. 25.

CHAPTER 2:   THE HUNDRED FLOWERS MOVEMENT AND THE HUNGARIAN REVOLUTION

1. A copy of Imre Nagy's political position paper, "In Defense of the New Course," was smuggled out of Hungary in the spring of 1957 and published in the West. In it Nagy offered his program for liberalization within the framework of a communist society. For the most part he explained his views on four subjects: industrialization, agriculture, foreign policy, and the problem of police terror and dictatorship. (See Imre Nagy, *On Communism, In Defense of the New Course* [New York, 1957].)

2. Nagy, *On Communism*, p. 22.

3. For further details, see François Fejtö, "Hungarian Communism," in William E. Griffith, ed., *Communism in Europe*, I (Cambridge, Mass., 1967), p. 242.

4. "He Ho Te-ching was satisfied, almost enthusiastic and hopeful, that his government would accept his point of view" (György Heltai, "Imre Nagy au Parlement," in Péter Gosztony, ed., *Histoire du soulèvement hongrois* [Paris, 1966], p. 183).

5. According to Fejtö, the representatives of the Soviet party, Mikoyan and Suslov, present at the 17 July 1956 Hungarian Politburo meeting, presumably took into account Kádár's popularity among the workers of Budapest when they ordered his appointment as a member of the Politburo and secretary of the party. See Fejtö, *Hungarian Communism*, p. 201. For further details, see also Váli, *Rift and Revolt, Hungary (Cambridge, Mass., 1961)*, p. 235.

6. Kádár was accompanied by Politburo member István Hidas and the chairman of the Institute of Cultural Relations, Zoltán Szántó. The delegation left Budapest on 9 September 1956. (See official Hungarian communiqué in *Szabad Nep*, 10 September 1956, p. 4.)

7. Liu Shao-ch'i, "Political Report," *People's China*, Supplement, 1 October 1956.

8. For a comprehensive analysis, see Dennis J. Doolin, *Communist China: The Politics of Student Opposition* (Stanford, Calif., 1964); and Roderick MacFarquhar, *The Hundred Flowers Campaign and the Chinese Intellectuals* (New York, 1960).

9. Mao Tse-tung, "On the Correct Handling of Contradictions Among the People, 27 February 1957" (Peking, Foreign Languages Press, 1960).

10. Doolin, *Communist China*, pp. 25-29.

11. New China News Agency, Peking, 12 July 1957.

12. *Jen-min Jih-pao* [People's Daily], 8 June 1957.

13. See Ferenc Páal, "Two-faced Intelligentsia," *Magyar Nemzet* [Newspaper of the Hungarian People's Patriotic Front], Budapest, 22 February 1959, p. 2. Páal visited China at the invitation of the Chinese government. His generally pro-Maoist article gives a description of the discontent of the Chinese intelligentsia. He noted, "It is undoubtedly true that the so-called Western outlook deeply penetrated the mentality of the Chinese intelligentsia." According to Páal, the majority (58 percent) of the teachers and assistant teachers of Shanghai University had studied in capitalist countries.

14. *I-chiu-liu-chi Fei-ching Nien Pao (1967 Yearbook on Communist Affairs)*, pp. 550-51, publ. by the Institute for the Study of Chinese Communist Problems in Taipei. See also *Fei-ching Yueh-pao* (Communist Affairs Monthly), August 1957, p. 32.

15. Hanyang is one of the three cities that make up Wuhan. The other two are Hankow and Wuchan.

16. For further details, see *Jen-min Jih-pao*, 6 and 8 August 1957, as cited by the *1967 Yearbook on Communist Affairs*, p. 550.

17. *Népszabadság*, 4 October 1957, p. 1.

18. See *Népszabadság*, 28 April to 8 May 1959. The author accompanied Münnich on this visit.

19. Liu Shao-ch'i had then been president of the Chinese People's Republic for only nine days.

20. This Chinese position was revealed later in the article, "The Origin and Development of Differences Between the Leadership of the C.P.S.U. and Ourselves," *Peking Review*, no. 37 (1963), pp. 9-10. Among other things, the article pointed out that "we Chinese insisted on the taking of all necessary measures to smash the counterrevolutionary rebellion in Hungary and firmly opposed the abandonment of socialist Hungary."

21. Mao described the Chinese people as sheets of blank paper whose leaders could write on them what they chose. The masses now ate twice a day, proving that two Chinese hands could produce more than one Chinese mouth could eat. This was imperative—even more significant than the Hundred Flowers Movement.

CHAPTER 3: DETERIORATION OF HUNGARIAN-AMERICAN RELATIONS

1. Cardinal Mindszenty had sought and had been granted asylum at the U.S. legation in Budapest on 4 November 1956 after the Soviet troops had returned there. He was fearful for his life and the Americans were anxious to save him.

2. "Protest to Hungary Concerning Communications with Budapest," *Department of State Bulletin*, 35, nos. 913 and 914 (1956), p. 980.

3. "United States Replies to Hungary on Postal Cancellation Stamp," *Department of State Bulletin*, 36, no. 935 (1957), pp. 849-50.

4. "U.S. to Reconsider Size of Legation Staff in Budapest," *Department of State Bulletin*, 37, no. 940 (1957), p. 30.

5. "U.S. Rejects Hungarian Charges Against Captain Gleason," *Department of State Bulletin*, 36, no. 934 (1957), p. 810-11.

6. See text of the note of the State Department in which First Lieutenant Károly Mészáros, Assistant Military and Air Attaché at the Legation of the People's Republic, was declared persona non grata in "United States Asks Departure of Hungarian Attaché," *Department of State Bulletin*, 36, no. 938 (1957), p. 983.

7. See White House statement and statement by Henry Cabot Lodge in *Department of State Bulletin*, 37 (1957): 748.

8. As part of the party control over government bodies, the Department of International Relations of the Party Central Committee supervised the activity of the Ministry of Foreign Affairs.

9. The cultural exchange program negotiations between the United States and the U.S.S.R. started on 28 October 1957. The agreement was concluded on 27 January 1958. See text of the agreement in "Joint Communique," *Department of State Bulletin*, 38, no. 973 (1958), p. 243.

10. See Communique of the Hungarian Mission to the United Nations, in *Népszabadság*, 25 October 1957, p. 1.

11. See "Report of the Credential Committee," 13 February 1957, and "Action taken by the General Assembly," United Nations General Assembly, *Official Records*, 11th Session, Annexes, Agenda item 3, pp. 1-2.

12. "Return of Minister Wailes from Budapest," *Department of State Bulletin*, 36, no. 925 (1957), p. 441.

13. *Ibid.*

CHAPTER 4: SUMMIT CONFERENCE DIPLOMACY AND THE EXECUTION OF IMRE NAGY

1. *Keesing's Contemporary Archives* (London), 15-22 March 1958, pp. 16069-74.

2. "The President to Premier Bulganin," *Department of State Bulletin*, 38, no. 970 (1958), pp. 122-30.

3. Bulganin pointed out to Eisenhower (in his letter of 1 February 1958) that "the events in Hungary have proven above all that the Hungarian people knew how to properly resist those elements which, acting on directives and with the support of certain circles from abroad, made an assault against the social system chosen by the people of Hungary." "Premier Bulganin to the President," *Department of State Bulletin*, 38, no. 976 (1958), p. 379; also, *Izvestia*, 2 February 1958, p. 1.

4. The Soviet government's agreement to a foreign ministers' meeting preparatory to a summit conference was conveyed by Soviet Foreign Minister Gromyko to the U.S. ambassador, Llewellyn Thompson, on 28 February in the form of an *aide mémoire* (*Pravda*, 1 March 1958, p. 1) and reaffirmed in Bulganin's letter of 6 March to President Eisenhower (*Pravda*, 7 March 1958, p. 1). See also "U.S. *Aide Mémoire* of March 6" and "Soviet *Aide Mémoire* of February 28," *Department of State Bulletin*, 38, no. 978 (1958), pp. 457-61.

5. See text of the Soviet government's proposals on 5 May 1958 and Western Agenda Proposal of 28 May 1958, Supplement to *New Times*, no. 26 (1958), pp. 7-16.

6. Considering that the Soviet Union decided on 21 December 1957 to reduce its armed forces by 300,000, this further cut meant a total reduction of 419,000. For details of Soviet troop reduction, see *New Times*, no. 2 (1958), p. 1 and no. 22 (1958), p. 1.

7. Message of N. S. Khrushchev, Chairman of the U.S.S.R. Council of Ministers, to President D. D. Eisenhower, in Supplement to *New Times*, no. 26 (June 1958).

8. See the text of the MTI announcement, in *Népszabadság*, 17 June 1958, p. 1.

9. The documents were "easily found." Nagy wrote the "secret documents" in defense of his new course policy against the Stalinist Rákosi regime and forwarded them to the Hungarian Communist Party Central Committee and to Khrushchev. The documents referred to in the sentence were published in the West after the revolution, as *Imre Nagy on Communism, in Defense of the New Course* (New York, 1957).

10. *Borba*, 23 June 1958, p. 1.

11. See the text of the State Department statement in the *New York Times*, 18 June 1958, p. 6.

12. *Yearbook of the United Nations 1958* (New York, 1959), p. 68.

13. President Eisenhower's Press Conference on 18 June 1958 in the *New York Times*, 19 June 1958, p. 20.

14. *New York Times*, 18 June 1958, p. 6.

15. Speech of Foreign Secretary Selwyn Lloyd in Cheshire, *New York Times*, 22 June 1958, p. 4.

16. See text of remarks by Hon. William P. Rogers, Attorney General of the United States, prepared for delivery at the Silver Knight Awards Chicago Youth Rally of the *Chicago Daily News*, Orchestra Hall, Chicago, Ill., Saturday, 21 June 1958, in *Congressional Record*, CIV, 85th Cong., 2d sess., p. 12996; and also "U.S. Rejects Soviet Protest on Attorney General's Speech," *Department of State Bulletin* 39, no. 996 (1958), pp. 150-52.

17. "Special Report of the Special Committee on the Problem of Hungary," United Nations General Assembly, N3849, 4 July 1958.

18. The second Middle East crisis, in 1958, resulted from the unleashing of the coordinated action program of the Arab nationalists and the Soviets. The movement was directed from Cairo and Damascus. President Nasser was the living symbol of Arab unity. The guerrilla war against Lebanon was carried out by Bedouin tribes trained and armed in Syria under the supervision of Colonel Abd el-Hamid Sarrag, head of

the Syrian II Bureau. The leaders of the Syrian and Lebanese Communist Party, Khalid Bakdash and Nicola Shawi, worked separately. The ultimate aim was to eliminate the pro-Western Lebanese government of Chamoun and the pro-British Hussein. In early summer 1958 fighting intensified in Lebanon and a nationalist take-over seemed imminent. However, the action in both countries fizzled out very quickly when, at the request of the Chamoun government, American troops landed in Beirut on 16 July and the British on the same day airlifted troops to Amman. The national revolution of Adbul Karim Kassem on 14 July that dethroned King Faisal and eliminated the Nuri Said government apparently was carried out independently from the Lebanese adventure.

19. U.S., Congress, Senate, "A Review of United States Foreign Policy and Operations," by Senator Allen J. Ellender, S. Doc. 78, 85th Cong., 2d Sess., 1958 (Washington, D.C.: Government Printing Office, 1958), pp. 206-208.

CHAPTER 5: KÁDÁR'S TWO-PRONGED PLAN OF ACTION

1. Every second week the members of the Politburo held a day-long meeting where relevant questions were discussed and appropriate decisions taken.

2. On 22 September 1958 Foreign Minister Dr. Endre Sik was able to get the floor in the United Nations and to deliver his speech. For text, see *Népszabadság*, 23 September 1958, p. 1.

3. For text of the Gyáros press conference, see *Népszabadság*, 13 September 1958, p. 3.

4. See text of the Hungarian note in *Népszabadság*, 21 September 1958, p. 1.

5. "U.S. Refutes Hungarian Charges of Improper Activities," *Department of State Bulletin*, 39, no. 1015 (1958), pp. 910-12.

6. "Developments in Hungary Brought to Attention of United Nations," *Department of State Bulletin*, 38, no. 967 (1958), pp. 33-34.

7. *New York Times*, 18 December 1957, p. 13.

8. *Ibid*.

9. "U.S. Questions Continuing Prosecution of Hungarian Patriots," *Department of State Bulletin*, 38, no. 980 (1958), pp. 581-82.

10. *Ibid*.

11. Endre Sik, *Histoire de l'Afrique Noire*, 2 vols. (Budapest, 1962).

12. Sándor Sik had suffered indignities earlier because of his Jewish ancestry.

13. I happened to be Dr. Sik's student at the Diplomatic Academy, and this biographical sketch of Dr. Sik is based on personal knowledge. Dr. Sik's recently published memoir (Endre Sik, *Bem Rakparti Évek*, Budapest, 1970) was also a valuable source of information.

14. See transcript of Dr. Endre Sik's speech in United Nations General Assembly, *Official Records*, 13th Session, 752nd meeting, (22 September 1958), pp. 51-52.

15. "U.N. to Seek Improvement of Situation in Hungary," *Department of State Bulletin*, 40, no. 1020 (1959), p. 59.

16. "U.S. Supports Inclusion of Item on Hungary," *Department of State Bulletin*, 39, no. 1007 (1958), p. 589.

17. "Special report of the Special Committee on the Problem of Hungary," United Nations General Assembly, A/3849, 14 July 1958.

18. "U.S. Cosponsors New Draft Resolution," *Department of State Bulletin*, 40, no. 1020 (1959), p. 62.

19. *Yearbook of the United Nations 1958* (New York, 1959), p. 69. An abbreviated

version of Péter's speech was published in the Hungarian newspaper *Népszabadság* 12 December 1958, p. 1.

20. The voting record on this resolution (United Nations General Assembly 13th Session, Resolution 1312), reproduced here, is in *Yearbook of the United Nations 1958* (New York, 1959), pp. 70-71; and also in "U. N. to seek improvement of Situation in Hungary," *Department of State Bulletin*, 40, no. 1020 (1959), p. 62.

In favor: Argentina, Australia, Austria, Belgium, Bolivia, Brazil, Burma, Cambodia, Canada, Chile, China, Colombia, Costa Rica, Cuba, Denmark, Dominican Republic, Ecuador, El Salvador, Federation of Malaya, France, Guatemala, Haiti, Honduras, Iceland, Iran, Ireland, Italy, Japan, Jordan, Laos, Liberia, Luxemburg, Mexico, Nepal, the Netherlands, New Zealand, Nicaragua, Norway, Pakistan, Panama, Paraguay, Peru, the Philippines, Portugal, Spain, Sweden, Thailand, Tunisia, Turkey, Union of South Africa, United Kingdom, United States, Uruguay, and Venezuela.

Against: Albania, Bulgaria, Byelorussian SSR, Czechoslovakia, Hungary, Poland, Rumania, Ukrainian SSR, USSR, Yugoslavia.

Abstaining: Afghanistan, Ceylon, Ethiopia, Finland, Ghana, Greece, India, Indonesia, Iraq, Lebanon, Libya, Morocco, Saudi Arabia, Sudan, United Arab Republic.

Absent: Israel, Yemen.

21. Press conference of Deputy Foreign Minister János Péter, in *Népszabadság*, 16 December 1958, p. 1.

CHAPTER 6: THE CAMPAIGN FOR RECOGNITION AT THE UNITED NATIONS

1. For further details of economic agreements between the U.A.R. and the U.S.S.R., see *Keesing's Contemporary Archives* (London), 1-14 June 1958, p. 16228.

2. Edgar O'Ballance, *The Greek Civil War 1944-1949* (New York, 1966), p. 169.

3. Sometimes referred to as EAM/ELAS; *ibid.*, p. 222.

4. After Stalin's death this city was renamed Dunaujváros.

5. The voting record on this resolution (United Nations General Assembly, 14th Session, Resolution 1454) is in *Yearbook of the United Nations 1959* (New York, 1960), p. 51.

CHAPTER 7: REORGANIZATION ON THE HOME FRONT

1. The Special Armed Forces operated with the Soviet Military Police to maintain public order, to enforce the curfew, etc. See *A Magyar Szocialista Munkáspárt határozatai és dokumentumai 1956-1962* (hereafter *M.SZ.M.P. határozatai és dokumentumai*) Resolutions and documents of the Hungarian Socialist Workers' Party (H.S.W.P.) 1956-1962 (Budapest, 1964), pp. 25-26.

2. For details, see François Fejtö, *Behind the Rape of Hungary* (New York, 1957), pp. 281-91.

3. *Népszabadság*, 17 November 1957, p. 1.

4. The martial law was introduced by Decree-Law No. 28; see *Magyar Közlöny* [Official Journal], 11 December 1956. This was repealed by Decree-Law No. 62; see *Magyar Közlöny*, 3 November 1957.

5. For complete material and detailed analysis, see *The Hungarian Situation and the Rule of Law*, International Commission of Jurists (The Hague, 1957).

6. The official name of the Politburo was at that time the Provisional Central Executive Committee.

7. *Népszabadság*, 3 January 1957, p. 3.

8. *M. SZ. M.P. határozatai és dokumentumai*, pp. 13-24.

9. *Népszabadság*, 6 January 1957, p. 1.

10. *Keesing's Contemporary Archives*, 30 March-6 April 1957, pp. 15463-64.

11. The Chinese economic assistance was revealed in a speech by State Minister György Marosán on 13 January, three days before Chou En-lai arrived in Budapest (*Népszabadság*, 15 January 1957).

12. With the arrival of the Chinese in Budapest, Kádár offered the following public explanation of his invitation: "When we learned that a Chinese government delegation would visit Poland, we conceived the idea of inviting this delegation to Budapest. And this delegation is now here. It is a special privilege for us that the Chinese comrades changed their original program to express their solidarity with our fight and with our people." (*Népszabadság*, 18 January 1957.) On 11 January Chou En-lai had left Moscow for Warsaw, where he publicly supported Władysław Gomułka's position on every question. Being aware of the tense relationship existing at the time between the Polish and Soviet leadership, Chou did not refer in the joint Chinese-Polish statement to the leading role of the Soviet Union in the socialist world. Nor did he mention the Soviet designation of the uprising in Hungary as a "counterrevolutionary movement instigated by Western powers." For a comprehensive analysis of Chou En-lai's visit to Eastern Europe in 1957, see Zbigniew K. Brzezinski, *The Soviet Bloc: Unity and Conflict* (Cambridge, Mass., 1967), pp. 279-84.

13. *Népszabadság*, 18 January 1957, p. 1.

14. See speech of Kádár, in *Népszabadság*, 17 January 1957, p. 1.

15. The Soviet Union and the other Communist countries delivered 900 million florins worth of commodity goods in the form of nonrepayable aid and assured 300 million dollars in credit commodities. The Soviet Union supplied the Hungarian National Bank with 60 million dollars, while China contributed 25 million dollars in hard currency; see *M.SZ.M.P. határozatai és dokumentumai*, p. 34.

16. Thomas Schreiber, "L'évolution politique et économique de la Hongrie 1956-1966," *Notes et Études Documentaires*, no. 3335 (Paris, 1966), p. 40.

17. "Resolution of the Hungarian Socialist Workers' Party," pp. 13-24.

18. Schreiber, "L'évolution politique," pp. 44-54.

19. The progressive Hungarian economists had to wait ten more years to introduce the "New Economic Mechanism" that started an overall reorganization.

20. The compulsory delivery of agricultural goods was abolished on 30 October 1956. The Kádár regime did not change this important decree of the revolution. For details, see Paul E. Zinner, *Revolution in Hungary* (New York and London, 1962), p. 287.

21. Thesis of the H.S.W.P.'s agrarian policy (July 1957), *M. SZ. M. P. határozatai és dokumentumai*. p. 102.

22. A similar treaty between the U.S.S.R. and Poland was signed in December 1956 (see *Pravda*, 18 December 1956, p. 1), between the U.S.S.R. and the German Democratic Republic in March 1957 (see *Izvestia*, 14 March 1957, p. 1), and between the U.S.S.R. and Rumania in April 1957 (see *Izvestia*, 17 April 1957, p. 1).

23. A group of Muscovite Hungarians led by Rákosi and Gerö arrived in Hungary with the Soviet army in 1945. Placed in leading political and economic positions, many became high-ranking officials in the police and army. During the 1956 revolution, many

of the Muscovite Hungarians fled to the Soviet Union, returning after the Soviet invasion to reoccupy secondary though still important positions. Kádár with sound reason considered them a potential danger and was able to convince Khrushchev that popular sentiment against the idea of dual citizenship had mounted within the party. Aware of the underlying reason for Kádár's concern, Khrushchev consented to a change in this arrangement.

24. *M.SZ.M.P. határozatai és dokumentumai*, p. 180.

25. Under Rákosi, collectivization had been characterized by open police terror and deportation.

26. In late spring of 1960, Ambassador Stikhov invited the members of the Politburo to his residence for a dinner party, during which he criticized the Hungarian three-year plan, maintaining that more emphasis should be placed on heavy industry. With regard to the agricultural campaign, he advised that more pressure should be exercised to achieve complete collectivization. He objected strongly to the incorporation of kulaks into collectives, arguing that it was particularly dangerous to allow them to occupy leading positions. Rejecting Stikhov's advice, Kádár informed the ambassador that he had discussed the whole matter with Khrushchev and abruptly left the party. It was soon after this that Stikhov was recalled.

27. *Népszabadság*, 8 March 1959, p. 2.

28. *M.SZ.M.P. határozatai és dokumentumai*, pp. 528-36.

29. *Népszabadság*, 17 February 1962, p. 3.

30. Dr. Egon Szabady, "Characteristics of Family Demography," *Statisztikai Szemle* [Journal of the Central Statistics Office], (Budapest, November 1966).

CHAPTER 8: THE NEW WAVE OF DE-STALINIZATION

1. For a detailed description of Khrushchev's personal policy, see Carl A. Linden, *Khrushchev and the Soviet Leadership 1957-1964* (Baltimore, 1966), pp. 119-28.

2. Richard Lowenthal, *World Communism: The Disintegration of a Secular Faith* (New York, 1964), pp. 219-24.

3. For further details, see "Archiv der Gegenwart" (Bonn-Vienna-Zurich, 17 October 1964), pp. 11482-83; also Roger Hilsman, *To Move a Nation* (New York, 1967), pp. 341-43.

4. N. S. Khrushchev, *Report on the Program of the C.P.S.U.*, II (New York, 1967), p. 107.

5. *Ibid.*

6. Harry Schwartz, ed., *Russia Enters the 1960s: A Documentary Report on the 22nd Congress of the Communist Party of the Soviet Union* (Philadelphia and New York, 1962), pp. 45-56.

7. *Ibid.*, pp. 28-35.

8. See "The Origin and Development of the Differences Between the Leadership of the C.P.S.U. and Ourselves," *Ren-min Ri-bao*, 6 September 1963, p. 1; in English, *Peking Review*, 13 September 1963, pp. 16-17.

9. *Pravda*, 24 October 1961, p. 1.

10. For further details, see Donald S. Zagoria, *The Sino-Soviet Conflict 1956-1961* (Princeton, N. J., 1962), pp. 370-83.

11. The central organ of the Albanian Workers' Party, *Zeri i Popullit*, published part of the Soviet Central Committee's letters. See text in English translation in William E. Griffith, *Albania and the Sino-Soviet Rift* (Cambridge, Mass., 1963), p. 342.

12. An Agence France press dispatch of 21 November 1961 reported the distribution of the Albanian documents.

13. The text of the Soviet and Albanian notes in connection with the diplomatic break was published in *Zeri i Popullit*, 10 December 1961. For the English text see Griffith, *Albania and the Sino-Soviet Rift*, pp. 278-87.

14. For further details, see Váli, *Rift and Revolt*, pp. 407-10.

15. The official monthly of the H.S.W.P. announced in January 1962 that on 5 December 1961 the Party's Central Committee had removed István Friss from his post as head of the Economic Department of the Party. Before his ouster, he had to apologize because in an article previously published, "he omitted to mention the mistakes of Stalinist planning, which were one of the causes of the 1956 uprising." See *Pártélet* Party Life , no. 1 (January 1962), p. 28.

16. Károly Kiss was ousted from the Politburo in August 1962 but remained a member of the Central Committee. His dismissal resulted from personal rather than from political causes.

17. Taking advantage of the experiences of the Twenty-second C.P.S.U. Congress, the H.S.W.P. "has to wipe out the traces of the old mistakes" and has to mount "impassible barriers in the way of its return" (M.SZ.M.P. *határozatai és dokumentumai*, p. 317). See also the communiqué issued after the August 1962 purge which pointed out that in 1961 a special committee had been set up to investigate the 1949-53 crimes of the Rákosi regime. *Népszabadság*, 19 August 1962, p. 3.)

18. "La documentation francaise," *Notes et Études Documentaires*, No. 2868 (13 March 1962).

19. *Népszabadság*, 10 December 1961, p. 1.

20. *Pravda*, 26 December 1961, p. 2.

21. *Népszabadság*, 4 March 1962, p. 2.

22. For further details, see "Experiences of the Party's Personal-Policy and its Directives," published in the ideological organ of the H.S.W.P., *Társadalmi Szemle*, no. 2 (1962), pp. 32-48.

23. In a major administrative reshuffle, six deputy ministers and twelve high executive officials were relieved of their posts. The changes affected mainly the ministries of Agriculture, Heavy Industry, Metallurgy, and Engineering, and the Economic Department of the Party. For further details, see *Hivatalos Közlöny* [Official Gazette], 11 February 1962, p. 1.

24. *Népszabadság*, 19 August 1962.

25. The quotations are from the memoir of Sándor Nográdi, *Uj Történet kezdödött* [The beginning of a new era], (Budapest, 1966), p. 177.

26. See full text in *Népszabadság*, 19 August 1962, p. 3.

27. It was an open secret that Soviet M.V.D. General Belkin of the Soviet Secret Police had personally conducted the interrogation of Laszló Rajk. For further details, see Molnár, *Victoire d'une défaite*, p. 46; see also Váli, *Rift and Revolt*, p. 213. According to reliable sources General Belkin disappeared in 1953 after Beria had been executed.

28. At the time of Stalin's death in 1953 the number of political prisoners (including internees, inmates of labor camps, and people uprooted from their homes and confined to some other locality) is estimated at 150,000, or one and a half percent of the entire population of Hungary. At least 2,000 are believed to have been executed. (Váli, *Rift and Revolt*, p. 64.)

29. The high-ranking police officer Colonel Gábor Rajnai, who had investigated and questioned Imre Nagy and had prepared his trial in 1957-58, was dismissed from the political police because of his participation in the Rajk show trial. He was transferred

to the Foreign Ministry and sent to the Hungarian embassy in Moscow. In 1967 Rajnai, with Soviet backing, was reassigned to the political police as head of the external intelligence service.

30. On 27 April 1970 Tanjug reported that the Central Committee of the H.S.W.P. had allowed Rákosi to return home on condition that he would not engage in any political activity (Belgrade, Tanjug International Service, 27 April 1970, in English). According to reports reaching the West, Rákosi returned to Hungary in the summer of 1970. He stayed there only a short time, then went back to the Soviet Union for medical treatment. On 5 February 1971 the official Hungarian news agency M.T.I. reported that Rákosi had died in the U.S.S.R. (Gorki) at the age of seventy-eight, after a prolonged illness. (*New York Times*, 6 February 1971.)

31. The Congress of the H.S.W.P. ended on 24 November. The new Secretariat (the inner circle of the Politburo) included Béla Biszku, who was relieved of his government post on 27 November. (*Népszabadság*, 28 November 1962, p. 1.)

CHAPTER 9: DIPLOMATIC THRUST AND PARRY

1. For text of the communiqué released on 27 September 1959 at the conclusion of talks between Eisenhower and Khrushchev at Camp David, Md., see *Department of State Bulletin*, 41, no. 1059 (1959), p. 499.

2. United Nations, General Assembly, Official Records, Fourteenth Session, 25 November 1959.

3. *Department of State Bulletin*, 41, no. 1068 (1959), p. 877; also 41, no. 1070 (1959), p. 943.

4. United Nations, General Assembly, *Official Records*, Fourteenth Session, Annexes, Agenda Item 74, Doc. 1454 (XIV), p. 8.

5. *Deadline Date of World Affairs* (New York), 31 March 1960, p. 16.

CHAPTER 10: THE NEW CHARGE'S CONTRADICTORY INSTRUCTIONS

1. On 25 November 1959, as has been mentioned, 51 delegates of the General Assembly voted to debate the Hungarian question, 10 opposed, and 15 abstained. (For further details, see *Yearbook of the United Nations 1959* New York, 1960 , p. 48.) A year later, on 10 October 1960, 54 voted in favor, 12 against, and the number of abstentions increased to 31. (For further details, see *Yearbook of the United Nations 1960* [New York, 1961], p. 180.)

2. *Yearbook of the United Nations 1960*, p. 180.

3. The voting record on this resolution (United Nations General Assembly, 16th Session, Resolution 1741), reproduced here, is to be found in *Yearbook of the United Nations 1961* (New York, 1963), p. 146.

In favor: Argentina, Australia, Austria, Belgium, Bolivia, Brazil, Canada, Chile, China, Colombia, Costa Rica, Cyprus, Dahomey, Denmark, Dominican Republic, Ecuador, El Salvador, Federation of Malaya, France, Greece, Guatemala, Haiti, Honduras, Iceland, Iran, Ireland, Italy, Japan, Laos, Luxembourg, Mexico, the Netherlands, New Zealand, Nicaragua, Norway, Pakistan, Panama, Paraguay, Peru, Philippines, South Africa, Spain, Sweden, Thailand, Turkey, United Kingdom, United States, Uruguay, Venezuela.

Against: Albania, Bulgaria, Byelorussia S.S.R., Ceylon, Cuba, Czechoslovakia, Guinea, Hungary, Indonesia, Iraq, Mali, Mongolia, Poland, Rumania, Ukrainian S.S.R., U.S.S.R., Yugoslavia.

Abstaining: Afghanistan, Burma, Cambodia, Cameroun, Central African Republic, Congo (Leopoldville), Ethiopia, Finland, Ghana, India, Israel, Ivory Coast, Jordan, Lebanon, Liberia, Libya, Madagascar, Mauritania, Morocco, Nepal, Niger, Nigeria, Senegal, Sierra Leone, Somalia, Sudan, Syria, Togo, Tunisia, United Arab Republic, Upper Volta, Yemen.

4. The U.S. Mission to the United Nations delivered to the Albanian, Hungarian, and Soviet Missions to the United Nations memorandums restricting the movements of the heads of their delegations to the U.N. General Assembly Fifteenth Session while they were in the United States. See text in "Albania, Hungary, U.S.S.R. Officials Restricted in Movements on U.N. Visit," *Department of State Bulletin*, 43, no. 1110 (1960), p. 521.

CHAPTER 11: AMNESTY BEFORE NORMALIZATION

1. *Népszabadság*, 1 January 1962.

CHAPTER 12: THE ROLES OF SENATOR ELLENDER AND SENATOR PELL

1. U.S., Congress, Senate, "A Review of United States Foreign Policy and Operations," by Senator Allen J. Ellender, S. Doc. 78, 85th Cong., 2d sess., 1958 (Washington, D.C.: Government Printing Office, 1958), pp. 206-208.

2. "Report on United States Foreign Operations," by Senator Ellender, p. 70.

3. U.S., Congress, House, Committee on Armed Services, "Statement of László Szabó in Hearings Before CIA Subcommittee," Armed Services Paper, no. 49, 89th Cong., 2d sess., 1966 (Washington, D.C.: Government Printing Office, 1966), pp. 5331-77.

4. Senator Pell became one of the promoters of an East-West détente, including the expansion of East-West trade. He visited the Soviet Union and many of the East European capitals and reported his findings to the Senate Foreign Relations Committee. See U.S., Congress, Senate, Committee on Foreign Relations, *Study Mission to East Berlin, Bulgaria, Rumania, Hungary, and Czechoslovakia*, Report by Senator Claiborne Pell to the Committee on Foreign Relations, United States Senate, 90th Cong., 1st sess., 1967 (Washington, D.C.: Government Printing Office, 1967); and U.S., Congress, Senate, Committee on Foreign Relations. *Czechoslovakia 1968*. Report to the Committee on Foreign Relations, United States Senate, by Senator Claiborne Pell, 90th Cong., 2d sess., 1968 (Washington, D.C.: Government Printing Office, 1968).

CHAPTER 13:   ANOTHER SHIFT IN HUNGARIAN FOREIGN POLICY

1. In his report to the Eighth Congress Kádár explained publicly the meaning of his famous slogan "He who is not against us is with us." He pointed out that "in ideology this slogan is useless. In ideology you cannot take your choice between hostile and not so hostile. All theories that are not Marxist-Leninist are hostile, for one cannot mix or reconcile ideologies." See Kádár, *Road to Socialism*, p. 117.

2. Cardinal Mindszenty has lived at the U.S. Embassy in Budapest since 1956, where, as mentioned earlier, he sought asylum when Soviet military intervention crushed the Hungarian revolution.

3. Radio Budapest, Domestic Service, in Hungarian, 12 December, 1961.

4. János Péter was not the real Hungarian foreign minister, although he held that title. In a socialist state the real power—legislative, executive, judicial—is held by the Politburo of the Communist Party itself, and János Péter was not a member of the Politburo. For several years previously, power in the area of foreign relations had rested with Dezsö Nemes, a member of the Politburo and secretary of the Central Committee for international relations.

5. *Népszabadság*, 17 May 1961, p. 1.

CHAPTER 14:   THE "PIECE OF PAPER"

1. "U.S. Requests Inclusion of Item on Hungary in G.A. Agenda," *Department of State Bulletin*, 47, no. 1211 (1962), pp. 394-95.

2. "Letter dated 25 September 1962 from Sir Leslie Munro, United Nations Special Representative on the question of Hungary, addressed to the President of the general assembly," and "Report of Sir Leslie Munro, United Nations Special Representative on the Question of Hungary," United Nations General Assembly, A/5236, 25 September 1962.

3. "Letter dated 28 September 1962 from the Permanent Representative of Hungary to the United Nations addressed to the President of the General Assembly," and "Statement of the Permanent Mission of the Hungarian People's Republic to the United Nations," United Nations General Assembly, A/5245, 29 September 1962.

4. United Nations General Assembly, 16th Session, Resolution 1741, was adopted by the General Assembly on 20 December 1961 by roll-call vote of 49 to 17 with 32 abstentions. *Yearbook of the United Nations 1961* (New York, 1963), p. 146.

CHAPTER 15:   THE CUBAN MISSILE CRISIS AND THE HUNGARIAN QUESTION

1. Address by the Chairman of the Council of Ministers of the U.S.S.R. (N. S. Khrushchev) Before the All-Russian Teachers' Congress, Moscow, 9 July 1960 (excerpts), in *Current Digest of the Soviet Press*, XII, no. 28 (10 August 1960), pp. 3-7.

2. *Izvestia*, 2 October 1962, p. 1.

3. For further details, see Robert F. Kennedy, *Thirteen Days* (New York, 1969), pp. 25-26.

4. In 1962 Aníbal Escalante was forced to leave Cuba and went to live in exile in Prague. After being recalled to Havana in 1967, he was arrested, tried, and sentenced to a long prison term for pro-Soviet activities. For further details, see *New York Times*, 22 December 1967, p. 9; also *Gramma*, weekly English edition, 11 February 1968, as quoted in the *Yearbook on International Communist Affairs 1968* (Stanford, Calif., 1969), p. 139.

5. In several later interviews Senator Keating elaborated on this question. For a good account, see *U.S. News and World Report*, 19 November 1962, pp. 86-89.

6. For a comprehensive description and analysis, see Elie Abel, *The Missile Crisis* (Philadelphia and New York, 1966), pp. 74-75; and Robert F. Kennedy, *Thirteen Days*, pp. 39-42.

7. After the Cuban crisis, unconfirmed rumors circulated in Washington to the effect that the Rumanian ambassador had assured the Americans that his country had played no role in the Cuban incident and that in case of war Rumania wished to remain neutral.

8. One can only speculate as to whether General Dubovik's remarks were of a personal or an official nature. In view of the rigid discipline under which communist diplomats operate, however, it is most likely that he acted under instructions from headquarters.

9. Hilsman, *To Move a Nation*, pp. 217-19.

10. Mohammed Hashim Maiwandwal became prime minister of Afghanistan in October 1965.

11. I was able to find no evidence to substantiate Mikoyan's statement. In other words, the punitive bombing of Quemoy and Matsu probably continued as usual, with neither interruption nor intensification.

12. Khrushchev's statement before the U.S.S.R. Supreme Soviet, *Pravda*, 13 December 1962, p. 1; also, "The Origin and Development of the Differences Between the Leadership of the C.P.S.U. and Ourselves," *Peking Review*, 13 September 1963, p. 18.

13. For Robert F. Kennedy's earlier remarks to Dobrynin on U.S. plans to dismantle the Turkish bases, see Kennedy, *Thirteen Days*, pp. 108-9. Announcement of the withdrawal of Jupiter missile bases from Italy and Turkey was made in January 1963.

14. Theodore C. Sorensen, *Kennedy* (New York, 1965), p. 726.

CHAPTER 16: THE COMPROMISE SOLUTION

1. *Népszabadság*, 9 November 1962, p. 1.

2. Associated Press, 9 November 1962.

3. "The Fearless Cuban People Are the Most Powerful Strategic Weapon," *Renmin Rih-bao*, 5 November 1962. The attempt to play the Munich scheme against the Cuban people ... is doomed to complete failure (cited in Griffith, *Albania and the Sino-Soviet Rift*, p. 160).

4. For text, see Kádár, *Road to Socialism*, pp. 43-128.

5. Kádár, *Road to Socialism*, p. 53.

6. To Peking, the neutrality on the Sino-Indian border dispute was caused by

cowardice before "American imperialism." For further details, see Griffith, *Albania and the Sino-Soviet Rift*, pp. 158-67.

7. Kádár, *Road to Socialism*, p. 55.

8. *Ibid*.

9. 4 December 1962, p. 7.

10. A summary of this U.S. Draft Resolution may be found in "Report of the Special Political Committee," United Nations General Assembly, 17th session, A/5388, 19 December 1962.

11. "U.N. Asks Secretary-General To Take Initiative on Hungary," *Department of State Bulletin*, 48, no. 1229 (1963), pp. 74-77.

12. See Ambassador Károly Csatordai's reply and the transcript of the debate, United Nations General Assembly, *Official Records*, 17th Session, Special Political Committee, 376th meeting, 18 December 1962, pp. 279-85.

13. United Nations General Assembly, *Official Records*, 17th Session, 1200th Meeting, 20 December 1962, p. 1206.

14. *Ibid*., p. 1208.

15. *Ibid*., p. 1209.

16. See text of Adlai E. Stevenson's press conference at the U.N. headquarters on 21 December 1962, in "The 17th Session of the U.N. General Assembly: Major Accomplishments," *Department of State Bulletin*, 48, no. 1231 (1963), p. 151.

17. "U.N. Asks Secretary-General To Take Initiative on Hungary," *Department of State Bulletin*, 48, no. 1229 (1963), p. 76.

18. United Nations General Assembly, *Official Records*, 17th Session, Special Political Committee, 376th meeting, 18 December 1962, p. 281.

19. The Report of the Credentials Committee was adopted by the General Assembly on 20 December 1962, 1202nd Meeting, by 73 votes to 4, with 23 abstentions. The voting record of the General Assembly did not reflect individual member states' stands on the question of the Hungarian credentials because the Assembly debated simultaneously the Chinese, Hungarian, and the Yemen Arab Republic's credentials (incorporated in the Committee's report). United Nations General Assembly, *Official Records*, 17th Session, 1201st and 1202nd meetings, 20 December 1962, pp. 1219-41.

20. On 12 February 1963 Senator Lausche strongly attacked U Thant for stopping radio broadcasts to Hungary. He stated that this news had been carried by the AP dated 5 January 1963, and he was informed by the State Department that such an order had been issued by the Secretary-General. See "The Changing Situation in Hungary," *Congressional Record*, CIX, 88th Cong., 1st sess., 15 May 1963, p. 8645. Congressman J.S. Monoghan attacked U Thant for the same reason in the House of Representatives. See "Our Policy on the Captive Nations of Europe," *Congressional Record*, CIX, 88th Cong., 1st sess., February 1963, pp. 1953-54.

21. Kádár, *Road to Socialism*, pp. 170-87.

22. For transcript of the report of the State Department issued on 9 May, see "Report on the Changing Situation in Hungary," *Congressional Record*, CIX, 88th Cong., Ist sess., 15 May 1963, p. 8646.

23. The "Report of the Changing Situation in Hungary" was used as the basis for answering various Congressional and public inquiries during the second half of 1963. See intervention of Congressman Kelly, in "The Question of Hungary," *Congressional Record*, CIX, 88th Cong., Ist sess., 5 June 1963, p. 10208; and Congressman Wyman's intervention in "United States-Hungarian Policy," *Congressional Record*, CIX, 88th Cong., Ist sess., 19 June 1963, p. 11218.

24. *Department of State Bulletin*, 49, no. 1253 (1963), p. 32.

25. To improve the relations between the United States and Hungary and to assure the presence of the American chargé d'affaires at the reception in the Parliament, the Kádár regime unexpectedly lifted the travel restriction on U.S. diplomats stationed in Hungary (see *New York Times*, 1 July 1963, p. 5).

26. Secretary-General U Thant's press conference in Rome, 11 July 1963, *Keesing's Contemporary Archives* (London), 9 November 1963.

Bibliography

PRIMARY SOURCES

Archives

"First Aid for Hungary." Correspondence of Herbert Hoover with President Eisenhower, Vice-President Nixon, and others in connection with the Hungarian refugees of 1956. Miscellaneous newspaper items and pamphlets relating to the revolution. 3 manuscript boxes, Hoover Institution.

Hungaricus. The complete text of the *Hungaricus* pamphlet written and disseminated secretly in Hungary in December 1956. Publ. by the Imre Nagy Institute for Political Research, Brussels, 1959. Part 1, 33 pp. Part 2, 21 pp.

"Theodore E. Kyriak Collection." Miscellaneous newspaper items, pamphlets, and proclamations published during the Hungarian revolution of 1956 with an accompanying list and index to the items in the collection. 1 manuscript box, Hoover Institution.

Monitoring Reports of Radio Broadcasts

Summary of World Broadcasts. 22 October 1956-30 June 1957.* Publ. by the Monitoring Service of the British Broadcasting Corporation (BBC). London, 1956-57.

A Magyar Forradalom és Szabadságharc a Hazai Rádióadások Tükrében (The Hungarian Revolution and the fight for freedom in the light of Hungarian broadcasts). 23 October-9 November 1956. New York: Free Europe Press.

Hungarian Government and Party Material

Primary Texts

Hatályos Jogszabályok Gyüjteménye, 1945-1958 (A compilation of Hungarian Laws, 1945-58). Budapest, 1960. Vol. 1.

Magyar Közlöny (Hungarian Gazette). The official gazette of the Hungarian People's Republic. Budapest.

Parlamenti Értesitő (Parliamentary Records). Verbatim records of the Hungarian Parliament. Vols. 1-51. 3 July 1953-26 September 1958. Budapest.

Daily Papers

Magyar Nemzet (The Hungarian Nation). The organ of the People's Patriotic Front. 1 January 1953-31 December 1963. Budapest.

Népszabadság (People's Freedom). Central organ of the Hungarian Socialist Workers' Party. 2 November 1956-31 December 1963. Budapest.

Szabad Nép (Free People). Central organ of the Hungarian Workers' Party. 1 January 1953-29 October 1956. Budapest.

Periodicals

Irodalmi Ujság (Literary News). Organ of the Hungarian Writers' Association. Weekly 1954-56. Last issue appeared 2 November 1956 in Budapest. From 1957 on, an organ of the Hungarian writers in exile in London and Paris.

Pártélet (Party Life). Monthly. Organ of the Hungarian Socialist Workers' Party Central Committee. Deals with internal party matters. January 1957-December 1963. Budapest.

Társadalmi Szemle (Social Review). Theoretical organ of the Hungarian Socialist Workers' Party Central Committee. January 1953-December 1963. Budapest.

Documents

A Magyar Szocialista Munkáspárt Országos Értekezletének Jegyzőkönyve. 1957, Junius 27-29 (Protocol of the National Conference of the Hungarian Socialist Workers' Party. 27 June-29 June 1957). Kossuth, Budapest, 1957. 302 pp.

A Magyar Szocialista Munkáspárt VII Kongresszusának Jegyzőkönyve. 1959, November 30-December 5 (Protocol of the Seventh Congress of the Hungarian Socialist Workers' Party. 30 November-5 December 1959). Kossuth, Budapest, 1960. 640 pp.

A Magyar Szocialista Munkáspárt VIII Kongresszusának Jegyzőkönyve. 1962, November 20-24. (Protocol of the Eighth Congress of the Hungarian Socialist Workers' Party. 20-24 November 1962). Kossuth, Budapest, 1963. 615 pp.

A Magyar Szocialista Munkáspárt határozatai és dokumentumai, 1956-1962 (Resolutions and documents of the Hungarian Socialist Workers' Party, 1956-1962). Kossuth, Budapest, 1964. 621 pp.

Ellenforradalmi Erők a Magyar Októberi Eseményekben (Counterrevolutionary forces as reflected in Hungarian events). Budapest, 1957-58. 4 vols.

Fontosabb adatok az 1956 október-december időszakról (Selected data concerning the October-December quarter of 1956). Budapest, Országos Statisztikai Hivatal, 1957. 81 pp.

Nagy Imre és Bűntársai Ellenforradalmi Összeesküvése (The counterrevolutionary conspiracy of Imre Nagy and his accomplices). A Magyar Népköztársaság Minisztertanácsa Tájćkoztató Hivatala, Budapest, 1958. 159 pp.

Tájékoztató az amnesztia rendeletről (Facts concerning the decree of amnesty). *Magyar Hirek*, Budapest, 1963. 47 pp.

United States Government Documents and Congressional Publications

Dulles, John Foster. "The Task of Waging Peace," *Department of State Bulletin*, 35 (5 November 1956): 695-99.

Eisenhower, Dwight D. "Developments in Eastern Europe and the Middle East," *Department of State Bulletin*, 35 (12 November 1956): 743-46.

Ellender, Allen J. *A Review of United States Foreign Policy and Operation.* S. Doc. 78, 85th Cong., 2d sess., 1958, pp. 205-21.

————. *A Report on the United States Foreign Operations.* S. Doc. 20, 87th Cong., 1st sess., 1961, pp. 67-77.

Kennedy, John F. "Remarks of the President at American University, Washington, D.C." Office of the White House Press Secretary, 10 June 1963. 5 pp.

Lodge, Henry Cabot. "United Nations General Assembly Condemns Role of U.S.S.R. in Hungary," *Department of State Bulletin*, 37 (30 September 1957): 515-24.

Nixon, Richard M. "In the Cause of Peace and Freedom," *Department of State Bulletin*, 35 (17 December 1956): 943-48.

"Report of the Changing Situation in Hungary," *Department of State Bulletin*, 9 May 1963. 2 pp.

Rowan, Carl T. "U.N. Asks Secretary-General to Take Initiative on Hungary," *Department of State Bulletin*, 48 (14 January 1963): 74-76.

U.S.S.R. Government and Party Documents
(in chronological order)

"Deklaratsiia Pravitel'stva Soiuza SSR ob osnovakh razvitiia i dal'neishego ukrepleniia druzhby i sotrudnichestva mezhdu Sovetskim Soiuzom i drugimi sotsialisticheskimi gosudarstvami" (Declaration on the bases for the development and further strengthening of friendship and cooperation between the Soviet Union and other socialist countries), *Pravda*, Moscow, 31 October 1956, p. 1.

"Negotiations for a Summit Meeting" (Documents), *Supplement to New Times*, no. 26, Moscow, 1958.

Address by the Chairman of the Council of Ministers of the U.S.S.R. N.S. Khrushchev before the All-Russian Teachers Congress, Moscow, 9 July 1960 (excerpts), *Current Digest of the Soviet Press*, 12, no. 28 (10 August 1960), pp. 3-7.

Documents of the 22nd Congress of the C.P.S.U. Vols. I-II. New York, 1961. 366 pp.

Khrushchev, N.S. "Sovremennoe mezhdunarodnoe polozhenie i vneshniiaja politika sovetskogo soiuza-Doklad N.C. Khrushcheva na sessii Verhovnogo Soveta SSSR" (Statement of N.S. Khrushchev on the Cuban crisis, the Sino-Indian border conflict, and relations with Yugoslavia and Albania), *Pravda*, 12 December 1962.

"Letters Exchanged Between the Central Committees of the C.P.C. and the C.P.S.U.," publ. in *Peking Review*, no. 37 (1963), pp. 1-21; and no. 19 (1964), pp. 7-21. Peking.

United Nations Documents
(in chronological order)

United Nations. Security Council, *Official Records*, 11th year, Supplement for October-December 1956, "Letter dated 28 October 1956 from the representative of Hungary to the Secretary-General, transmitting a declaration of the Government of the Hungarian People's Republic," S/3691, 28 October 1956, pp. 100-101.

United Nations. Security Council, *Official Records*, 11th year, Supplement for October-December 1956, "United States of America: draft resolution," S/3710, 30 October 1956, p. 110.

United Nations Security Council, *Official Records*, 11th year, 746th-754th Meeting, 28 October-4 November 1956.

United Nations General Assembly. First Emergency Special Session (1-10 November 1956), "Cablegram dated 1 November 1956 from the President of the Council of Ministers of the Hungarian People's Republic addressed to the Secretary-General." A/3251, 1 November 1956.

United Nations. Security Council, *Official Records*, 11th year, Supplement for October-December 1956, "Note dated 2 November 1956 from the permanent mission of the Hungarian People's Republic to the United Nations, transmitting a letter dated 2 November 1956 from the President of the Council of Ministers and Acting Minister for Foreign Affairs of the Hungarian People's Republic addressed to the Secretary-General," S/3726, 2 November 1956, pp. 119-20.

United Nations. Security Council, *Official Records*, 11th year, Supplement for October-December 1956, "Report by the Secretary-General to the President of the Security Council concerning the credentials of the Representative of Hungary to the Security Council," S/3729, 3 November 1956, p. 125.

United Nations. Security Council, *Official Records*, 11th year, Supplement for October-December 1956, "United States of America: Revised draft resolution," S/3730 and S/3730/Rev. 1, 4 November 1956, pp. 125-26.

United Nations General Assembly, *Official Records*, Second Emergency Special Session (4-10 November 1956), 564th-573rd Meeting, 4-10 November 1956.

United Nations General Assembly, 11th Session. "Report of the Secretary-General," A/3403, 30 November 1956.

United Nations General Assembly, 11th Session. "Note by the Secretary-General," A/3435, 7 December 1956.

United Nations General Assembly, 11th Session. "Note verbale dated 12 December 1956 from the Permanent Mission of Hungary to the United Nations, addressed to the Secretary-General, A/3435/Add. 6, 12 December 1956.

United Nations Security Council, *Official Records*, 11th year. Supplement for October-December 1956, pp. 100-01.

Yearbook of the United Nations 1956, New York, 1957.

United Nations General Assembly, *Official Records*, 11th Session, Annexes, Agenda item 3. "Report of the Credentials Committee," A/3536, 13 February 1957.

United Nations General Assembly, 11th Session. "Interim report of the Special Committee on the Problem of Hungary," A/3546, 20 February 1957.

United Nations General Assembly. "Note verbale dated 26 March 1957 from the Permanent Representative of Hungary to the United Nations, addressed to the Secretary-General, 29 March 1957," A/3573, 1 April 1957.

United Nations General Assembly, *Official Records*, 11th Session, 669th-677th Meeting, 10-14 September 1957.

United Nations General Assembly, *Official Records*, 11th Session, Supplement 18 (A/3592) 12 June 1957. "Report of the Special Committee on the Problem of Hungary."

United Nations General Assembly, *Official Records*, 12th Session, Annexes, Agenda item 3. "Report of the Credentials Committee," A/3773, 9 December 1957.

Yearbook of the United Nations 1957. New York, 1958.

United Nations General Assembly. "Special Report of the Special Committee on the Problem of Hungary," A/3849, 14 July 1958.

United Nations General Assembly, *Official Records*, 13th Session, 752nd Meeting, 22 September 1958.

Yearbook of the United Nations 1958. New York, 1959.

United Nations General Assembly, 14th Session. "Letter dated 16 November 1959 from the Special Representative on the Question of Hungary addressed to the Secretary-General," A/4258, 17 November 1959.

Yearbook of the United Nations 1959. New York, 1960.

United Nations General Assembly, *Official Records*, 15th Session. "Report of the United Nations Representative on Hungary," A/4606, 1 December 1960.

Yearbook of the United Nations 1960. New York, 1961.

Yearbook of the United Nations 1961. New York, 1963.

United Nations General Assembly. "Report of Sir Leslie Munro, United Nations Special Representative on the Question of Hungary," A/5236, 25 September 1962.

United Nations General Assembly. "Letter dated 28 September 1962 from the Permanent Representative of Hungary to the United Nations addressed to the President of the General Assembly" and "Statement of the Permanent Mission of the Hungarian People's Republic to the United Nations," A/5245, 29 September 1962.

United Nations General Assembly, *Official Records*, 17th Session, Special Political Committee, 376th Meeting, 18 December 1962.

United Nations General Assembly, 17th Session. "Report of the Special Political Committee," A/5388, 19 December 1962.

United Nations General Assembly, *Official Records*, 17th Session, 1200th-1202nd Meeting, 20 December 1962.

Articles

Abel, Elie. "Out of Hungary, the Defiant Exiles," *New York Times Magazine*, 25 November 1956, pp. 9-11.

Aladár, Tamás. "A Hungarian View of the October 1956 Disturbances," *Foreign Affairs Reports* (India), no. 6 (1957), pp. 121-30.

Aron, Raymond. "The Meaning of Hungary," *The New Leader*, 24 March 1958, pp. 5-19.

Bain, L. B. "How We Failed in Hungary," *Reporter*, 24 January 1956, pp. 26-28.

————. "Aftermath in Hungary," *Reporter*, 21 March 1957, pp. 18-22.

Ball,.George W. "NATO and the Cuban Crisis," *Department of State Bulletin*, 47 (1962): 830-31.

Barton, Paul. "Les revendications ouvrières dans la Révolution Hongroise," *Saturne*, 2, no. 10 (December 1956), pp. 31-38.

Bernal, J. D. "Hungary Revisited," *New Statesman*, no. 53 (1957), p. 641.

Bernard, Théo. "L'affaire hongroise aux Nations Unies," *Saturne*, 2, no. 10, (December 1956), pp. 5-17.

Bialer, Seweryn. "I Chose Truth," *News From Behind the Iron Curtain*, October 1956, pp. 3-15.

————. "The Three Schools of Kremlin Policy," *The New Leader*, 29 July 1957, pp. 11-12.

Birecki, Henrick. "Le mécanisme de formation de la politique étrangère dans les pays des democraties populaires," *Politique Etrangère*, no. 2 (1970), pp. 197-210.

Cleveland, Harlan. "A Most Dangerous Time," *Department of State Bulletin*, 47 (1962): 875-76.

Cotrell, A. J., and J. E. Dougherty. "Hungary and the Soviet Idea of War," *Russian Review*, October 1957, pp. 17-26.

Deutscher, Isaac. "Crisis in Moscow," *Reporter*, 15 November 1959, pp. 6-9.

Fanfani, Amintore. "How Deep Is the Crisis of Communism?" *Christian Democratic Review*, no. 7 (1957), pp. 11-15.

Farmer, Gene. "Doubtful Future for the Russian Tyranny," *Life*, no. 41 (1956), pp. 46-48.

Farrell, Barry. "Foreign Policy Formation in the Communist Countries of Eastern Europe," *East European Quarterly*, March 1967, pp. 39-74.

Fejtő, François. "La Hongrie, cinq ans après," *Preuves*, no. 129 (November 1961), pp. 3-11.

Figuères, Léo. "Sur les événements de Hongrie," *Cahiers du Communisme*, November 1956, pp. 1119-32.

Glassman, Jon D. "Soviet Foreign Policy Decision-Making," *Columbia Essays in International Affairs*, 3 (1967): 373-402.

Gömöri, George. "Cultural and Literary Developments: Poland and Hungary," in *Annals of the American Academy of Political and Social Sciences*, May 1958, pp. 317-52.

Griffith, William E. "The Revolt Reconsidered," *East Europe*, July 1960, pp. 12-20.

Havas, Gábor. "Workers' Council in Hungary," *Free Labor World*, May 1957, pp. 26-30.

Hoffman, Stanley. "Sisyphus and the Avalanche: the United Nations, Egypt and Hungary," *International Organizations*, no. 11 (Summer 1957), pp. 446-69.

Horelick, L. Arnold. "The Cuban Missile Crisis," *World Politics*, 16, no. 3 (April 1964), pp. 381-89.

Ignotus, Paul. "The A.V.H." (Államvédelmi Hatóság, or State Security Police), *Problems of Communism*, no. 6 (1957), pp. 19-25.

Jásay, A. E. "Russia's Indirect Rule in Hungary," *Contemporary Review*, no. 191 (1957), pp. 328-30.

Kertész, Stephen D. "Political Solution for Hungary," *Current History*, no. 33 (July 1957), pp. 7-15.

Király, Béla. "Hungary's Army: Its Part in the Revolt," *East Europe*, June 1958, pp. 11-14.

Kósa, J. "Költők Forradalma" (Revolution of the poets), *American Slavic and East European Review*, no. 17 (1958), pp. 578-79.

Kulski, W. W. "Soviet Diplomatic Techniques," *Russian Review*, no. 3 (July 1960), pp. 217-26.

Kuznetsov, Vasily V. "Stop Using United Nations in the Interest of Inspirers of Counterrevolutionary Putsch in Hungary," *Soviet News*, January 1957, pp. 16-17.

Láncos, János. "Ties of Friendship," *Free Hungarian Trade Unions*, April 1957, pp. 1-3.

Laudy, Paul. "Hungary since the Revolution," *Problems of Communism*, no. 6 (1957), pp. 8-15.

Lengyel, Emile. "Hungarian Revolution and the U.N." *Foreign Policy Bulletin*, no. 36 (1957), pp. 57-58.

Lindley, E. K. "Hungary and the U.N.," *Newsweek*, no. 50 (1957), pp. 40-42.

Lowenthal, Richard. "Hungary: Were We Helpless?" *New Republic*, no. 135 (1956), pp. 10-15.

————. "Revolution over Eastern Europe," *Twentieth Century*, no. 160 (1956), pp. 483-93.

Mende, Gerhard von. "Policy-Making in the Communist Camp Today," *Modern World*, 1963/64, pp. 53-74.

Mikes, George. "Hungary after the Revolution," *Royal Commonwealth Society Journal*, May-June 1958, pp. 104-108.

Molnár, Miklós. "Überlegungen zur Ungarnfrage," *Gewerkschaftliche Monatshefte*, no. 9 (2 February 1958), pp. 75-80.

Morris, Bernard. "Soviet Policy Toward National Communism: The Limits of Diversity," *American Political Science Review*, March 1959, pp. 128-37.

Munro, Leslie. "Hungary and Suez, Problems in World Order," *Record of Association of the Bar of the City of New York*, January 1957, pp. 12-29.

————. "No Evidence of any Basic Change in the Hungarian Situation," *United Nations Review*, no. 6 (January 1960), pp. 23-26.

Murphy, Robert. "U.S. Views on Problems of Hungary and the Middle East," *Department of State Bulletin*, 35 (10 December 1956): 907-11.

Nemes, Dezső. "Die 'Ideen' von Imre Nagy und die ideologische Vorbereitung des Verrats," *Einheit*, February 1958, pp. 211-29.

Páloczi-Horváth, György. "Case of János Kádár," *Catholic Digest*, 21 August 1957, pp. 22-28.

————. "The Life and Times of János Kádár," *New Leader*, 8 April 1957, pp. 16-20.

Savarius, Vincent. "The Silent Writers of Hungary," *Survey*, July-September 1958, pp. 11-16.

Schapiro, Leonard. "Has Russia Changed?" *Foreign Affairs*, April 1960, pp. 391-401.

Schreiber, Thomas. "L'évolution politique et économique de la Hongrie, 1956-1966," *Notes et Etudes Documentaires*, no. 3335 (8 November 1966), Paris, 1966, 99 pp.

Seton-Watson, Hugh. "Five Years after October," *Problems of Communism*, no. 5 (1961), p. 15.

Sik, Endre. "The Foreign Policy of the People's Republic of Hungary," *International Affairs* (Moscow), March 1960, pp. 17-25.

Szász, A. M. "Kádár's Politics," *East Europe*, October 1962, pp. 2-11.

Toma, Peter A. "Revival of a Communist Party in Hungary," *Western Political Quarterly*, March 1961, pp. 87-103.

Ustor, Endre. "Les pleins pouvoirs des représentants de la Hongrie à l'O.N.U. et dans les autres organisations internationales," *Revue de Droit Hongrois*, no. 3 (1959), pp. 5-39.

Váli, Ferenc A. "The Hungarian Revolution and International Law," *Fletcher Review*, Summer 1959, pp. 9-25.

Wadsworth, J. J. "Hungary: Our Continuing Responsibility," *Department of State Bulletin*, 37 (1957): 192-95.

Zinner, Paul E. "Hungary's Imre Nagy," *Columbia University Forum*, no. 2 (Fall 1958), pp. 6-10.

―――――. "Should U.S. Have Helped Hungary More?" *Foreign Policy Bulletin*, no. 36 (1957), pp. 132-35.

Bibliographies

Bako, Elemér. "Selected References on the Hungarian Revolution of 1956," in *Society for the Investigation of Human Ecology, Inc., New York:* "The Hungarian Revolution of October 1956." Second Seminar, 6 June 1958, Columbia University Men's Faculty Club. New York, 1958. Bibliography, pp. 90-100.

Barlay, Stephen. "Bibliography of the Hungarian Revolution," Appendix I in *Ten Years After*. New York, Chicago, San Francisco, 1966, pp. 209-32.

Gosztonyi, Péter. *Die ungarische Revolution von 1956*. Frankfurt am Main, 1963, pp. 604-33. (Books and articles—320 entries.)

Hálasz de Beky, I. L. *A Bibliography of the Hungarian Revolution*. Toronto, 1963. 179 pp. (Entries total 2,136—428 books and pamphlets, 12 motion pictures, 88 monitored broadcasts, and 1,608 articles—covering the period October 1956 to December 1960. Index.)

Molnár, János. *Ellenforradalom Magyarországon 1956-ban*. (Counterrevolution in Hungary in 1956). Budapest, 1958, pp. 299-305.

Sztáray, Zoltán. *Books on the Hungarian Revolution: A Bibliography*. Brussels, 1960, 14 pp. (Entries total 218, plus 20 bibliographies.)

*Dates in annotations (here, as well as in all the entries that follow) represent dates for which the particular items were used or consulted and do not reflect the publishing dates of the material (unless so indicated).

SECONDARY SOURCES

Books and Pamphlets

Abel, Elie. *The Missile Crisis.* Philadelphia and New York, 1966. 220 pp.

Aczél, Tamás, and Tibor Méray. *The Revolt of the Mind.* New York, 1959. 449 pp.

Aptheker, Herbert. *The Truth about Hungary.* New York, 1957. 256 pp.

Bain, Leslie Balogh. *The Reluctant Satellites.* New York, 1960. 233 pp.

Bak, István, ed. *A Magyar Mezőgazdaság az Ellenforradalom után* (Hungarian agriculture after the counterrevolution). Budapest, 1958. 288 pp.

Benedek, Eugen. *Einige juristische Aspecte der "ungarischen Frage."* Budapest, 1957. 31 pp.

Bibó, István. *Harmadik Ut* (The third road). London, 1960. 380 pp.

Borsody, Stephen. *The Tragedy of Central Europe.* New York, 1960. 288 pp.

Brzezinski, Zbigniew K. *The Soviet Bloc: Unity and Conflict.* Cambridge, Mass., 1967. 599 pp.

Craig, Gordon A., ed. *The Diplomats.* Princeton, 1953. 700 pp.

————. *War, Politics and Diplomacy: Selected Essays.* New York, 297 pp.

Dallin, Alexander, ed. *Soviet Conduct of World Affairs.* New York, 1960. 318 pp.

Daniels, Robert V., ed. *A Documentary History of Communism,* Vol. 2. New York, 1960.

Doolin, Dennis J. *Communist China: The Politics of Student Opposition.* Stanford, Calif., 1964. 70 pp.

Eden, Sir Anthony. *Full Circle.* London, 1960. 336 pp.

Eisenhower, Dwight D. *Waging Peace 1956-1961.* Garden City, N. Y., 1965. 741 pp.

Fejtő, François. *Behind the Rape of Hungary.* New York, 1957. 335 pp.

————. "Hungarian Communism," in *Communism in Europe*, Vol. I. Ed. by William E. Griffith. Cambridge, Mass., 1967.

Finer, Herman. *Dulles over Suez.* Chicago, 1964. 538 pp.

Fryer, Peter. *The Hungarian Tragedy.* London, 1956. 96 pp.

Gosztonyi, Péter. *Der ungarische Volksaufstand in Augenzeugenberichten.* Dusseldorf, 1966. 461 pp.

Griffith, William E. *Albania and the Sino-Soviet Rift.* Cambridge, Mass., 1963. 508 pp.

Hilsman, Roger. *To Move a Nation.* New York, 1967. 602 pp.

Kádár, János. *On the Road to Socialism*. Budapest, 1965. 284 pp.

————. *Szilárd Népi Hatalom: Független Magyarország*. (A collection of speeches and interviews on independent Hungary). Budapest, 1959. 429 pp.

Kállai, Gyula. *A Magyarországi Ellenforradalom a Marxismus-Leninizmus Fényében*. (The Hungarian counterrevolution as seen in the light of Marxism-Leninism). Budapest, 1957. 38 pp.

Kecskemeti, Paul. *The Unexpected Revolution*. Stanford, Calif., 1961. 178 pp.

————. *Strategic Surrender: The Politics of Victory and Defeat*. Stanford, Calif., 1958. 287 pp.

Kennedy, Robert F. *Thirteen Days*. New York, 1969. 224 pp.

Kertész, Stephen D., ed. *East Central Europe and the World: Developments in the Post-Stalin Era*. Notre Dame, Ind., 1962. 386 pp.

Kovacs, Imre, ed. *Facts about Hungary*. New York, 1959. 280 pp.

Lasky, Melvin J., ed. *The Hungarian Revolution*. New York, 1957. 318 pp.

Lederer, Ivo J., ed. *Russian Foreign Policy: Essays in Historical Perspectives*. New Haven, Conn., 1962. 620 pp.

Linden, Carl A. *Khrushchev and the Soviet Leadership 1957-1964*. Baltimore, Md., 1966. 270 pp.

Love, Kennett. *Suez: The Twice-Fought War*. New York and Toronto, 1969. 767 pp.

Lowenthal, Richard. *World Communism: The Disintegration of a Secular Faith*. New York, 1964. 296 pp.

Lukacs, John. *A New History of the Cold War*. New York, 1966. 426 pp.

MacFarquhar, Roderick. *The Hundred Flowers Campaign and the Chinese Intellectuals*. New York, 1960. 324 pp.

Méray, Tibor. *Thirteen Days That Shook the Kremlin*. New York, 1959. 290 pp.

Mezerik, A. G. "Hungary and the United Nations," in *International Review Service*, 4, no. 40. New York, 1958. 51 pp.

Molnár, Miklós. *Victoire d'une défaite–Budapest 1956*. Paris, 1968. 363 pp.

————, and László Nagy. *Imre Nagy: Réformateur ou Révolutionnaire?* Geneva-Paris, 1959. 256 pp.

Murphy, Robert. *Diplomat among Warriors*. New York, 1964. 525 pp.

Nagy, Imre. *Imre Nagy On Communism: In Defense of the New Course*. New York, 1957. 306 pp.

Nográdi, Sándor. *Uj Történet Kezdődött* (The beginning of a new era). Budapest, 1966. 241 pp.

O'Ballance, Edgar. *The Greek Civil War 1944-1949*. New York, 1966. 237 pp.

Paige, Glenn D. *The Korean Decision.* New York, 1968. 394 pp.

Páloczi-Horváth, György. *Khrushchev: The Making of a Dictator.* Boston, 1960. 314 pp.

Polgár, Dénes. *A Szuezi Haború és Magyarország* (Suez and Hungary). Budapest, 1957. 31 pp.

Sager, Peter. *Refusal of a Compromise: Document Concerning the Indian Attempts to Mediate in Hungary.* Bern, December 1956. 12 pp.

Schwartz, Harry, ed. *Russia Enters the 1960s: A Documentary Report on the 22nd Congress of the Communist Party of the Soviet Union.* Philadelphia and New York, 1962. 278 pp.

Seton-Watson, Hugh. *The East European Revolution.* London, 1956. 435 pp.

————. *Neither War Nor Peace.* New York, 1960. 504 pp.

Sik, Endre. *Bem Rakparti Évek* (My years in the Foreign Ministry). Budapest, 1970. 286 pp.

————. *Histoire de l'Afrique Noire.* Budapest, 1962. 2 vols.

Sinor, Denis. *History of Hungary.* New York, 1959. 310 pp.

Snyder, R. C., H. W. Bruck, and Burton Sapin, eds. *Foreign Policy Decision-Making.* New York, 1962. 274 pp.

Sorensen, Theodore C. *Kennedy.* New York, 1965. 783 pp.

Szabó, Bálint. *A Szocializmus Utján: A Felszabadulást Követő Negyedszázad Kronológiája* (On the path of Socialism: a chronological account). Budapest, 1970. 410 pp.

Szikszóy, J. Alexander. *The Legal Aspect of the Hungarian Question.* Ambilly-Annemasse, 1963. 219 pp.

Váli, Ferenc A. *Rift and Revolt in Hungary.* Cambridge, Mass., 1961. 590 pp.

Vass, Henrik. *A Magyarországi 1956 Oktoberi Ellenforradalom Történetének Néhány Kérdése* (History of the 1956 Hungarian counterrevolution). Budapest, 1958. 223 pp.

Zagoria, Donald S. *The Sino-Soviet Conflict 1956-1961.* Princeton, N. J., 1962. 484 pp.

Zinner, Paul E. *Revolution in Hungary.* New York and London, 1962. 380 pp.

Index

Ackerson, Garret G., 104
Aczél, György, 66, 78-79
Adjei, Ako, 54
Afghanistan, 18, 50, 52, 132
Africa, 17, 47, 50, 89, 91, 133-34; in
U.N., 89, 118, 148, 149
Agriculture: Hungarian development,
102; Kádár's appointments, 60;
U.S.S.R. aid to Cuba, 127. *See also*
Farms, collectivization of
Aid, economic:
—from China to Hungary, 62
—from Hungary to Egypt, 53
—from U.S.: to Africa, 89; to Europe,
101
—from U.S.S.R.: to Africa, 89; to
Ceylon, 52; to Cuba, 122, 139; to
Egypt, 52; to Hungary, 6, 62-63, 65;
to Korea, 139
Aid, military: from U.S., 11; from
U.S.S.R., 122-27 *passim*, 139
Albania, 54, 71-75, 140, 142
Albanian Workers' Party, 71, 73, 74,
142
Algeria, 148
American Draft Resolution (U.N.), 146-
47, 149
American History Research Institute in
Munich, 44
Amnesty, 6, 85-86, 92-101, 104, 108-
116, 141-51 *passim*; and the Hungar-
ian question, 113, 114, 116. *See also*

Hungarian-U.S. relations; Normaliza-
tion
Anderson, Major Rudolf, Jr., 125
Andropov, Yuri, 13-14, 22
Anti-Strike Decree, 59
Apró, Antal, 60
Arab countries, 38, 52, 53, 57, 90, 118,
134. *See also countries by name*
Asia, 17, 50, 73, 134, 148, 149; Péter's
goodwill tour of, 53, 90, 91; U.N.
votes, 89, 118. *See also countries by
name*
Australia, 10, 18, 146
Austria, 20, 32, 35, 44, 146
Austro-Hungarian monarchy, 152
A.V.H., 5, 7, 58-59, 75, 78, 79, 85

Bălăceanu, Petre, 126, 129
Balance of power. *See* Superpowers
Báli, Sándor, 59
Baltica, 93
Bandung Conference, 22, 62
Bank, National, of Hungary, 67
Bay of Pigs, 86, 95, 121-24 *passim*
Beck, János, 123-24
Belgium, 10
Belgrade, Declaration of, 4
Belkin, General Fjédor, 79
"Bem Square", 43
Benites, Leopoldo, 145
Bibó, Istvan, 46, 47, 150
Biszku, Béla, 58, 60, 67, 78, 79, 81